Preserving Local Writers, Genealogy, Photographs, Newspapers, and Related Materials

EDITED BY CAROL SMALLWOOD
AND ELAINE WILLIAMS

THE SCARECROW PRESS, INC.
Lanham • Toronto • Plymouth, UK
2012

Published by Scarecrow Press, Inc.
A wholly owned subsidiary of The Rowman & Littlefield Publishing Group, Inc.
4501 Forbes Boulevard, Suite 200, Lanham, Maryland 20706
www.rowman.com

10 Thornbury Road, Plymouth PL6 7PP, United Kingdom

British Library Cataloguing in Publication Information Available

Library of Congress Cataloging-in-Publication Data
Preserving local writers, genealogy, photographs, newspapers, and related materials / edited by Carol Smallwood and Elaine Williams.
     p. cm.
  Includes bibliographical references and index.
  ISBN 978-0-8108-8358-1 (pbk. : alk. paper) — ISBN 978-0-8108-8359-8 (ebook)
  1. Libraries—Special collections—Local history materials. 2. Libraries—United States—Special collections—Local history materials. 3. Local history materials—Conservation and restoration. I. Smallwood, Carol, 1939– II. Williams, Elaine, 1968–
  Z688.L8P74 2012
  025.8'4—dc23   2011045068

Printed in the United States of America

Contents

Foreword   vii
     Barbara B. Eden

Acknowledgments   ix

Introduction   xi

PART I: BASICS

1   Band-Aids and Superglue for the Cash-Strapped Local History
Preservation Librarian   3
    Chad Leinaweaver
2   Basic In-House Book and Paper Repair   11
    Karen E. K. Brown
3   Emergency Preparedness   22
    Dyani Feige
4   You Can't Keep It All   35
    Rochelle LeMaster

PART II: NEWSPAPERS

5   Balancing Selection and Digitization: Selecting Nineteenth-
and Early Twentieth-Century Newspaper Titles for Online Access   47
    Athena Jackson

 6   Indexing Your Local Newspapers on Microfilm   55
     Kelly Zackmann
 7   Newspaper Preservation in Developing Countries: Issues and
     Strategies for Intervention   63
     Goodluck Israel Ifijeh

PART III: SCRAPBOOKS

 8   How to Get Scrapbooks into the Hands of Users   75
     Anastasia S. Weigle
 9   Keeping Scrapbooks Secure and Available   86
     Erin Foley
10   Physical Properties of Scrapbooks   94
     Jennifer Hain Teper

PART IV: LOCAL HISTORY

11   Creating Local History Collection Development Guidelines   105
     William Helling
12   Keeping a Past: Preservation Issues in Local History   116
     Nancy Richey
13   Minimizing Privacy and Copyright Concerns with Online
     Local History Collections   127
     David Gwynn
14   Lavaca County Records Retention Project   137
     Brenda Lincke Fisseler
15   Managing Archives in Local History Collections   146
     Sarah Welland

PART V: GENEALOGY

16   Partnering with Local Genealogical Societies   159
     Lisa Fraser
17   Patron-Driven Family History Preservation   169
     Howard C. Bybee

PART VI: PHOTOGRAPHS

18   Collecting and Preserving Photographic Materials   179
     Amanda Drost
19   Organizing and Indexing Photo Collections   189
     Rose Fortier

20   Photograph Selection, Access, and Preservation for the
     Public Librarian   199
     Rebekah Tabah

PART VII: DIGITAL

21   Digital Preservation of the Emilie Davis Diaries   213
     Alexia Hudson
22   Preserving and "Publishing" Local Biographies   223
     Elizabeth B. Cooksey
23   Promoting Local History through the Catablog   234
     Cyndi Harbeson
24   Reinventing the Obituary File for the Digital Age   243
     Kerry A. FitzGerald

PART VIII: ORAL HISTORIES

25   Preserving Born-Digital Oral Histories   257
     Juliana Nykolaiszyn
26   Preserving Indiana Women's Voices: A University Oral
     History Project   266
     Theresa McDevitt
27   Steps in Preserving Oral Histories   275
     Suellyn Lathrop

PART IX: APPROACHES TO PRESERVATION

28   Affiliation Agreements   287
     Tomaro I. Taylor
29   Educating the Community: Preserving Tomorrow's
     Treasures Today   296
     Jessica Phillips
30   Historical Sheet Music Collections: Practical Wisdom,
     Racial Sensitivity   305
     Karl Madden
31   Tracing History through Nontraditional Methods   316
     Emily Griffin

Afterword   325
     Aline Soules

Index   327

About the Editors and Contributors   337

Foreword

As library trends evolve, the current thinking on preservation of the collections held at cultural institutions views collection care as a holistic continuum. As a result of this rationale, preventative maintenance emerges at the top of the list of priorities. These include important topics such as disaster planning, environmental controls, proper lighting, protective enclosures, and other nonintrusive means of preserving materials.

This anthology addresses preservation issues associated with a wide range of cultural institutions. What they all have in common is that they provide all users with a wealth of resources and are faced with the daunting task of serving as the custodians of history. The majority of these institutions are underfunded. There are countless local historical societies, museums, small public libraries, and reading rooms. All are faced with the conflict between the need to preserve their collections and the reality of dwindling resources. How do you determine which priorities to choose when all of these institutions are filled with documents and objects that are unique and frequently serve as the cultural memory for a community? Can you confidently predict usage trends? Is it more important to use your precious funds to preserve these collections, or to keep the building open and staff the circulation desk? Are providing reference service, funding collection development, and offering programming higher priorities? Do we purchase computers for the public or focus our funds on conservation of an important collection? Are you prepared to make a decision between preservation and access? In the twenty-first century, we are also faced with the preservation of born-digital objects. For example, many genealogists are using databases to track their findings. How will a small cultural institution respond to a CD of information that is donated to them? Is there a digital preservation plan in place? All of these questions and numerous others need to be carefully analyzed and decisions made.

When you are fortunate enough to have external funding made available for preservation, there are choices to be made that include digitization. For example, should a damaged scrapbook be repaired, or is it better off being digitized as is and having the original placed in a dark print archive? Which is the preferred choice?

All cultural institutions should have a mission and a strategic plan. Management and planning provide the infrastructure through which an institution implements its mission. The building blocks for any preservation program involve the preservation-related tasks that librarians and archivists perform on a daily basis that affect the way collections are handled and shelved, the environment in which they are stored and displayed, and the preventative measures that must be taken to ensure their protection and survival.

This publication is very timely. We have many challenges as we resolve concerns over limited funds and the pressing need for preservation.

Preserving Local Writers, Genealogy, Photographs, Newspapers, and Related Materials will help stewards of collections answer these and further important questions. You will be provided the intellectual and practical stimulus to begin planning the course of action.

—Barbara B. Eden, Director, Department of Preservation and Collection
Maintenance, Cornell University Library, Ithaca, New York

Acknowledgments

The co-editors wish to thank the following librarians for writing reviews:

Jeanne Munn Bracken, reference librarian, retired, Lincoln Public Library, and curator of the Lincoln, Massachusetts, Town Archives; *Children with Cancer: A Comprehensive Reference Guide for Parents* (2010, 2nd ed.)

Craig Bunch, librarian, Hamilton Middle School, Houston; 2011 H. W. Wilson Foundation Research Award, Art Libraries Society of North America

Sandra Cortese, reference librarian, Jonathan Bourne Public Library, Bourne, Massachusetts

Larry Grieco, director, Gilpin County Public Library, Black Hawk, Colorado; contributor to *Bringing the Arts into the Library* (forthcoming)

Greg MacAyeal, assistant head, Northwestern University Music Library, Evanston, Illinois

Nancy Kalikow Maxwell, author of the forthcoming *Library Grant Collaboration: How Libraries Can Benefit from Other People's Money*

Mary Jo McKeon, visiting librarian, The Sage Colleges Libraries, Albany, New York

Sarah Naumann, library literacy instructor, Berkeley Public Library, Berkeley, California; circulation assistant, Academy of Art University Library, San Francisco, California

Sarah Passonneau, assistant professor and assistant to the dean/assessment librarian, Iowa State University

Mary Redmond, special liaison for the New York State Library

Sue Samson, humanities librarian, University of Montana, Missoula

Catherine Wilson, executive director, Greene County Ohio Historical Society, Xenia, Ohio; *Historic Greene County* (2010)

Introduction

The purpose of *Preserving Local Writers, Genealogy, Photographs, Newspapers, and Related Materials* is to help public, academic, special, and school librarians, LIS faculty, library board members, historical societies, and others who are not professional archivists to preserve their local culture. In these pages, readers will find tips on preserving primary sources, guidelines for collection development and organization of materials, and basic terms of cooperation between agencies that share an interest in local history. Contributors responded from across the United States as well as abroad. Aline Soules, a library faculty member at California State University, East Bay, in her afterword notes: "Many studied history, but their backgrounds also include African American studies, anthropology, English literature, fine arts, French, information technology, and music, all of which inform their perspectives on this complex topic." This anthology is for beginners in preservation as well as those with experience.

The anthology's thirty-one chapters are divided into: part I: Basics; part II: Newspapers; part III: Scrapbooks; part IV: Local History; part V: Genealogy; part VI: Photographs; part VII: Digital; part VIII: Oral Histories; part IX: Approaches to Preservation.

We hope that you will find the information presented here to be practical and relevant to your efforts in preserving your community's history. Our thanks to the thirty-one librarian and archivist contributors from public, academic, and special libraries, preservation groups, and LIS classrooms, who graciously shared their knowledge.

PART I

BASICS

Band-Aids and Superglue for the Cash-Strapped Local History Preservation Librarian

Chad Leinaweaver

At present, very few institutions are the beneficiaries of huge budgets to run even their basic cataloging and reference work, so preservation initiatives—from purchasing archival supplies to upgrading their climate control—are often scrapped when money runs tight. What are special collections librarians to do when budget constraints challenge their ability to perform their jobs professionally? There are helpful initiatives—even if they are not optimal—in order to achieve the best results possible in collection preservation. Low-cost options for collections care, alternatives for maintaining a constant collection environment, preventative measures for collections safety, and other considerations can be of immense use to librarians with limited budgets.

Collections Care

When it comes to preserving collection materials, some librarians are predisposed to rebind, clean, or repair a choice item in lieu of the general preservation care of all collection material. Prioritization for collections care is certainly important, but when institutional money is scarce, the best decision is the rehousing of an entire collection, rather than the high-cost conservation of only one. This approach ensures that the majority of a collection is preserved. If a rare book requires care, creating a phase box for the volume is an important first consideration since it will invariably be used *even if* the book is conserved. But for most institutions, conservation is not even financially possible, so many only employ basic preservation methods to deter further degradation of the collection items. Thus, there are several rehousing and minor activities librarians can undertake to meet their collection needs.

What repository has not received donations of posters tightly rolled up in rubber bands? Luckily, if the paper is not brittle or heavily torn, these posters can be flattened at minimal cost. The rolled items should be placed into a tall plastic bucket (e.g., five gallons) and placed within a standard, plastic garbage drum. The bucket should be surrounded with large sheets of blotting paper sprayed with water. Closing the garbage drum with a firm-fitting lid will create enough humid air for the posters to absorb when left overnight. Once removed, the posters can be flattened between dry blotting paper and foamcore and underneath weights for about twenty-four hours depending upon the extent of the poster's curling.

If books suffer from page curling, separated covers, or even red rot, phase boxes are one of the fundamental approaches employed. However, constructing original phase boxes is often outside the normal purview of most librarians. Thankfully, many library preservation suppliers have various-sized book boxes with scored edges so that the librarian can simply fold the box to fit the size of the book. A phase box should have a close fit to its book; otherwise the inner movement will cause additional damage. Thus, for homemade boxes with gaps, spacers made from spare strips of acid-free board work great to properly support books. For ambitious librarians with some spare time, there are great instructions online for constructing simple phase boxes.

Polyethylene (or "poly") bags and acid-free tissue are cheap and can be wrapped around dirty or red-rot books in lieu of polyester covers or phase boxes. Though polyester covers and boxes are ideal, some libraries may need to rehouse a bulk of materials quickly or have a limited budget. Poly-bagged books need to be retrieved and shelved carefully, however, as a shelf of slippery poly bags can make it easier for materials to drop on the floor; staff shelvers should be warned of the potential danger. Poly bags are also useful for books with separated covers, loose pages, or a lot of accompanying material (e.g., announcements, clippings, etc.) that are uncataloged. Though acid-free tissue will not last forever, it can be used to wrap low-use books in the short term as long as the outside is properly labeled (with book call number, author, and title) to prevent constant wrapping and unwrapping.

At times diplomas, prints, posters, and other items may be donated inside a wooden or metal frame that may hasten further deterioration. Older wooden frames and support material are generally acidic and metal fasteners often rust, all of which can cause staining. Before removal, if the framed item appears attached or stuck to the glass or frame, *only* a conservator should remove the item. Otherwise, back dustcovers and the frame nails or metal inserts can be removed carefully (so as not to dent or puncture the item with any sharp edges) with a microspatula and needle-nose pliers, respectively. Many times the print or document may be attached to the matting material, so each layer requires careful lifting and placement upon clean matboard, foamcore, or blotters while working. In addition, any dust cover or support material that contains writing, stamps of the framing company, gallery, or artist information should be retained.

For generations, scrapbooks have been a major challenge for librarians. Many of them contain acidic newspaper clippings, ephemera, and photographic items all glued to—and sandwiched between—highly acidic pages. Though modern-day scrapbooking insists on acid-free pages, binders, and glues, most nineteenth- and twentieth-century scrapbooks are really beyond most conservation techniques. Thus, many libraries can only box the original scrapbooks and document them via reformatting in order to preserve the original order and information (e.g., this would document photograph captions written on the scrapbook pages rather than on the versos of loose or removed photographs). Microfilming is not always an affordable option, but color copying or scanning is less expensive for libraries and can provide a service or archival copies.

Scrapbooks as well as rare books and manuscripts may have pages with stray marks or dirt. Though a widely held belief among conservators was to use standard erasers to remove these marks, they can leave small eraser particles within the paper (or book pages), some of which are not chemically inert. The Northeast Document Conservation Center suggests rubbing carefully and lightly on the page or sheet with a vulcanized rubber dry-cleaning sponge (nonchemical), though areas with notations, signatures, and notes should never be erased. However, if the paper is quite brittle, *only* a professional conservator should perform any cleaning. Books printed from the 1860s through the early twentieth century often were made from wood pulp, which yellows and becomes extremely brittle over time. Refrain from erasing brown-edged or overly brittle paper.

For more intensive collection and shelf cleaning, HEPA (high-efficiency particulate air) vacuums are the best option, but are not an immediate purchase for most institutions. Decent vacuums are affordable and are preferable to no cleaning at all, though only HEPA vacuums will prevent the redistribution of dust back into clean air. Regular dusting and vacuuming is great preventative maintenance, keeping dust and red rot of deteriorating materials from migrating to more stable collections. Magnetic wiping cloths (such as Dust Bunny and Preserve It) gather in dust rather than simply stirring it up and are preferred for cleaning tasks.

Environment and Storage Space

Many institutions simply cannot afford a complete HVAC (heating, ventilation, and air conditioning) system, so librarians need to examine other options to maintain ideal collection environments. Since most buildings can produce adequate heat in colder weather, decent air conditioners are the most obvious need. The units are a minor investment, so grants are ideal for their purchase, especially with many grantors willing to fund capital expenses. In order to retain heat in storage areas in the winter, windows and doors should always be closed, windows should be sealed with plastic sheeting, and doors should be weather-stripped. Windows should never be opened as this will enable humidity, which is very limited in winter months, to escape. Materials should not reside in direct line with heat registers or air conditioners; if they cannot be moved, it may be necessary to block them.

Humidifiers and dehumidifiers are also cheaper than entire HVAC systems (though again, they can be a minor investment) and can be another good grant capital expense. Room sizes should be considered with the purchase of these machines, so that the needed climate can be maintained without immense stress on the unit. These machines do involve ongoing maintenance: emptying water (in the case of dehumidifiers) and consistently changing or cleaning filters to eliminate any pollutants from reentering the air. In the case of high humidity, desiccants (e.g., Damp Rid, silica gels) can also soak up excess water in the air within storage areas, exhibition cases, or boxes packed with collections for shipping. Other than some color-indicating silica gels, these desiccants are inexpensive, will last a few months, and can be a short-term solution. Ultimately, dehumidifiers or an HVAC system work much better for larger storage areas.

For institutions with windows in collection areas or large numbers of fluorescent lighting fixtures, the presence of collection-fading ultraviolet (UV) light can be a problem. Depending upon the window size and number of lighting fixtures, UV film is relatively inexpensive and is one of the best options. Window shades can block outside light (so long as staff are trained to draw the shades during the brightest parts of the day), but for some institutions (particularly public and academic libraries constructed in the mid- to late twentieth century), the windows can be so large that shades and UV film are prohibitively expensive. Other suggestions to limit light levels include removing unneeded light fixtures (or at least lightbulbs), replacing needed lightbulbs with lower wattage bulbs, or, if possible, keeping collections stored in windowless rooms.

Preventative Measures

The best prevention involves relocating collections away from potential problem areas. The cost in prevention is minimal compared to the cleanup when disaster strikes. If possible, store collections away from sinks, bathrooms, or other plumbing sources and certainly not underneath overhead pipes (noting that some overhead pipes may be hidden by ceiling tiles or Sheetrock).

The collections area should always be free of potential extrinsic problems. New donations should be separated from existing collections until the items can be inspected for any mold, pests, or other problems that could enter the collection areas. For many institutions with limited space, it is as difficult to keep new acquisitions in a separate room as it is to keep the collection room free of any food, due to limited (or no) designated staff eating areas. Bagging all food waste separately, utilizing a trashcan that can be sealed, and keeping it away from the collections can help to deter the entrance of pests to the collections themselves. After any event where there is food, staff should thoroughly vacuum all areas, wipe down all surfaces, and remove all food waste completely from the building. Plants, though attractive, can also be considered food for a variety of pests and should not be situated in any collections area.

Security measures can be inexpensive to implement. Staff can create pull sheets to document collection retrieval, can have registration forms for users (with users providing identification), and have collection return inspection procedures in place. If the reading room is staffed only part-time by extradepartmental staff, collection access should be set up through appointment-only scheduling so that staff can be present to monitor collection use. Staff can document the most valuable collections through keeping files, photographing items (or photographing distinguishing marks), and discreetly marking collection items with some institutional identification.

Developing an institutional preservation program enables administration to have greater awareness of preservation issues but also acts as a constant reminder for collection staff. Carolyn Clark Morrow provides an excellent checklist for a preservation program in her chapter from *Defining the Library Preservation Program*. Certainly not everything on the checklist will be completed at the start, let alone several years into such a preservation program, but it provides reminders such as routine cleaning, pest inspection, the addition of UV filters to lighting fixtures, and regular monitoring of environmental conditions.

Other Considerations

Within reason, take care of preservation issues when initially encountered. Once an item is boxed or shelved, it could reside there for a near eternity. On the other hand, some repositories could easily expend all available staff time rehousing items and making book covers. Therefore, rehouse or address preservation concerns when an item is requested by patrons. This approach ensures the most retrieved items receive preservation care and prevents a stalemate of preservation efforts. For most time-limited staff, the extra minute spent with a pulled collection item's preservation is easier to manage than a larger, full-scale effort involving boxes of materials.

The extra-minute preservation approach could also be applied to new collection acquisitions, especially archival and ephemeral collections, by minimally processing them at time of acquisition. Few librarians can fully process a collection immediately and many new acquisitions sit for years unprocessed, but rehousing and removing potentially damaging items (e.g., paper clips, sticky notes, etc.) ensures at least a safely stored collection. When doing minimal processing, several considerations should be heeded. Label folders appropriately (or at least retain old folders in order) so that any original collection order or identifying information is retained. If material is stapled or paper-clipped together, utilize plastic paper clips or microfolders so that the collocation of that material is documented. Certainly, some complex collections are beyond this approach given their organization or the sheer number of folders. When in doubt, adhere to full processing and proper documentation (creation of finding guides or inventory lists).

A clear collections policy saves librarians the trouble of preserving formats or subject material that really falls outside the institutional scope. Keeping a list or bookmarking websites of related-subject organizations are great for patron referrals. Selection of materials for acquisition is sometimes difficult because not everything can or should be saved.

Since every collection brought into the institution will consume staff time in processing, cataloging, retrieving, and reformatting, in times of tight budgets, it is important to consider how valuable the possible donation is to the mission of the repository.

Clean scraps of purchased archival supplies can be reused to save on supply costs. A small piece of polyester film is excellent for sliding underneath to remove staples or paper clips from manuscript items without tearing the paper. Used but clean acid-free boxes or folders can be cut up for use as spacers within less-than-full collection boxes to prevent any drooping or curling folders. Scraps of acid-free folders can also be cut up for call number bookmarks in lieu of sticky spine labels. Bricks or marble slabs wrapped in acid-free paper work great as weights for flattening items. Smaller (and relatively light) stones work great in this fashion as book weights and supports. Although many archives print collection box labels, using a pencil to inscribe collection information neatly on the archival box allows for it to be erased and reused in the future. This can save on the mass purchasing of sheet labels and printer ink, given that humidity changes can cause stickers to peel off over time, perhaps resulting in misplaced collection boxes or incorrect items being placed therein. If the repository constructs exhibits and there is storage space, consider saving the mounts, props, book cradles, and lifts to utilize for future exhibits. Defective exhibition supports should not be reused if they could damage or not properly sustain a collection item.

Conclusion

There is no substitute for following established preservation methods to prolong the life of an institution's collections. However, the past twenty years have seen a steady decline in budgets for archives and libraries, to a point where optimal conditions are not being maintained, no matter what the situation. When cataloging and reference services are compromised, normal preservation operations such as dusting, vacuuming, planning, and rehousing projects are simply put aside. Thus, any simplified or cost-saving measures that can be taken until financial situations improve need to be considered so long as they do not endanger the collections and follow preservation standards as much as possible. Certainly some preservation is better than none at all.

Bibliography

"ACRL/RBMS Standards and Guidelines." Association of College and Research Libraries, Rare Book and Manuscripts Section, 2009. www.rbms.info/standards/index.shtml (accessed January 13, 2011).

Balloffet, Nelly, Jenny Hille, and Judith Reed. *Preservation and Conservation for Libraries and Archives.* Chicago: American Library Association, 2005.

Banks, Paul N., and Roberta Pilette, eds. *Preservation: Issues and Planning.* Chicago: American Library Association, 2000.

Bell, Nancy, and David McPhail. "Managing Change: Preserving History." *Materials Today* 10 (2007): 50–56.

Brown, William E., Jr., and Laura Stalker, eds. *Getting Ready for the Nineteenth Century: Strategies and Solutions for Rare Book and Special Collections Librarians. Proceedings of the Thirty-Ninth Annual Preconference of the Rare Books and Manuscripts Section, Association of College and Research Libraries, Washington, D.C., June 23–26, 1998.* Chicago: Association of College and Research Libraries, 2000.

Clarke, Rachel. "Preservation of Mixed-Format Archival Collections: A Case Study of the Ann Getty Fashion Collection at the Fashion Institute of Design and Merchandising." *American Archivist* 72 (2009): 185–96.

Gorman, G. E., and Sydney J. Shep, eds. *Preservation Management for Libraries, Archives and Museums.* London: Facet Publishing, 2006.

Greene, Mark A. "MPLP: It's Not Just for Processing Anymore." *American Archivist* 73 (2010): 175–203.

Hain, Jennifer E. "A Brief Look at Recent Developments in the Preservation and Conservation of Special Collections." *Library Trends* 52 (2003): 112–17.

Lavender, Kenneth. *Book Repair.* 2nd ed. How-to-do-it Manual, no. 107. New York: Neal-Schuman, 2001.

Lull, William. "Low Cost/No Cost Improvements in Climate Control." Preservation Leaflet, 2.6. Andover, Mass.: NEDCC, 2007. www.nedcc.org/resources/leaflets/2The_Environment/06LowCostNoCost.php (accessed January 14, 2011).

MacDonald, Eric. "Creating a Preservation Department from Existing Staff Resources: The UC Irvine Experience." *Conservation Administration News* 55 (1993): 6–7.

Morrow, Carolyn Clark. *Defining the Library Program: Policies and Organizations in Preservation Issues and Planning.* Chicago: ALA, 2000.

Ogden, Sherelyn. "Cleaning Books and Shelves." Rev. ed. Preservation Leaflet, 4.3. Andover, Mass.: NEDCC, 2007. www.nedcc.org/resources/leaflets/4Storage_and_Handling/03CleaningBooksAndShelves.php (accessed January 7, 2011).

"Priority Actions for Preservation." Preservation Leaflet, 1.6. Andover, Mass.: NEDCC, 2007. http://www.nedcc.org/resources/leaflets/1Planning_and_Prioritizing/06PriorityActions.php (accessed November 23, 2010).

Ritzenthaler, Mary Lynn. *Photographs: Archival Care and Management.* Chicago: Society of American Archivists, 2006.

———. *Preserving Archives and Manuscripts.* 2nd ed. Chicago: Society of American Archivists, 2010.

"Surface Cleaning of Paper." Preservation Leaflet, 7.2. Andover, Mass.: NEDCC, 2007. http://www.nedcc.org/resources/leaflets/7Conservation_Procedures02SurfaceCleaning.php (accessed January 7, 2011).

CHAPTER 2

Basic In-House Book and Paper Repair

Karen E. K. Brown

Conservators and other preservation professionals have long been concerned with the ethics of training nonspecialists to repair objects that may have enduring significance. The familiar axiom "A little bit of knowledge is a dangerous thing" is one way of saying that insufficient information can lead to wrong conclusions or simply bad decisions. In the realm of caring for valued cultural collections, there is a serious risk of causing irreversible damage if inappropriate materials or methods are used in any attempt at item stabilization. Larger historical societies, libraries, and museums can support expertly staffed and well-equipped in-house conservation facilities. However, the cost of doing so in medium- and smaller-sized institutions is not always feasible, even when collections are especially valuable. The emphasis, regardless of organizational size, should be on the prevention of damage through actions such as control of the environment, emergency planning, proper storage and handling, and security. Nevertheless, smaller cultural organizations still need access to treatment services. What is the framework for setting up an in-house book and paper repair program, and how can it be done responsibly?

To start, curators and others charged with protecting collections from unnecessary damage need to become familiar with the range of services offered by outside vendors such as commercial binders, reformatting services, and trained conservators. In addition to this array of options, an in-house repair operation can be extremely valuable, especially if the focus is on simple, effective, and efficient processes that can be sustained with minimal resources.

In-house repair has many advantages:

- Valuable, fragile material can remain in the safety of the home institution.
- Minimal intervention can prevent or lessen damage.
- Basic treatments can obviate the need for more complex and expensive treatments.
- The cost can be less than contracting with an outside vendor.
- The "turnaround" time can be shorter than when materials are sent off-site.
- The appearance of the collection can be improved, both on the shelf and on exhibit.
- The condition of the collection can be improved, extending its useful life.
- Access to the collection can be enhanced.

For an in-house repair program to be truly effective, its value to the institution must be measured and documented, to determine if it mitigates damage, improves collection condition and access, and is economical and faster than off-site conservation services. If an in-house program is established, an annual examination of the work performed and the workflows established will determine the quality, suitability, and expense of in-house treatment operations. Since staff time can be very expensive and repairs may take time away from other duties, it is essential to assess the costs and benefits of the in-house operations. Clearly, success will depend on excellent training and program oversight. This cannot be overemphasized.

The Importance of Training

Those who will be mending, rehousing, or reformatting collections must have adequate training and supervision in order to maximize program benefits and ensure work is of the highest quality. In many cases, these individuals will be technicians, not professional conservators, but they must have a serious interest in and aptitude for careful, tactile activity. Optimally, institutional directors and curators will gain heightened preservation awareness by engaging in some basic training. This is important because curators and conservation technicians must work in partnership to determine the most reasonable stabilization option for the item at hand.

During the past twenty years I have given innumerable workshops on the many facets of collections care, including the organization and management of in-house repair programs for smaller libraries, archives, and historical societies. With respect to hands-on treatment, the primary goal has always been to convey the importance of responsible custodianship, highlighting the idea that individuals and institutions must learn where to draw the line in terms of what types of conservation treatment they can safely perform. It is perhaps more reasonable to show workshop participants how to do a simple paper mend correctly than to not offer a workshop at all, knowing there is the chance that some may reach instead for "archival" tape if they do not know there are better options. Damage from the use of poor-quality materials and inappropriate techniques is preventable and should be avoided at all costs. The objective of all treatment must be to extend the useful life of all collection materials for as long as they are needed to support the goals of the institution. In other words, whether a practitioner has very limited skills or is highly trained, the Code of Ethics of the American Institute for Conservation of Historic and Artistic Works should apply equally to everyone. Item IV states the following: "The conservation professional shall practice within the limits of personal competence and education as well as within the limits of the available facilities."[1]

Establishing an in-house repair program is worth the investment when the plan includes support for ongoing staff training in preservation/conservation, sufficient funding to set up the workspace, and a regular line item in the budget for purchasing supplies.

Preservation/Conservation Training Guidelines

- Provide support for staff responsible for preservation to attend workshops whenever possible. Regional centers such as Lyrasis and the Northeast Document Conservation Center regularly offer preservation and conservation workshops, including book and paper repair. The Conservation DistList, a monitored listserv, is an excellent resource for learning about upcoming offerings (cool.conservation-us.org/byform/mailing-lists/cdl/aboutcdl.shtml). Attending hands-on repair training programs is essential. This is fundamental to building skill sets.
- Establish a book and paper repair reference library. Refer to published articles and manuals to help refine techniques and procedures.
- Practice hand skills on less valuable materials. Take good notes and photographs and carefully monitor personal progress. Document routine procedures. Work with a supervisor to gauge the quality of all treatments.

Selection for Preservation

A preservation program must establish a workflow to identify damaged objects that may be candidates for preservation action. This can be based on condition problems noted on the shelf or in storage, during processing or use, or as part of a formalized survey process to evaluate the preservation needs of an entire collection. For example, staff may observe that the binding of a book is damaged or deteriorated, or that the paper is brittle; a recently donated collection of negatives may have a funny smell; or a set of old local maps is so tightly rolled that the collection cannot be used without causing damage. A note about the problem can be made in the bibliographic record or on a form kept with the object itself, and/or the materials can be set aside for further evaluation.

Each institution must then develop criteria for determining what preservation actions are most appropriate for the item at hand, depending on the service options at their disposal. During initial screening, one might determine that the object or collection is a good candidate for (1) commercial binding, (2) in-house treatment, or (3) conservation services, or that it is (4) irreparable (i.e., reformatting or replacement strategies are the only options). Table 2.1 summarizes these options and the issues to be considered. See the online dictionary "Bookbinding and the Conservation of Books" by Matt T. Roberts and Don Etherington listed under Resources to help in understanding some of the terminology.

The risk of inaction must also be considered. For example, if deteriorating negatives, newspapers, or building plans are not stabilized or copied in a timely fashion, the images and information may be lost forever. However, "doing nothing" can be a responsible choice if the object or collection is extremely fragile, rare, or significant. Perhaps the only use of these types of materials should be limited to facsimiles. This is a warning that invasive treatment (something that will alter the original) should be attempted only by a professional conservator.

Other criteria that may influence decisions might include past, present, or future use; size of a collection; research value; and the availability of other copies. Consider if the damaged objects under review have an aesthetic quality, physical form, age, or some other value that makes them important or unique. Discussion among staff and perhaps other stakeholders regarding value, risk, and use will also help determine which items or collections are a priority for treatment.

The literature on assigning value to collections and preservation decision-making is extensive; much of it is discipline specific. Choices regarding conservation treatment must be made within the context of individual organizational missions and policies. A few key resources are listed at the end of this chapter to help in developing conscientious strategies for deciding what to preserve and how to preserve it, sometimes referred to as "selection for preservation."

Table 2.1. Preservation/Conservation Service Options

Option	Rationale	Services	Notes
Commercial Binding	• Cover is worn/badly damaged • Textblock is broken; pages are loose or detached • No artifactual value; machine-made binding with no physical or aesthetic value that makes it unique • Paper in good condition • Plenty of gutter margin to allow for rebinding	• Recase only (new cover only) • Consolidate textblock (sew through the fold, double fan adhesive binding, etc.) and recase • Custom boxing, photocopying, digitization, and book conservation services may be available	• Smaller institutions may not have the volume for reduced pricing (consider going through a cooperative) • Regular funding and staff time required to support this service option • Quality is very strong and durable
In-House Treatment	• Artifactual value; need to preserve original item in original form • Simple cleaning, rehousing, or mending is all that is required	• Custom enclosures • Surface cleaning • Humidification and pressing • Minor mending of books and paper • Pamphlet binding • Paperback stiffening	• Trained conservation technicians and proper supplies and equipment are essential if repairs are to be done correctly and efficiently • Plenty of flexibility in terms of service options • Can be expensive (especially staff time/overhead)
Conservation Services	• Fragile, unique, significant holdings	• Full range of services, from the most basic and noninvasive to complex and highly skilled	• For the most valuable, most important objects in your collection • Can be very expensive • Turnaround time may be slow • Select your conservator with care
Irreparable	• Brittle paper • Extensive loss (missing illustrations, pages, etc.) • Mold damage • Not enough gutter margin to rebind	• Reformat (microfilm, photocopy, digitize, etc.) • Replace (published material; reprints, digital reproductions, etc.) • Can enclose and return to the shelf (but this will not solve the problem) • Withdraw	• Curators and subject specialists make the final decision about disposition • Reformatting options can be very expensive • Decide if originals are to be retained after copying

What Stabilization Procedures Should You Use?

A stepwise approach to learning about book and paper repair is highly recommended. While some procedures are considered "basic," it is critical that conservation technicians understand as much as possible about the history, technology, and manufacture of the collections in their care before attempting any type of preservation action. For example, before mending a torn blueprint, it is important to know about grain direction in paper. In addition, it is good to know that blueprints sometimes fade rapidly when exposed to light, so it is best to handle them facedown and to keep them covered whenever possible. They are also sensitive to alkalinity and can turn brown unless they are stored in pH neutral, unbuffered enclosures. Some maps and many manuscripts will have water-soluble inks, and many writing inks (such as iron gall) have both particulate and soluble components that could be compromised if water is introduced during treatment, even as little as what is used when mending with Japanese tissue and wheat paste. Simply stated, knowing how a book, photograph, or print is created will help make certain that repairs are sympathetic to the original. Table 2.2 outlines the knowledge and skill sets that are fundamental to conservation technician training. It features three topics: paper care and repair, enclosures, and book repair. The units within each topic progress from the most basic to the more demanding expertise for each activity listed within that topic.

Equipment, Space, Materials, and Suppliers

Selecting a workspace and deciding what equipment, tools, and supplies are needed are intimately related to the treatments to be accomplished. For example, paper mends and minor book repairs can be made with simple hand tools and small weights to assist drying. A large paper cutter will speed up many routine operations and should be considered if efficiency is a key objective. If workers intend to build phase boxes, then more space and larger equipment will be needed (e.g., flat storage space for barrier board, workspace for assembling and drying, board shears, and a board creaser). If large rolls of bookcloth or polyester sheeting will be purchased, consider how these will be stored. Boards for pressing (9 × 12 inches) and heavy weights and/or a standing press will be required for many book repair operations. Consider what the situation might be in five to ten years. It is possible you will have more staff and/or will be performing more complex treatments in the future. In addition, be sure to designate space for administrative work.

Table 2.2. Stabilization Procedures

	Topic I: Paper Care and Repair	
Unit	Objective/s	Skills and Knowledge
The Nature of Paper and Board	• History of Western and Asian papermaking • Permanent paper	• Learn how paper is made (hand and machine), its physical characteristics (grain direction, absorbency, surface qualities, strength, etc.), and chemical characteristics (pH, presence of lignin) • Handle a variety of papers and consider their applicability for repair/rehousing
Dry Cleaning	• Removal of surface dirt and debris	• Test media and supports for sensitivity in order to prevent loss and damage • Learn about different types of eraser products; practice techniques using solid and ground eraser • Understand vacuum methods for cleaning books and paper
Adhesives	• Properties and applicability of various vegetable, protein, and synthetic adhesives	• Become familiar with the chemical and physical properties of adhesives used in conservation, considering their use and reversibility • Work with wheat paste, cellulose ethers, and white glues (especially PVA); know their preparation; study the use and limitations of pressure-sensitive and heat-set adhesives
Simple Torn Paper Repairs	• Characterizing damage (tear, puncture, loss, etc.) • Use of Japanese paper and wheat paste	• Become sensitive to the quality of the original object (media and support); choose the right repair method and practice techniques

Table 2.2. (continued)

Unit	Objective/s	Skills and Knowledge
Humidification and Pressing	• Reduce planar deformations (usually from rolled storage)	• Learn to examine the object for surface dirt; identify risks such as weakness from mold damage; watch for supports and media that are water sensitive; consider the problem of attachments such as applied seals • Learn various techniques for controlling the movement of moisture into the object and gentle methods of pressing
	Topic II: Enclosures	
Encapsulation	• Provide support for flat paper objects	• Understand the use of clear polyester to "encapsulate" a flat paper object to provide additional support and protection during handling • Learn about the materials, tools, and techniques, as well as optional equipment such as heat and ultrasonic welders, corner rounders, etc.
Portfolios	• A three- or four-flap container used to house small books, pamphlets, and other items such as CDs and DVDs	• Learn to size, cut, glue, and assemble a simple container (paper, board, white glue) • May be adhered inside stiff boards (advisable if the item is from a general collection)
Boxing	• Phase boxes, drop-spine boxes	• Learn to construct custom-sized boxes to protect fragile books and other objects

Topic III: Book Repair

History of the Book and Book Structures	• The history of book structures and printing technologies	• Learn about methods of constructing books (historical to current) • Become familiar with the terminology (e.g., the parts of a book) • Become sensitive to aesthetic quality, physical form, age, and other values that make an item important or unique • Learn about printing methods and media
Simple Book Repairs	• Guarding, tipping in, hinge tightening	• Learn simple methods of reattaching loose or replacement pages and for tightening a cover that is pulling away from the textblock
Corner Reinforcement	• Repairing worn corners	• Use bookcloth and adhesive to neatly reinforce corners
Rebacking	• Replacing a damaged book spine	• Learn how to build a new spine and fit it properly to the book
Paperback Stiffening	• Reinforce flimsy book covers	• Stiffen weak or damaged covers using folder stock
Pamphlet Binding	• Sew a small (less than 1/4" thick) pamphlet and adhere within stiff covers	• Practice various techniques of sewing small books to a hinge and protecting it within boards • Move to more advanced methods for side-sewing loose sheets and attaching multiple signatures
Odors, Bugs, and Wet Books	• Salvaging damaged books	• Become familiar with safe options for reducing odor in books, treating them for pests without the use of chemicals, and stabilizing and salvaging a few wet books or wet paper

The workspace does not need to be a separate room, but it should be divided off enough to ensure that staff can work comfortably and that materials can be safely handled. An 8 × 12 foot space or larger should be ample to get started. There should be a large work surface (a sturdy table, roughly 3 × 6 feet at a height of 36 to 40 inches), shelf storage, and optional book trucks. Movable furniture will provide flexibility in how the space is used. Good lighting is essential. Use natural light when possible, with both overhead lighting and one or two task lights. Flooring should be easy to clean, as should all surfaces. Overall, the area should be clean and dry, with temperatures at or below 74 degrees F. Environmental conditions in attics and basements are usually not well suited to conservation work. Some measure of security must be considered. Lockable cabinets are good for storing valuable materials awaiting treatment, for after hours, and for when the space is not occupied.

High-quality tools and best-quality materials are vital components of conservation work. Purchase your supplies, tools, and equipment from reputable vendors. Read catalog descriptions and look for indicators of quality. Expect good customer service if you have questions or problems with your purchases. It is recommended that you buy small quantities and samples of materials to test and examine before making a big purchase. Do not overlook the many options and products available from archival suppliers for housing and rehousing collections, including folders, envelopes, boxes, and other storage systems. If possible, seek advice from a preservation professional or conservator whenever you are unsure about what to buy.

Conclusion

There are many advantages to setting up an in-house repair operation, but there are considerable challenges as well. Ongoing training, conscientious selection, familiarity with service options, and careful consideration of space, material, and equipment needs must be supported by a respect for what each institution can accomplish, even if training and resources are minimal. By recognizing strengths and acknowledging limitations, it is possible to set up a successful in-house operation that is both efficient and effective.

Resources

Balloffet, Nelly, and Jenny Hille. *Preservation and Conservation for Libraries and Archives.* Chicago: American Library Association, 2005.
Gertz, Janet. "Preservation and Selection for Digitization." Preservation Leaflet 6.6. Andover, Mass.: Northeast Document Conservation Center, 2007. www.nedcc.org/

resources/leaflets/6Reformatting/06PreservationAndSelection.php (accessed January 14, 2011).

Harris, Carolyn. "Selection for Preservation." In *Preservation Issues and Planning*, edited by Paul N. Banks and Roberta Pilette, 206–24. Chicago: American Library Association, 2000.

Library Binding. ANSI/NISO/LBI Z39.78-2000. Bethesda, Md.: NISO Press, 2000. www.lbibinders.org/mc/page.do?sitePageId=112541&orgId=hbi#lbiPublications (accessed January 14, 2011).

Merrill-Oldham, Jan, and Paul Parisi. *Guide to the ANSI/NISO/LBI Binding Standard*. Chicago: American Library Association, 2000.

Morrow, Carolyn Clark, and Carole Dyal. *Conservation Treatment Procedures*. Littleton, Colo.: Libraries Unlimited, 1986.

Nathanson, David, and Diane Vogt-O'Connor. "What Makes a Book Rare?" Conserve O Gram 19/1. Washington, D.C.: National Park Service, July 1993. www.nps.gov/history/museum/publications/conserveogram/cons_toc.html (accessed January 14, 2011).

Northeast Document Conservation Center. "Exploring Selection for Preservation." Andover, Mass.: Northeast Document Conservation Center, 2006. www.preservation101.org/session1/expl_selection.asp (accessed January 14, 2011).

Paris, Jan. "Choosing and Working with a Conservator." Preservation Leaflet 7.7. Andover, Mass.: Northeast Document Conservation Center, 2010. www.nedcc.org/resources/leaflets/7Conservation_Procedures /07ChoosingAConservator.php (accessed January 14, 2011).

Roberts, Matt T., and Don Etherington. "Bookbinding and the Conservation of Books: A Dictionary of Descriptive Terminology." Last modified 1994. cool.conservation-us .org/don/don.html (accessed January 28, 2011).

Vogt-O'Connor, Diane. "Reformatting for Preservation and Access: Prioritizing Materials for Duplication." Conserve O Gram 19/10. Washington, D.C.: National Park Service, July 1995. www.nps.gov/history/museum/publications/conserveogram/cons_toc.html (accessed January 14, 2011).

Note

1. American Institute for Conservation of Historic and Artistic Works, *Directory, 2010* (Washington, D.C.: AIC, 2010): 21.

CHAPTER 3

Emergency Preparedness

Dyani Feige

One of the most important steps any institution can take to safeguard its collections is to be prepared in the event of an emergency or disaster. Although emergencies and disasters are, by definition, unanticipated, it can be possible to minimize some of the most devastating potential outcomes by having a plan in place. Emergency preparedness and response plans offer a framework for organized response, recovery, and continuity of operations. Having a plan in place can ensure safekeeping of collections, minimize collection damage and loss, and limit costs for recovery.

Emergency planning is vital for any size institution—small or large. Whether your historical society has a staff of one or your museum is run entirely by volunteers, so long as there is a collection and a space in which it is located, this chapter is for you.

An *emergency* is "an unanticipated event or series of events that requires immediate action,"[1] but might not escalate into a catastrophic situation, major loss of collections, or damage to the site. A contained pipe leak or a onetime insect infestation is an emergency.

A *disaster* is much more serious: "an event that results in significant loss, damage, or destruction. An emergency can become a disaster if immediate action is not taken to protect staff, visitors, and the collection."[2] A fire that destroys part of the building or a severe flood is a disaster.

There are several types of emergencies or disasters:

- natural disaster, extreme weather
- environmental problems: heating, ventilation, and air conditioning (HVAC) failure, power failure, mold bloom

- pest infestation
- building-related: leak, construction damage (roof collapse, etc.)
- human-caused: intentional (theft, vandalism, arson) or unintentional (mishandling of collections, damage during construction)

Assessing Risks

The first step in emergency preparedness is to identify the risks that are already present for an institution and its collections. Analyze these threats to determine which ones have the greatest likelihood of occurring and the greatest potential impact on your organization and its collections. Once threats are known, explore mitigation strategies that can be put in place to reduce risk. A survey and analysis of any known or possible risks is called a *risk assessment* or *vulnerability assessment*.

A risk assessment can be conducted in-house by an institution's staff and/ or volunteers, or a consultant can visit the site(s) and complete an assessment. A consultant will often deliver a written report that states his or her findings in terms of present or potential risks and associated mitigation strategies. Both options have benefits and drawbacks.

If your institution decides to work with a consultant, find a qualified professional to complete the assessment by posting a query on a relevant listserv, contacting the American Institute for Conservation, or asking other institutions who have recently gone through the process. Seek out grants that might fund such a consultation.

If you decide to conduct the assessment in-house, several tools are available for guidance:

- Canadian Conservation Institute (CCI). "Emergency Preparedness for Cultural Institutions: Identifying and Reducing Hazards." CCI Notes 14/2. Ottawa: Canadian Conservation Institute (CCI), 1995. www.cci-icc.gc.ca/publications/ccinotes/enotes-pdf/14-2_e.pdf. Although CCI has not updated this technical note since 1995, they remain a highly trusted institution and this publication is still very relevant today.
- Heritage Preservation. Risk Evaluation and Planning Program. www.heritagepreservation.org/REPP/TGS.html.
- Federal Emergency Management Agency (FEMA). *Integrating Historic Property and Cultural Resource Considerations into Hazard Mitigation Planning.* 2005. www.fema.gov/pdf/fima/386-6_Book.pdf. See "Phase 2: Assess Risks," pp. 2-1–2-39.
- LYRASIS "Disaster Prevention and Protection Checklist." LYRASIS Preservation Services Leaflet. www.lyrasis.org/Products-and-Services/Digital-and-Preservation-Services/~/media/Files/Lyrasis/Preservation%20Files/disasterprevention.ashx.

Table 3.1.

	Pros	Cons
In-House Risk Assessment	• Less costly • Staff members who have an intimate knowledge of the collections and site can pay special attention to issues that a consultant might fail to see • May provide for more flexibility in terms of scheduling • May have an established relationship with local first responders, who can participate in the assessment	• Requires time commitment • Day-to-day work with a collection may cause staff members to become overly familiar, overlooking issues that could be evident to an outside expert
Consultant-Conducted Risk Assessment	• Brings an outside perspective, knowledge, expertise, and experience with conducting risk assessments • Can be seen as an authoritative voice to an institution's director, administration, or board of directors • Can advocate for financial support—excerpts from the report can be included in grant applications or other funding requests	• Consultants almost always charge a fee • Not intimately familiar with the collections • May be scheduling constraints

When assessing your institution, consider these risks:

- Location: Is your building located near a river with low banks? In a neighborhood with a high crime rate? Near highways, railroad tracks, or a nuclear power plant?
- Weather in the region: Is the region prone to heavy snowfall and/or ice storms? Tornados? Earthquakes?

- Building: Is it a historic structure? Does it have a flat roof? Is the basement below the water table? Is construction planned in or around the building? Are there known problems that have not been addressed (e.g., weak floors in the attic or moisture accumulation in the basement)?
- HVAC and other mechanical systems: Are systems antiquated? Are temperature and relative humidity adequately controlled?
- Fire: Does the building have a fire suppression system? Are fire extinguishers on hand, and is staff trained in their use?
- Pests: Are fresh flowers or food allowed in the same areas of the building where collections are used and/or stored? Are there points of entry for insects, rodents, or birds around windows, doors, through the chimney, and so on?
- Security: Is the building alarmed? Are collections storage areas kept locked, with key access only given to certain staff members or volunteers? Do researchers ever use collections without supervision? Are tours self-guided, and if so, are there security cameras to monitor visitors?
- Policies, planning, and records: Are the collections fully inventoried? Are policies and plans in place to govern all aspects of safe stewardship, from collections management to exhibition to theft or damage reporting?
- What has occurred to your institution or similar institutions in the past? Does your building have mold blooms toward the end of each summer? Do your gutters or downspouts get clogged after periods of leaf fall? Have nearby historic sites been recent targets for break-ins or vandalism?

These questions are just examples; possible concerns are extensive. Every institution's list of risks or vulnerabilities will be unique.

Developing an Emergency Plan

Emergency preparedness is not the responsibility of just one person in an institution; rather, all levels of staff, volunteers, and the board must be aware of the plan and should be involved to some extent. Anticipate investing a substantial amount of time in the development of the plan—it is a necessary commitment. Emergency preparedness is not necessarily an expensive endeavor, but will most likely involve some financial investment.

When you develop your plan, always remember that human safety is the most important consideration in any and all situations! Protection of collections and continuity of the institution come second. Do not begin to consider these factors until all individuals have been accounted for, possible injuries assessed, and medical help sought if necessary.

A complete emergency preparedness and response plan should, at a minimum, contain the following information:

A. Table of contents
B. Introduction (use of the document, revision schedule, general facility information)
C. Emergency information sheet
D. Telephone chain and contact information
E. Response outline
F. Collection priorities for recovery
G. Supply lists and recovery/equipment vendors
H. Response tips, handling and salvage techniques
I. Continuity plans for resuming operations and conservation treatment
J. Appendixes (floor plans annotated with the locations of emergency exits, fire extinguishers, emergency and first aid supplies, water shut-off valves, electrical panels, and controls for the HVAC systems; forms; technical bulletins or detailed articles on salvage)

Emergency Information Sheet

It can be very useful to have the most vital emergency preparedness information available on just one sheet so that responders can quickly find important phone numbers without paging through a document. The quick-response sheet can be posted throughout the site in clearly visible locations, such as near fire extinguishers and telephones. Key responders can even carry copies of the sheet with them at all times in a purse or wallet, as well as in their vehicle.

The Council of State Archivists (COSA) developed a one-sheet emergency response tool called the Pocket Response Plan (PReP), which fits on two sides of a legal sheet of paper and can be folded to the size of a credit card. PReP templates for different types of repositories are available here: www.statearchivists .org/prepare/framework/prep.htm.

This sheet should include, at a minimum, phone numbers for local fire departments, police departments, hospitals, and utility companies; a brief list of emergency responders with phone numbers; and emergency shut-off locations within the building. The sheet can also include basic instructions for response and salvage, recovery services, and anything else your institution needs to have available at a glance.

Telephone Chain and Contact Information

In the event of an emergency or disaster, it is very important that all staff and, depending on the institution, possibly all volunteers and board members are reachable.

One staff person, ideally someone with both the authority to make operational decisions and a good knowledge of collections, should be designated head of the chain of command. This person will likely also be the incident commander, the person responsible for overall management of the incident, the response, and overseeing all personnel involved.

Of course the head of the chain will not always be the first to discover an emergency. Perhaps the caretaker of a historic home may notice a building problem in the middle of the night, or a volunteer will notice a leaking pipe while she is reshelving collections. He/she should first call 911 (if the situation involves a crime or a threat to life safety, such as a building collapse, fire, or other hazard to humans) and then notify the head of the chain. The head will notify the next on the list, who will notify the next, and so on. If you call someone and do not reach him or her, leave a message and call the next person on the list.

Ensuring that everyone's contact information is up to date may be one of the most important and overlooked aspects of the plan. Circulate the phone chain on a regular basis, at least annually, so that everyone can check for accuracy, and then be sure to distribute updated copies to everyone if there are changes. Update the chain whenever staff members or volunteers begin or cease employment. It is advisable to collect home addresses as well, but at a minimum list all phone numbers.

It is essential that copies of the phone chain are stored off-site and kept at the homes of key responders. A list of contact information is useless if it is not readily available.

Response Outline

In advance, identify staff members or designated volunteers who will be responsible for the following tasks. Depending on the size of the institution, the magnitude of the incident, and the number of responders on hand, some individuals may need to take on multiple roles.

In a disaster, someone will first need to deem the building safe to enter or reenter. The incident commander should communicate with first responders such as firefighters to ascertain when assessment and recovery can begin.

- Incident commander: All leaders (those responsible for the tasks described below) report to the incident commander; leaders will assign tasks to all other responders. FEMA's Emergency Management Institute has developed the ICS 100, a free online training program that defines in-depth the roles of the incident commander and explains functions of other responders: emilms.fema .gov/IS100b/index.htm.
- Assess the situation: Estimate the type and extent of the damage, the number of personnel needed to complete the work, how long recovery will take, and how much recovery can be done in-house vs. with a commercial disaster recovery service. Ensure proper documentation of the damage (photos, written descriptions, etc.).
- Organize efforts: Deploy work teams. Supervise responders in terms of proper salvage techniques and personal safety.
- Deal with building issues: Evaluate extent and type of damage to site structures and repairs needed. Coordinate all issues leading up to the eventual restoration of the building(s) to normal. Identify locations for response and salvage activities.
- Control the environment: Monitor temperature and relative humidity, if possible. Preventing mold growth is a key consideration.
- Deal with the media: Only one person should communicate with the media. Prepare a simple statement in advance, stating that the institution has implemented its emergency preparedness and response plan.
- Obtain emergency funding/supplies: Someone on the response team should have access to the institution's budget, bank account, and insurance information.
- Provide security: Especially if police have not responded, someone will need to make sure the site is secure.
- Provide human comforts: Responders will need food and drinks throughout the day and will need adequate breaks. Make sure responders are properly dressed and have sufficient personal protective equipment (gloves, protective eyewear, hard hats, etc.).

Collections Priorities

Institutions must develop a prioritized list of collections items that, given accessibility, should be salvaged first in an emergency or disaster. This list can speed recovery and will be especially useful for external responders who are not familiar with the collection.

Consider the following when determining priorities:

- emphasis in collecting area
- current needs to support programs

- difficulty/cost of replacement
- format of material
- historic importance/value
- items on loan

In the midst of recovery, unforeseeable factors will be important to consider. Responders should always consider their own personal safety: even if an object is top on the institution's priority list, do not attempt to salvage it if doing so would be dangerous. When it is safe to do so, responders should focus attention on materials that are at the greatest risk (e.g., boxes of documents sitting in a puddle of water).

Record a list of these priorities with locations, and identify them on floor plans. It can be helpful to include photographs of the objects with this list, so that first responders can quickly recognize the objects.

It is also very important that vital records are either salvaged in the recovery process or available elsewhere. Duplicate copies of essential records, such as telephone lists, personnel information, building floor plans, service contracts, insurance policies, and records documenting collections (inventories, accession records, donor files) should always be stored off-site or backed up electronically to an external hard drive or tape backup that is stored off-site. Relevant staff, volunteers, and board members should keep copies of the full emergency preparedness and response plan at home and in their vehicles.

Supplies

Supplies dedicated for emergency response should be kept on-site in a centralized location, gathered together in a waterproof container or on a cart. If the building is large, the institution may wish to have several of these kits on hand. Determine a safe location with easy access where the supplies will be stored. Be sure to identify their location(s) on a floor plan. For supplies that are not consolidated into response kits (such as vacuum cleaners, ladders, and other large items), compile a list identifying where these items are located.

The Conservation Center for Art & Historic Artifacts (CCAHA) publishes the *Mid-Atlantic Resource Guide for Disaster Preparedness*, which includes a comprehensive list of supplies institutions should have on hand to begin a recovery effort: www.ccaha.org/publications/emergency-resource-guide.

Identify vendors where these supplies can be purchased, in bulk if necessary. Some vendors sell emergency supply kits already compiled, with names like "disaster preparation kit," "collections protection kit," or React Pak. Check archival vendors such as Gaylord (www.gaylord.com) or University Products (www.universityproducts.com).

Set a schedule for checking and replenishing the supplies. Batteries expire; electronic equipment should be plugged in on a regular basis to make sure it still works. Staff must resist the temptation to "borrow" supplies from these kits, even commonly used items such as paper towels or sponges. All supplies necessary for day-to-day cleaning and basic first aid should be readily available elsewhere on-site.

Vendor/Assistance Contacts

Compile a list of all the vendors you may need to contact in an emergency or disaster, with phone numbers. If you have the opportunity, meet and form relationships with experts like conservators, and develop contractual agreements with key vendors in advance. This may expedite purchasing and response time in the moment of need.

The *Mid-Atlantic Resource Guide for Disaster Preparedness* lists numerous types of supplier resources and vendors. Although focus is on the Mid-Atlantic region, the guide is national in scope: www.ccaha.org/publications/emergency-resource-guide.

Response and Basic Salvage Techniques

The plan should include simple instructions for response based on the type of emergency or disaster. This may include contingency plans for bomb threats, storms, electrical failure, fire, medical emergencies, and other possible emergency scenarios.

Also include basic handling and salvage techniques for collections, based on the types of materials the institution collects. When in doubt, always call a conservator, but it will be helpful to know ways of moving, stabilizing, packing, and gently cleaning various formats of collections.

The following is a list of resources for salvage information:

- CCAHA Technical Bulletins and Preservation Resources: www.ccaha.org/publications/technical-bulletins and www.ccaha.org/services/philadelphia-stewardship-resource-center/preservation-resources.
- National Park Service Conserve-O-Grams, Section 21, Disaster Response and Recovery: www.nps.gov/history/museum/publications/conserveogram/cons_toc.html.
- Northeast Document Conservation Center (NEDCC) Preservation Leaflets, Section 3, Emergency Management: www.nedcc.org/resources/leaflets.list.php.

Forming Partnerships

Are there other small historic sites, societies, or museums in your institution's area? Small institutions can benefit from collaboration and resource sharing in many areas, including emergency preparedness. Consider forming a network with other local sites so that you can build upon one another's strengths. This might begin as a simple meeting among staff, volunteers, and/or board members, and has the potential to grow into a strong planning entity.

Institutions can assist each other in the following ways:

- Buy shared supplies.
- Build a network of responders.
- Organize joint training sessions and disaster response exercises.
- Pool resources to rent a cooperative off-site storage space that can be used in the event of a disaster.
- Foster relationships as a network with local first responders.
- Apply for grants together to fund emergency preparedness projects.

Heritage Preservation sponsors the Alliance for Response, a network of local forums for emergency and disaster response that connects cultural heritage institutions with first responders. Consult their website to see what activities and opportunities there are in your area, or for information on forming your own Alliance for Response Network: www.heritagepreservation.org/AfR/index.html.

Testing the Plan and Training

Any policy or plan only exists on paper until it is tested, so training is a major component of emergency preparedness. All staff, volunteers, board members, and anyone else listed in the plan as a responder should be aware of their roles in the plan, know what to do if they are the first on the scene of an emergency, and know evacuation procedures.

One simple, effective way to test the plan is by holding a tabletop exercise. In this type of exercise, an emergency scenario is presented to staff in the form of a narrative. Participants, consulting their institution's plan, must decide what actions to take. The exercise is discussion-based and does not involve hands-on salvage, and therefore can be done at any time. FEMA has sample tabletop exercises available online at www.fema.gov/privatesector/exercises.shtm, as does the California Preservation Program: www.calpreservation.org/disasters/exercise.html.

Other types of essential exercises, like evacuation procedures, must be acted out to be effective. Take a walk through the space to see where fire extinguishers and exits are located. Active fire extinguisher training is messy, but there is a good animated training exercise at www.fireextinguisher.com. If your institution has the space and resources on- or off-site, practice salvage techniques like packing wet books into boxes.

Reviewing and Updating the Plan

An emergency preparedness and response plan will be of little use if the phone chain includes departed employees, the floor plans indicate collections storage locations before a move, or the contact sheet lists companies that have gone out of business.

The plan should be updated on a regular basis, ideally once a year. Set a schedule for review and update, then stick to it. Make sure responders' roles will remain the same, insurance policies are accurate, institutional partnerships and agreements still hold, and handling and salvage information is up-to-date.

At a minimum, update the phone chain, collection priorities, and supply list on a regular basis.

Consistently reviewing the plan will keep its contents fresh in staff members' minds. After all, the best-case scenario is that this plan will never need to be used!

Additional Resources:

California Preservation Program
www.calpreservation.org/disasters
Plan templates, disaster planning exercises, and other resources.

Conservation OnLine
cool.conservation-us.org/bytopic/disasters
Links to publications, supply lists, sample plans, case studies, and more resources.

Coordinated Statewide Emergency Preparedness (COSTEP)
www.nedcc.org/disaster/costep.php
"A planning tool designed to bring together cultural resource institutions with emergency management agencies and first responders."

Council of State Archivists (COSA)
www.statearchivists.org/prepare/framework/prep.htm

The PReP mentioned previously is just one component of COSA's Framework for Emergency Preparedness.

Disaster Mitigation Planning Assistance
matrix.msu.edu/~disaster
A database that allows users to search by region to find services, supplies, and experts for emergency and disaster assistance. Also includes sample plans.

dPlan: The Online Disaster Planning Tool
www.dPlan.org
Developed by NEDCC, dPlan is a free tool that walks you through the steps of writing and updating an emergency preparedness and response plan. Enter information about your institution using the comprehensive fill-in-the-blank template.

Getty Conservation Institute
Dorge, Valerie, and Sharon L. Jones, eds. *Building an Emergency Plan: A Guide for Museums and Other Cultural Institutions.* Los Angeles: The Getty Conservation Institute, 1999. www.getty.edu/conservation/publications/pdf_publications/emergency_plan.pdf.
This helpful book is available full-text online. Regardless of its publication date, the GCI and this book are still considered trusted authorities in the field.

Heritage Preservation
www.heritagepreservation.org
Along with the many resources mentioned above, Heritage Preservation sells helpful quick-reference tools like the *Field Guide to Emergency Response* and *Emergency Response Salvage Wheel.*

Library of Congress
www.loc.gov/preservation/emergprep/index.html
Articles on insurance/risk management, planning, and recovery, as well as an extensive list of links to more resources.

Regional Alliance for Preservation
www.preservecollections.org
A national network of conservation centers that provide information about conservation, preservation, and disaster response. The website includes bibliographies on numerous related topics, including emergency preparedness.

Western State & Territories Preservation Assistance Service (WESTPAS)
http://westpas.org/course_docs.html

Documents used for the WESTPAS "Protecting Library & Archive Collections: Disaster Preparedness, Response & Recovery" workshops, including sample forms.

Notes

1. Dorge, Valerie, and Sharon L. Jones, eds. *Building an Emergency Plan: A Guide for Museums and Other Cultural Institutions*. Los Angeles: The Getty Conservation Institute, 1999.

2. Ibid.

CHAPTER 4

You Can't Keep It All

Rochelle LeMaster

When faced with a plethora of family history items, and nowhere to store them, people often look to donate their own personal pieces of history. Libraries and historical societies of all kinds are often awarded the burden of accepting those donations that may or may not be of some historical or cultural significance. But how does one know? How does an institution determine what stays and what goes? What can be sacrificed and what must be preserved?

In an effort to provide a certain level of transparency, every institution responsible for taking donations, or "gifts," should have a gifts policy in place. A gifts policy used in conjunction with your mission statement not only provides guidance to staff but also protects your institution from certain issues when it comes to housing, handling, and ownership rights.

What to Keep

The purpose of a gifts policy is to clarify the items that you will and will not bring into your collection. When accepting donations, the following should be considered: preservation environment, item condition, budget, space, purpose, and ownership rights.

ASSESSMENT 1. PRESERVATION ENVIRONMENT:
A BOOK IS NOT A PHOTOGRAPH

What can you save? The emphasis here is on *can*. Do you have access to cold storage? Is your institution equipped with a special room for film? Temperature and humidity levels for film storage should be constant, at a maximum of 50 degrees F and 50 percent RH. If you cannot provide this specialized type of environment, then there should be a clear statement in your gifts policy that states you cannot accept or preserve film. Many a donor will have reel-to-reel film containing homemade family movies, and will believe it to be in the best interest of the community to donate those items to your institution for future generations. Look at your environment and be truthful with potential donors. Don't accept items you can't properly house.

This step alone will begin to define your gifts policy, stating clearly to you, your staff, and the public what formats you can and cannot accept.

Preservation environment includes:

- temperature and humidity control
- shelving options
- lighting
- cleanliness of storage area
- care and handling

Environmental Requirements

For all formats: A dark environment is best. Indoor lights, if fluorescent, should be glazed to prevent UV damage. Window glass can also be glazed if needed. A constant temperature and RH are always desired. Dusting and cleaning should be a regularly scheduled activity. Clean cotton gloves are preferred when handling any fragile items.

Books: Stood on end and not packed too tightly on shelves, books do well in temperatures 75 degrees F or lower, with a 50 percent RH. Store away from windows. Steel or metal shelving is preferred. Wood shelves may be used if they have been properly sealed.

Cassette tapes, open reels, discs: For medium-term storage, temperature should be set between 65 and 70 degrees F and 45 to 50 percent RH. If long-term storage is planned, then these levels change to 45 or 50 degrees F and 20 to 30 percent RH. These items should always stand upright, on end, and be checked regularly for certain levels of deterioration.

Motion picture film and slides: These items should be kept constant, at a maximum of 50 degrees F and 50 percent RH. Films should not be wound too tightly. Store film and slides in metal cases or plastic containers when possible.

Laid flat, film should not be stacked more than twelve inches high. Because of the wide variety of film types, it is wise to contact the International Federation of Film Archives (FIAF) for specifics on varying types of deterioration. Slides can be stored in PVC-free and acid-free sheeting, or stood on end in archival containers.

Photographs: Temperature should be at a constant 68 percent F and a 30 to 40 percent RH. If cold storage is a possibility, color photographs should be stored at 40 degrees F or below to ensure the longest life. Each photograph should be stood on end and stored in nonacidic containers. Clean cotton gloves are recommended when handling. PVC-free plastic sheeting of archival quality is appropriate for family albums. If possible, keep negatives and print materials separate. All tape, paperclips, and rubber bands should be removed.

Blueprints: Store laid flat, separated by archival sheeting, preferably in appropriate shallow steel drawers.

Maps, posters, documents, manuscripts: House at a temperature of 72 degrees F, and 35 percent (or below) RH. These items are best stored when laid flat or hung and housed in dark, cool, and dry locations.

Newspapers: Stack neatly in shallow boxes with lids to keep clear of dust and sunlight. Store boxes up off the floor, and away from exterior walls to keep away from moisture.

Once you have decided which formats your organization can keep, it is then necessary to look at the condition of those incoming items.

ASSESSMENT 2. CONDITION: CORRESPONDENCE AND OTHER SCRAPS OF PAPER

What defines culture? What defines a historical relic that one day may help to explain the whole of our society to future civilizations? Is it good enough to save? While these questions are laced with ethical and moral concerns, we must remember one thing: it's not about what you want to keep; it's about what you can afford to keep. The condition of every single item you allow into your collection must be considered.

- If the item is damaged, are you or the organization you work for in the position to conserve or digitize this important piece of history immediately?
- Can you find a less damaged example worth saving?
- How much will it cost to keep (digitize, migrate to a new format, store)?
- Has another institution already restored/conserved/digitized this item?
- Is it a piece of war correspondence of which you already have more than two hundred examples? What makes this item a better specimen of our society, or at least the society you are trying to preserve?

- Is it local? First and foremost, as an institution it is your responsibility to preserve those items that are local to your community. As other institutions will do the same, there is no need to take in items from some distance away.
- Is it moldy or in a state of deterioration that would require either attention or specific housing requirements (e.g., archival box or plastic)?

Once answered, these questions should help you decide whether to keep the item. If it is a history of one of your town's founding families, and you have the means to either store it appropriately in a controlled environment or digitize it, then accept the item in its less than fair condition, knowing that you must conserve the item before preserving.

ASSESSMENT 3. BUDGET: WHAT CAN YOU AFFORD?

While budget is often the most unpleasant aspect of collection development to address, it is often the easiest to answer. Again, here, the emphasis is on *can*. Chances are you can preserve items to some degree.

To preserve something in a library or historical society, the primary concern, and often the cheapest, is a controlled environment. Set the thermostat, and

Bare Bones: What to Keep When You Don't Have Money

While money is needed for many things, there are some items that will require very little actual money after acquisition, as long as a proper stable environment is provided.

- Books: Books have a life span of about forty to sixty years before deterioration is complete and require little more than not being packed onto a shelf too tightly. Regular dusting and placing books away from direct light also help to prolong their life.
- Newspapers: Apart from offering an excellent history of your community, newspapers are easily kept in shallow boxes and, unless your organization is undertaking conservation efforts, fairly low-cost to keep.
- Realia: Items such as ticket stubs from your local theater, coins, election pins, textiles, and the like tend to be one-of-a-kind items. While your institution may not be in the position to conserve those items, they will draw attention to your collection.

Remember to keep a stable environment, dust the shelves, keep items oriented in the right way (e.g., books standing up, newspapers laid flat), keep items away from light, and handle them gently. If all this is done, you will be able to maintain your collection for a very long time on very little cost.

keep it constant. Adjust the lighting, dust the shelves, and make sure each item in your collection is housed the right way.

If you have obtained monies with which to preserve this collection and can afford digitization, then it is wise to do so. Keep in mind, however, that once you have reached the capability of digitization, you have also committed yourself to the consistent migration of the content with which you work. While the paper copy of a World War II letter may only live for forty years, a digital copy will be out of date and possibly inaccessible in ten years' time.

ASSESSMENT 4. SPACE: WHEN THERE IS TOO MUCH STUFF

When it comes down to space, a different aspect of the items you intend to keep must be considered. Up until this point we've assessed the containers and the proper environment required to preserve that item, the issue of space requires a look at content. Consider:

- Is anyone else saving this content already? Are you or the organization you work for the repository for your county? Or state? The blueprints of the town hall and original maps of your community are more than likely already being housed at other local offices.
- Call local colleges, university libraries, historical societies, special libraries, and organizations to make sure they have not already digitized the items you are considering for inclusion into your collection.
- Is there a clause in your gifts policy on duplication of material or similar materials? How many color slides does one need of a rosebush specimen?
- By including a clause regarding duplication of content, in conjunction with a full waiver of rights, you are then able to discard items as you wish if the need has already been met. Are you keeping more than one copy of a local author's book, a family history, a commercially available title about the county in which you live?
- You have acquired a large box of photographs containing mostly people and portraits. Are the people in the photographs identified? If not, then it is up to you and your organization to decide how to handle unidentified photos. Keep in mind that if there is no plan to identify the subjects in those photographs, they will provide little to future generations.
- Are all items in your collection in accordance with the organization's mission statement?
- Are your large bound family histories available through the LDS Family History Library? If the family is well researched, the information may already be available through another reliable source.

If your mission statement allows, and your gifts policy supports, consider keeping the following formats.

Books: Maintain a good representation of your local history. This includes complete family histories, photographs of the community (new buildings and roads), samples of brochures for the community theater, newspaper articles about elections, and ticket stubs from a local amusement park or theater. Complete histories of local disasters should also be saved if possible.

Cassette tapes, open reels, discs, motion picture film, and slides: These items deteriorate quickly. Artistic material from local recording artists and performers should be considered for acquisition. Footage of any news-related items should also be considered if it can be migrated to a more stable format.

Photographs: Through the American Memory Project, headed by the Library of Congress, much of our nation's photographic history is already being preserved digitally. The steadfast rule for photos is that if you cannot identify the people or place in the picture after some research, then the photo should not be kept. Photos require a particular environment in which to live and should not be kept unless there is space, budget, and purpose.

Blueprints: A history of the development of building styles in your locality should be saved. Note that these items may already be preserved through your local engineer or map office.

Bare Bones: What to Keep When You Don't Have Space

- Do you have the right preservation environment available to house this item?
- Do you have money to conserve the item, if needed?
- Do you have the money to migrate the item to a new format if and when needed?
- Do you plan to include the item in a special collection to be highlighted or viewed by the public?
- Is the item of local origin?
- Is this the only item of its kind in your collection?

If you answered yes to all of these questions, then you can keep the item you are considering for accession. These questions should apply to all of the items in your collection. Essentially it comes down to what you *can* keep. Think of your cherished pieces of history and culture as pets. If you can't afford to feed your pet, then you can't keep it. If you can't provide a comfortable place for your pet to live, then you can't keep it. If you're going to keep your pet locked up in a cage where no one can see it, then you probably shouldn't have it.

Maps, posters, documents, manuscripts: Keep local maps and items highlighting local authors or celebrities.

Newspapers: Local elections are top on the priority list in this category and should be kept. Be aware, though, that there is a mass movement to digitize and microfilm newspapers through the United States Newspaper Program (USNP). It is probable that the paper you are striving to save has already been digitized and you can now get rid of its deteriorated container.

ASSESSMENT 5. PURPOSE: ARE YOU SAVING CONTENT OR CONTAINER?

It is important to understand what you are saving and why. This should be addressed in your organization's mission statement, but a clear definition of what you are saving is a key component to your gifts policy. Do you live in the town where the first wax cylinder was made? If not, chances are you don't need to save an actual wax cylinder. Do you live in the town where a famous composer recorded his first opus on wax cylinder? If so, then by all means attempt to retrieve that important audio content from the wax cylinder. A digital copy of the sound you are able to retrieve will be far more important that the actual container when the container itself is so difficult to properly preserve.

The same goes for many audiovisual items. Magnetic media such as reel-to-reel film, VHS tapes, and cassette tapes are susceptible to varying levels of deterioration if not properly stored. In smaller establishments, especially, it is best to make it a priority to migrate content from unstable containers as soon as possible. Consider why you are saving the items you allow to be donated, and then provide the environment required for those items.

ASSESSMENT 6. DE-ACCESSIONING AND RIGHTS: WHAT DO YOU MEAN YOU THREW IT AWAY?

Often we are faced with boxes and trunks full of various family items the donor is certain we can use in some capacity. With a gifts policy in place, you can simply and easily go through the box and pull all the formats you do not acquire for your collection and return them to the owner or discard them. Then you can check the items that are left for condition, assessing each one based on the criteria mentioned above. It is important to remember that a gifts policy is put in place to outline what you *can* keep. The items that you *want* to keep, or believe to be important, cannot be kept if you have not considered the following stipulations:

- Can you provide the proper preservation environment?
- Is the item condition satisfactory?
- Have ownership rights been waived?
- Do you have the budget to take in the item?
- Do you have space?

But what do you do with the stuff you can't use?

It is difficult for professionals in our field to stomach, but if the item does not fit into the parameters of your gifts policy, then you should throw it away. I know it's difficult. If you find that a valuable item you cannot keep is too good to throw away, it is best to offer it to interested institutions. Conservatories, universities, and larger organizations are sometimes able to take on historical documents or items of interest. Quite often, though, you'll find that not all items need to be saved. Physical objects aren't meant to last forever. It is simply our job to see that some of what we see now is able to be passed on.

A good gifts policy always has a statement about ownership rights. Provide each donor with a waiver form to sign over all rights to your organization. Some donors may feel uncomfortable with this. It is always in the best interest of the organization to not have exceptions to this rule, for then insurance and extra liability issues (security, safety, borrowing, handling, etc.) would have to be considered. Exceptions, however, are yours to make if necessary.

Ideally, a waiver will be needed for every donation. A waiver will:

- provide the organization with the rights to conserve, preserve, and/or migrate the item content if needed;
- give the organization rights to de-accession the items if they are in poor condition or no longer in accordance with the mission statement, at any time.

Structuring a Gifts Policy

Decide and define what is important to your organization and the community. Use the aforementioned assessments to determine what you can keep.

Begin by including a simple statement about content; for example: "We will strive to collect local family histories, as well as items concerning local elections, the A. I. Root Company, and items documenting the physical development of our community."

The above statement is clear, but vague enough for some legroom. It does not state *all* local family histories, so you are able to de-accession items in poor condition. It also does not state what election items you aim to collect, so if you do not have the proper storage environment for newspapers or buttons, you are not obligated to keep them. Note the mention of a company, which may or may not have its own historical collection already in place. You always want to make sure that you are not duplicating someone else's efforts. It is also important to understand, as an organization that preserves history, the necessity of keeping items related to bridges, buildings, streets, and landmarks. Again, it would be wise to check with other area offices, preserving this history so that your organization does not duplicate this effort.

In addition to the above statement, you will also want to include at least one sentence on item types or formats, depending on the physical capabilities of your establishment. Include a simple statement on format; for example: "We are unable to house blueprints, reel-to-reel film, illuminated manuscripts, and 35mm color film."

By providing a statement addressing the content and format type, you allow for a smooth acquisition process of all donated items, and make clear to the donor what you cannot take.

Last, include a simple statement on ownership rights; for example: "All ownership rights are surrendered to the organization at time of donation."

The gifts policy is meant to be part of your organization's mission statement and, when structured as mentioned here, will be able to provide your organization with a clear, concise outline for the accession and de-accession of donations.

PART II

NEWSPAPERS

CHAPTER 5

Balancing Selection and Digitization: Selecting Nineteenth- and Early Twentieth-Century Newspaper Titles for Online Access

Athena Jackson

When embarking on a mass historical newspaper digitization project, three basic points must immediately be considered:

1. It is of utmost importance to define the parameters and goals of the online newspaper collection.
2. The level of access desired will dictate much of the behind-the-scenes work required to digitize a collection.
3. Given the amount of digital storage and maintenance, the amount of titles that will be digitized may vary. Because of this potential limitation, number 1 becomes more important to the integrity of the project.

Overarching all of these points should be the concern that the titles chosen best represent the mission of the project and are historically relevant to researchers and scholars.

This chapter will suggest tips for working with ad hoc historical committees or advisory boards in historical newspaper title selection to ensure historical relevancy and incorporating digitization specifications into the final selection process. It closes with some considerations of the implications of offering a curated and sample corpus online and ways we can make certain our users are aware of those newspapers not yet introduced to the digital realm.

Challenges such as organizing the work of a geographically disparate advisory board, prioritizing microfilm reel analysis based on both the board's selections and digitization compliance, and ensuring temporal coverage of the state's history were met with diverse results, but all were opportunities to learn and develop expertise. From this experience, our team accrued valuable insight into curating the historical and digitization selection of nineteenth- and early twentieth-century newspapers for online access. It is with this in mind that we hope to impart useful tips for similarly derived projects of any scale.

Background: National Digital Newspaper Program at Louisiana

Preservation of newspapers in the United States received a digital upgrade with the creation of the National Digital Newspaper Program (NDNP).[1] This program continues the efforts of its predecessor, the United States Newspaper Project (USNP), which empowered states to identify, collate, and microfilm extant newspapers in their holdings. NDNP furthers this activity by supporting, via grant funds, the digitization of a more curated selection (one hundred thousand pages per award cycle) of microfilmed newspapers from each awarded state. The benefits of digitizing newspapers include not only preservation of the content but also enabling a level of access that microfilm and/or print copies may not often provide, particularly if the digitization includes making the newspapers keyword searchable or provides searchable metadata that bolsters researchers' potential to identify useful content for their work. With such efforts, though, comes the challenge to ensure that the titles selected best reflect a region's history, since not all newspapers will be digitized in the first go-round.

For NDNP, participants are required to seek the advice of an advisory board made up of scholars and librarians familiar with the awarded state's history. From the start, we were faced with many questions. How do we go about prioritizing and identifying the candidate titles for inclusion while at the same time remaining cognizant of the technical limitations of digitizing a hard-to-read microfilm reel? What if a hard-to-read reel had some of the most desirable snippets of history on its fragile film? What, then, are the implications of not including a title just because the integrity of the film did not lend itself to digitization? Is there a solution to ensuring the online collection will accurately reflect our state's history?

Defining the Online Collection

Most online collections have an all-encompassing theme or purpose to guide the collection makeup. For our project, we were given clear instructions by our grant providers: digitize a collection of historically valuable, microfilmed, English-language newspaper titles from Louisiana that covered the years 1860 to 1922 and that were also Optical Character Recognition–friendly.[2] As in the case for NDNP, defining your digital collection may include determining such specifications as: page and/or title count, longevity, date ranges, language(s), temporal breadth, and geographic coverage. This is particularly important if your project is not going to be an all-inclusive project (that is, leaving no print newspaper behind). If not dictated by an external party (e.g., grant specification), determining these boundaries is best suited for a committee of scholars and/or librarians who are well versed in the regional history and the newspaper collection's extent.

Remember, making these decisions early may reduce the potential for scope creep as the project progresses. Once your parameters are set, you can begin equipping your advisory board with the materials they may require to appraise the content of individual titles. Indeed, if they do not have access to an actual reel of microfilmed newspaper, this reference source becomes even more important to their selection process.

Picking Your Advisory Board Members

Typically your historical advisory board should be drawn from a pool of scholars familiar with regional and/or state history. For most historical newspaper digitization projects, a good sample of practitioners would be: historians, journalists, genealogists, educators, and librarians/archivists. Overall, make sure your board is:

• composed of a diverse group from many communities of practice, and
• balanced in research strengths to make certain that important historical events are familiar to at least one member of your board.

Tips for Working with Advisory Boards

Where does one start when working with your historical advisory committee for this kind of project? Is it better to choose the most digitization-friendly microfilmed newspapers as their first options for selection? Would offering the entire list of newspaper holdings regardless of digitization readiness be a more inclusive way to ensure a comprehensive assessment? Remember that resources, cost, and time play a crucial role in getting to a final list. In a perfect world, it would be most prudent to allow a comprehensive review of all titles. However, if your parameters are such that you can preselect titles for the advisory board to consider, it would not detract from the overall mission of the project. For example, we were able to filter out titles whose date ranges extended outside the 1860–1922 range, as well as those that included non-English languages, because the goals for the project were clearly defined. Bottom line: consider your goals and what you hope to accomplish up against the amount of time you have to carefully review viable candidate titles. Once you have your title list ready for review, you can begin preparing reference materials for your advisory board to use when evaluating individual titles.

In this day and age, a committee is most often composed of individuals from geographically disparate regions. Deploying online community technologies can become your best tools for ensuring that your team remains focused on a project in a similar fashion, regardless of where they live. Since our advisory board was from all points of the compass, we opted to use a free wiki service[3] to disseminate information for their reference. Remember, when choosing an online apparatus for communication, you must build in time to acquaint those who have never used wikis or any other form of online discussion tools to their features and uses. On the wiki (or any portal you choose for disseminating information) keep the following in mind:

- Let your advisory board think broadly in terms of historical evaluation, but explicitly define boundaries and note the potential digitization limitations early.
  - List every parameter you designed for your project. Historical consultants may suggest alternate titles they prefer based on individual research. It is always good practice to point intrepid advisory board members to the list of parameters as a reminder of what boundaries were set for the project.
  - Explain plainly the challenges of digitization specifications and meeting them vis-à-vis older materials that may have suffered deterioration over time. While advisory board members are encouraged to consider all titles in terms of selection, not all of those chosen titles will make it into the online project. Look to the digitization specifications set forth by the project team and share these details with your historical consultants.
- Enable access or create references specific to aiding in the title selection process. Keep in mind that every resource should provide information to support the final objectives for selection, particularly with regard to securing historical relevancy in your final collection. For any project consider including some or all of the following:
  - an advisory board roster and contact information for project staff;
  - a comprehensive list of newspaper titles on microfilm for the targeted dates or a filtered list in which titles that do not meet the basic criteria for the project are removed (prelabel titles with as many qualifiers as possible; we identified such aspects as which titles were commercially digitized, which were too scattered/too short, those at an alternate location, and titles missing or borrowed from the collection);

- a timeline of major events;
- historical information about as many newspapers and major regions as available;
- access and links to any resources available online that may describe the historical eras or newspaper content;
- a list or map of major towns and cities the newspapers cover;
- the OCLC bibliographic record;
- the title selection criteria clearly stated, such as your project's main boundaries and digitization expectations; and
- any publicity announcements and links to articles regarding mention of the project. It is good to keep any reference to the project on the board's radar to reaffirm the value of their work to the general public.

Incorporating Digitization Specifications into the Selection Process

With regard to access, migration from analog to digital brings its own challenges as online researcher expectations must be considered. For example, having the ability to search the text by keyword or to receive a legible image for browsing of online materials may be specific goals outlined for the online collection. Will simply putting the newspaper images online with basic bibliographic information be enough? Will enabling keyword searching or subject indexing be supported by the resources allotted for the project? The more features applied to the project, the more one must ensure that the digitized pages will be able to be manipulated and explored at the most advanced level of searching. These concerns should be addressed at the onset of the project because they will guide what you choose for the selection pool of titles.

Title Assessment: A Survey

After you supply your advisory board with reference resources, the title selection process can commence. For our group, we decided to deploy a survey. Because our committee was from different parts of Louisiana (and two were out of state), we opted to use an online survey that would enable each member to evaluate a title and respond via a Likert Scale option (basically, 1 to 5). We linked the survey to our project wiki; all resources were available while the advisory board members reviewed titles.

Why a survey? Statistics can open a whole new level of justification for title selection. One need not be an expert statistician to capture just the basic data that would illustrate how the newspapers are ordered for inclusion into an online collection. By quantifying where possible, you are able to point to an understandable and plain data set that can be referenced when questions arise (which they inevitably will) as to why certain titles are or are not on the final cut.

When dealing with a large corpus of materials, only a fraction may be chosen for inclusion in your digitization project. For example, of the 578 total titles reviewed, approximately 56 were chosen for our 2009–2011 project. As well, we were confined by our grant provider's parameters: a specific range of years, English only, and preference for those titles that had yet to see the light of a scanner, hence our notation of commercially digitized titles. Being able to justify why the titles were chosen becomes more crucial when your resulting online collection represents only a small portion of your overall holdings.

Survey Methodology

As a new participant, our methodology in choosing titles was deliberate. We decided to purchase (for less than $100) a short-term subscription to Survey Monkey.[4] Utilizing this tool, the advisory board rated the titles on a Likert Scale according to each title's geographic and research value and its representation of diverse communities throughout Louisiana's history. The language for our survey was pulled directly from the project's goals, as we wanted to quickly review data that revealed the most historically relevant titles that fit the mission of the project.

Phrase your questions so that each title can be assessed for its own merit. We provided the board with detailed instructions on how to complete the surveys. The titles were divided into multiple surveys according to parish (county), and board members could save their survey responses and return to complete them when convenient. Because we had the additional challenge of ensuring that we included mostly long-running titles while not overlooking the gems in a shorter-run newspaper, we separated the shorter-running titles and allowed the board to evaluate those as well. Along with the Likert Scale question/response format for each title, we provided the reviewers a space for comments that might have illuminated their ranking (e.g., identifying a title with a unique political perspective or noticing an industry-focused periodical).

When you have a knowledgeable advisory board (those who are aware of the regional history and geography), using a scale for measuring contextual value may prove an ideal exercise. It is with this understanding that you will not assemble a board that will need basic instruction on the history of your region or the basic content of your newspapers.

After the titles review, it will be time to choose among the top-ranked newspapers those items that are digitization-ready. Always adhere to the specifications required by a given project considering electronic format and delivery. Is it just going to be a scan or is it intended to be keyword searchable? A few basic rules of thumb to use when plainly explaining to board why a certain title will not be acceptable for digitization:

- When it comes to historical newspapers, most content will be on microfilm. Even if you are primarily using print source materials, you will have to consider that search-friendly source materials may be a challenge to identify. Historical newspapers are, well, old. Therefore, when you are thinking about a digitized historical newspaper, try to refrain from assuming it will be as easy as scanning the daily that drops on your doorstep every morning.
- If it is in microfilm format, you will have to consider all of the physical aspects of the reel. What is the composition of the film? What's the reduction ratio? Look to standards set by other digitization projects to establish your own parameters based on your resources and project's expectations.
- If it is in print, then consider the physical state of the paper and the type of scanner you will be using. For example, how will the imaging work with oversized newspapers if all you have is a small flatbed scanner?

One major tip to take away from our experience is to remember that if a title is widely regarded for its research value, it should usually trump any concerns over its digitization readiness. Therefore, there will be times when you may make the executive decision to digitize a not-so-pretty image of a newspaper; it could be torn, fragmented, or merely too dark to be searchable by keyword. Of course, this should not be the rule for all titles, as we aim to always make certain our online collections are capable of being searched. However, when your advisory board is unanimous in selecting a title, it would be incumbent upon the team to do its best to make its digital surrogate available for searching.

After Digitization—What to Do with the Digitization-*Un*friendly

While exceptions to the rules are expected, many titles will not see the light of a scanner. This does not mean that they do not contain inherently historically valuable content. It is vital to the integrity of the collection that the team devises a way to shed light on those titles that may only remain available in print or microfilm format for the foreseeable future.

Our team has come up with a few ways to inform our users of those newspapers not yet introduced to the digital realm:

- Bridge the digitization project to the larger landscape of available materials. Linking to catalog records of related titles, generating detailed subject guides, and soliciting collaboration projects with scholars are currently on our radar.
- Identify funding streams to continue digitization. We have recently been awarded a renewal grant to digitize an additional one hundred thousand pages that will allow us to go as far back as 1836 in this new cycle. As well, the new grant specifications include acceptance of non-English titles, and we are thrilled to add important French-language newspapers from Louisiana.
- Incorporate caveats at your project website. Make sure your public knows this is only a selection of newspapers, carefully vetted for research value by reputable scholars. Nonetheless, many more titles are available for review and encouraged for use.

Conclusion

Historical newspapers are invaluable to our collective memory as a nation. It is an understatement to remind readers that the more our users depend on online resources for research, the more we must do our best to provide access to information that best suits their typical needs. In the digital realm, librarians must continue to educate our users that while we want to continue enabling access and use from the comfort of a computer (or PDA) screen, there is more to our collection than meets the eye. Providing links to information about our collective holdings within these digital spaces will make this very fact more apparent to our researchers.

We learned a lot from this project. And we continue to think of ways to enhance our digital collection by noting the valuable material still available in analog format. Someday we may be able to access almost everything online. But in a world that straddles the digital and analog realms, what we decide to make available online must be carefully considered and enriching to our users. Having a strong historical advisory committee that also understands the challenges of digitization is a best first step forward.

Notes

1. www.neh.gov/projects/ndnp.html.
2. OCR enables keyword searching, but depending on the clarity of the original image, the mileage may vary.
3. We used PBWorks: pbworks.com.
4. www.surveymonkey.com.

CHAPTER 6

Indexing Your Local Newspapers on Microfilm

Kelly Zackmann

Newspapers are an invaluable source of information on the history of a town because they record events as they happen. Delving into newspaper microfilm provides a researcher the opportunity to go back in time and relive events using a primary source of information. The newspaper provides information for journalists, authors, genealogists, or the general public interested in researching local history.

While microfilmed newspapers provide this wonderful opportunity, anyone who has done research with microfilmed newspapers knows that without an index, it is a most wearisome task. Unless the researcher has exact dates of events, microfilmed newspapers can be overwhelming and nearly impossible to navigate because they are a resource that cannot be keyword searched or filtered. A newspaper index entry contains an article's title, the date it was published, the page number where it appeared, the name of the newspaper, and any subject headings specifically related to the article.

Indexing a backlog of a microfilmed daily press takes years. It creates invaluable efficiency when an organization is unable to obtain a digital archive of a newspaper. Indexing a newspaper can also be done with minimal technology and training and can be accomplished utilizing volunteer staff.

Before the computer age, newspapers were indexed into card catalogs. This required a lot of index cards and typing ribbon. Nowadays, we can use computers to streamline the indexing process. While the data for your index can be gathered into an expensive library database, it is not altogether necessary. Instead, it can be gathered into a simple spreadsheet or out-of-the-box database that is either standard on most computers or available via open access. Data can also be gathered in a simple word processing document and formatted into portable document format (PDF) that can be uploaded to a website and shared with the community remotely. There is no need to spend a lot of money. All you need is time and patience to gather the data. Once the data is gathered, it can be migrated into different and updated applications.

Process for Developing Your Index

WHAT DO YOU WANT TO INDEX?

Before assigning staff and volunteers to the project, you must set up the process and determine a few things. The backbone of your project will be determining what data to gather. Generally, you will index all local articles and obituaries. Do not waste time and storage space on articles about world or regional events because these articles will be archived or indexed by major newspapers and others. You should only focus on those articles that will not be picked up by other entities, such as those affecting your local community and articles written by local journalists. You may also want to include other vital statistics such as birth notices and wedding announcements, as oftentimes these can be as informative as an obituary. Newspapers often cover weddings with photos and full-length articles, providing information such as the names of those who attended and their relationship to the couple. You should always index articles that cover specific people within the community, specific places and landmarks, unusual or major crimes and accidents, local politics, economic and statistical reports, major sporting events, and any feature articles about your community's history.

Do not index incidental items such as upcoming event announcements, weather reports, gardening columns, crime briefs, fanciful stories, routine notices, and other such material unless the items specifically affect your community in some way. For example, include any articles about the weather that might have made a significant impact on a neighborhood or family, such as major flooding or windstorms. You may also wish to include a routine column if it is written by a well-known local personality. If you decide to do this, be sure to also index the columnist's name.

GEOGRAPHIC AREA

In addition to determining the type of information you will gather, you must also determine the geographic area of focus. If there is another newspaper in a nearby community that covers local news for that area, and there is another library or historical society that should be responsible for that area, you may want to omit articles relating to that area from your index. You may want to focus only on the area stated in your collection development policy for local materials. Narrowing down your focus will help you achieve your goal faster, but later you may wish you had included surrounding communities. In any case, once you make the decision, stick with it, as consistency is important in your indexing project.

HOW MANY NEWSPAPERS DO YOU NEED TO INDEX?

You also need to determine which newspapers you will include in your index. If you have multiple microfilmed newspapers in your collection, you will have to decide which of those newspapers your community will want to access. Determine if any other entities are already indexing newspapers, and if so omit those titles. If no other entity is currently indexing any of your holdings, you may wish to include them all. This determination will also help you decide on the geographic area you will include in your index.

SUBJECT HEADINGS

Once you have decided which newspapers you will index, the data you will gather, and the geographic area to include, you must then get to the heart of your index: subject headings. Good indexing is accomplished by ensuring that your subject headings are consistent, relevant, and specific. You do not have to predict all the subject headings that you will ever need because you can add new headings as needs arise. However, you should develop a good basic list before you begin the actual indexing. Your subject heading list is necessary to guide your staff and any volunteers who may contribute to your indexing project.

There are many sources you can use to determine subject headings. Some indexers recommend traditional sources such as *Anglo-American Cataloging Rules* and *Sears Subject Headings*. The Library of Congress Subject Authority Headings (authorities.loc.gov/) is another source and is available online for free. You can also consult with other organizations that have already created a subject authority file to help you determine headings for your index. However, be sure to create subject headings that are specific to your community. While the above-mentioned sources are good places to start, do not rely on them to perfectly fit your particular project. These sources are designed for cataloging books, not indexing newspapers, and oftentimes the headings can appear ambiguous to the general library user. The Library of Congress Subject Authority File can indicate how to format your subject headings, but be sure to modify them to meet your specific needs. For example, consider an article about a local school named Washington High School. If your community is small you may decide to format your subject heading as it would likely appear in the Library of Congress headings: Schools—High Schools—Washington High School. However, if you have a larger community with dozens of schools, you may wish to create a separate subject heading for each individual school, simply calling this one Washington High School. This may also fit if you have a very small community with only one high school. Determine how you will format subheadings for other subjects with specific names such as businesses, clubs and organizations, buildings, and airports. Also understand that an article about a specific person will require a subject heading for that person.

Once you are ready to create your basic list of subject headings, organize it as a word processing document and keep it safe. You will need to provide a copy of this list to all indexers involved in your project. Then you must make sure someone is assigned the task of keeping the file up to date. As times change, so does our language, so headings must be kept contemporary and relevant. There should be one person or position assigned to update headings to reflect contemporary language and also to add new headings as necessary. Too many people with this authority can cause problems with heading format and consistency.

Who Will Gather the Data, and How Will It Be Done?

Now that you have the basis for your index, you must determine who will and how to physically gather the data. In order to index a newspaper, individuals will be assigned to comb through the newspaper microfilm and note what will be added to the index. You may want to assign different aspects of indexing to different individuals. For example, you may decide to assign article indexing to individuals who can effectively determine subject headings without personal bias. You can assign individuals who are unfamiliar with subject headings to the task of indexing obituaries and other vital statistics because the only subjects that will be assigned to these entries are the type of vital statistic (obituary, birth, or marriage) and the names of the individuals in the article. It will be like filling out a form, so there will not need to be any interpretation of a written article.

If you are able to view microfilm on a computer, you may want to have an indexer enter data right into a database or spreadsheet simultaneously if possible. Using two windows on a screen can accomplish this, if the indexer can see both windows clearly and comfortably. If you are only able to view microfilm on a microfilm reader or in a single computer window, then you may want to create a preprinted form or blank spreadsheet and have the data gatherers manually transcribe information from the microfilm for later entry. Such forms will have to include fields for the article title, the publication name, the date the item was published, the page number, and subject headings. While this method sounds tedious, you will find that as the process moves forward and the gatherers become accustomed, the process will become relatively simple.

You Know What Data to Gather. Now What?

Once you have data gathered, you have to put it someplace. Hopefully, you have determined where you will be putting your data at least for the time being. Remember, you can migrate the data into different applications or databases once it is gathered, so there is no need to re-index a newspaper in the future unless you fail to back up the data or to keep a paper copy in a safe place.

SPREADSHEETS

One simple way to organize your data is by entering it into a simple spreadsheet. This can be a nice way to organize data, particularly if you plan to provide your index in a paper format for public use. You can sort your index by date range or alphabetically by subject and print copies to compile into simple binders that can be cataloged and shelved. You can also sort your indexes by subject or by date and convert them into PDF files that can be uploaded to your organization's website. Spreadsheets are generally easy to import into other applications as well, so you can migrate your documents into newer file formats or newer applications, and the data can usually be imported into a database. The main drawback to gathering your data into spreadsheets is that you may need to limit the number of subject headings allowed for each article to keep the size of your spreadsheet manageable, because each subject heading will require a separate entry for the article on an additional row.

WORD PROCESSING SOFTWARE

Another data gathering option is the word processing document. It is possible to create an index using columns or by inserting tables into a document. While this option may be a bit awkward and clunky, it is an option for an organization lacking funds for an elaborate database setup. It is also easy to print and easy to migrate to newer formats, and a simple text file can be kept as a backup; should the file be neglected over the years, it should still be readable with any computer at a later date. You can also easily convert the file into PDF format using free software or scan the index using optical character recognition (OCR) technology that will make the index searchable by keyword. Also, a PDF file can be uploaded to your organization's website very easily.

DATABASES

Most computers are preloaded with a simple relational database. These databases sometimes look much like a spreadsheet, but relational databases are designed specifically to be manipulated to create data-sorted reports. These reports can be uploaded to the Internet and can be searched very efficiently. You can also print reports to bind and place on a shelf. If you are unfamiliar with such an application, and your library is equipped with an information systems or information technology department, you probably have professionals who can assist you with your database creation. You can ask your IT department if they have the ability to create a dedicated database that could be accessed through your organization's website by the public. If not, they should be able to help you format an out-of-the-box database for your project.

If you have an IT department at your disposal, you will need to work with them closely to help them understand your project so that they can customize a database for you. They will need to know how many different resources are being indexed, and you will share with them your subject authority file and discuss which fields will be searchable. You may also have to help them determine the size of the database. It is relatively simple to estimate the total amount of items you will likely index over the course of the project. You will need to take a sample of your newspaper(s) and count the number of articles and vital statistics you will index. Because cities and towns grow over time, a good representation can be made by taking a sample from each decade. Follow these steps for your estimate:

- Gather one reel of film from each decade.
- Count the number of local articles and vital statistics for one week from each decade.
  - Multiply that number by 52.
  - Multiply that number by 10.
  - This is your total for each decade.
- Add up the number of articles and statistics for each decade.
- This is a rough estimate for your backlog of newspapers.

Next, project how much space you will need for the future by taking a count from your recent newspapers and projecting the next ten years. You only need a rough estimate so that you can give yourself and your IT department an idea of the size the database may be expected to reach.

Another database option is utilizing your current integrated library system (ILS). Some companies that develop ILS systems for libraries also develop specific modules that cater to libraries with local history collections. If available, your ILS system support team should be able to help you set this up. Inquire with your ILS system support team to determine if there is an available add-on or module that can be modified into an index for newspapers. Sometimes such modules work similarly to an existing cataloging module within that database. Each article or vital statistic to be indexed is created as a separate bibliographic record using a special MARC-style work form. When considering this option, consult with your library's cataloger for input on setting up the ILS database. Also, it is most effective if the database is kept separate from your regular library catalog so that customers looking for books and materials are not overwhelmed with bibliographic records for newspaper articles and vital statistics.

If your library is planning an ILS upgrade or change in the future, get involved with planning your library's needs. Be sure to ask ILS representatives if there are options for local history components in their system that can be used for indexing, and ask if your current indexes (spreadsheets, word processing files, or databases) can be integrated into their system.

Keeping Current and Managing the Backlog

Once you have dedicated your organization to an indexing project, it is important to keep it current. You will need staff and volunteers to work on both current and old newspapers. Start your indexing project with today's newspaper. Keeping up with the current edition will save you time in the future. Do not wait until the newspaper arrives on microfilm; instead, work on the paper edition of today's newspaper. Do not start with the oldest newspapers and work toward the front and put off the current newspaper. It is best to assign an indexer to index the current newspaper daily. Once today's paper is indexed, that indexer can work on the backlog.

Remember, when a subject heading is updated or changed, the person you have assigned to be responsible for updating the authority file must also update the existing index. This means finding all articles already indexed under a specific subject heading and physically editing the existing heading to reflect the change.

THE BACKLOG OF NEWSPAPERS ON MICROFILM

If you have more than one title to index, index one newspaper at a time. For the backlog of newspapers, you may want to begin with the newspaper that had the smallest run. Of course, that depends on your research demands. You may determine that more information is requested from another longer-running newspaper, so it would be more practical to begin with that newspaper.

If you have more than one indexer on board for your project, it might be a good idea to assign one person to index the current newspaper and others to index the backlog. When indexing the backlog of newspapers, start with the oldest date available. Have only one indexer work on the backlog at a time if possible. This way, one indexer can begin working on a date and note the date that he or she ends. Then the next indexer to work on the project can pick up on the date following where the last indexer left off. To streamline and avoid a potential overlap, you can create an indexing log for the indexers to write in the last date completed.

If you have an abundance of indexers to participate in the project and they may be working at the same time, create an assignment sheet and have indexers work on one year at a time, with each indexer being assigned a specific month for that year. Then check off the months completed on the assignment sheet. It would be unwise to assign individual indexers to a span longer than one month because should you lose an indexer, you will have to assign the unfinished portion to another indexer's current batch to catch it up. The idea is to assign the project to indexers in manageable portions that can be completed fairly quickly. As each month is completed, the indexer can begin a new batch. This will keep your project manageable and also provide your indexers with a sense of accomplishment that will encourage them to continue with the project. If you are relying on volunteers to do your indexing, consider some incentives or rewards for completion of their assigned portions. If you periodically honor your volunteers with a special event, you can tally up the months or years each volunteer has completed as part of honoring their contributions.

Indexing your local newspapers can add richness to your local history collections by creating a searchable resource for genealogists and researchers. While it is a long-term project that requires a commitment, once it is broken down into small portions, the project becomes quite manageable. It is a great opportunity for volunteers to get involved in preserving the history of a community, adding a sense of pride and accomplishment to their hard work, especially as they witness the index in use by the public. The end result will last indefinitely as long as the index is kept safe and migrated to newer digital formats or a paper copy backup is kept in a safe place. An indexed local newspaper is an invaluable resource that will continue to be utilized by future generations.

CHAPTER 7

Newspaper Preservation in Developing Countries: Issues and Strategies for Intervention

Goodluck Israel Ifijeh

Newspaper preservation has a long history in developing countries, especially in Africa (Alegbeleye 2002). However, it is gaining more attention in recent times. Highlighting the various preservation methods, this chapter defines newspapers, explores their importance and the need to preserve them, and outlines ways through which newspapers can be better preserved in sub-Saharan Africa, comprising countries in western, eastern, and southern Africa.

A newspaper is a regularly scheduled publication containing news, information, and advertising. As of 2007, there were 6,508 daily newspapers in the world, selling 395 million copies a day (Joseph 2010). Wikipedia (an online encyclopedia) attributes this high selling rate to the fact that newspapers publish stories on local and national political events, personalities, crime, business, entertainment, society, and sports. They also feature editorials, columns, classified advertising, comics, and inserts from local business enterprises.

Generally, newspapers meet the following four criteria:

Universality: They cover a wide range of topics.
Periodicity: They are published at regular intervals.
Currency: They contain up-to-date information.
Publicity: Their content should be accessible to the public.

Newspapers may be categorized as daily or weekly and local, national, or international, depending on publication time interval and scope. In terms of format, they are available in hard copies, on compact discs (CDs), and on the Internet. All of these formats are available for use in developing countries.

Modern newspapers come in one of these sizes:

Broadsheets: 600 mm by 800 mm (23 1/2 by 15 inches)
Tabloids: 380 mm by 300 mm (15 by 11 3/4 inches)
Midi or Berliner: 470 mm by 315 mm (18 1/2 by 12 1/4 inches)

The importance of newspapers cannot be overemphasized. They constitute an important source of information in literate societies. Newspapers owe their existence to peoples' desire to know about themselves, their governments, and their economy. All over the world, researchers consult both retrospective and current newspapers to keep abreast of developments in the past and present, in order to correctly draw scientific conclusions. The increasing relationship between information and the economy of nations and multinationals has given rise to the insatiable need for information. Increasing the quality of information in the decision-making process of organizations definitely improves productivity. Therefore, information is vital to the socioeconomic and technological transformation of developing countries. Thus, newspapers are always in high demand among the various categories of library users. Users' demand for newspapers has not only justified the need for their acquisition; it has also created the need to evolve effective means to preserve them for current and future use.

Librarians in developing countries are often faced with peculiar challenges in their quest to acquire newspapers. Ordinarily, libraries would like to acquire as many available newspapers as possible. This has not been achieved, partly because these libraries are located within depressed economies (Mohammed 1989). Most national and state governments are faced with the enormous challenge posed by the global economic recession. This has necessitated a cut in library budgets. Most affected are public libraries, which are run by state and regional governments. There have been cuts in the number of newspaper titles acquired by libraries (Aguolu 1996). The costs of newsprint (material with which newspapers are produced) affects the production of newspapers, which in turn affects the subscription rate. The advent of the structural adjustment program (SAP) adopted by many governments in developing countries made prices of major production materials go up by more than 500 percent (Olorunsola 1997). This has caused libraries to cut their newspaper lists, while some libraries have suspended subscriptions altogether. Sporadic interruptions in the publication of some newspaper titles have also posed a challenge to the acquisition of newspapers. Such interruptions are occasioned mainly by political instability, wars, and military and civilian dictatorships in government. There have been reported incidents where newspapers were seized by agents of governments, thus hindering the acquisition and provision of such titles in libraries (Olorunsola 1997).

These factors have made libraries go all out to preserve the number of titles they can afford, using appropriate preservation methods as budgets will allow.

"Developing country" is a term generally used to describe a nation with low-level material wealth. Levels of development may vary, with some developing countries having high average standards of living (O'Sullivan and Sheffrin 2003). These countries are found in Africa, parts of Eastern Europe, Asia, and South America.

The concept of librarianship in developing countries is not fundamentally different from that in the developed world. The main differences lie in the economic, geographical, sociocultural, and technological contexts. No doubt these factors play key roles in the development of any nation's library system. However, libraries and librarians in developing countries have evolved survival strategies in their professional practice in order to effectively and efficiently serve the needs of clients.

The Difficulty of Newspaper Preservation

One of the most complex problems libraries all over the world face today is how best to preserve the materials that constitute their collections. The preservation of newspapers is complicated by the nature of their composition and structure. Fortunately, librarians, manufacturers, and publishers are becoming more aware of issues relating to preservation and, as such, are searching for solutions.

Ritzenthaler (1993) defined preservation as the activities associated with maintaining library and archived materials for use either in their original form or in some other usable way. Generally, the objective of preservation is to ensure that information is accessible and used for as long as is required by users. The importance of information to the economy of nations justifies the enormous cost and burden of newspaper preservation. Newspapers are media through which important information is accessed. Therefore, libraries cannot afford to allow these papers to deteriorate and become inaccessible to researchers and other library clienteles.

Information professionals in these countries cannot wave aside the obvious fact that libraries stand the imminent risk of losing much of their valuable documented information in consequence of the deterioration of the paper on which they are printed (Ola 2004). Newspapers are made from newsprint, which is very low in archival quality. It is made using ground wood fibers and retains impurities after processing, including resins, tannin, and lignin. Lignin promotes acidic reactions when exposed to heat, light, high humidity, or atmospheric pollutants. Acid causes newspapers to become brittle and deteriorate quickly.

The environmental conditions of sub-Saharan Africa are primary factors that call for the need to preserve newspapers. The three most important factors in environmental control are humidity, temperature, and light; others are dust and air pollution (contaminants in the atmosphere). If newspapers are not properly stored and preserved, these conditions could make them deteriorate rather quickly. The relatively high temperature and sunlight in western and eastern countries of Africa contribute to the quick deterioration of papers. Some of these factors are beyond control, but it is advisable to work toward best practices.

Newspapers need to be preserved against the destructive effects of micro- and macroorganisms such as bacteria, fungi, insects, and rodents. These organisms breed easily in the swamp and rainforest regions. While the vegetation encourages the breeding of these organisms, the eating habits of library staff and users attract them to the library. Micro- and macroorganisms either eat up pages of newspapers or leave stains on them. Proper preservation methods are therefore necessary to keep the activities of these destructive agents in check, especially with regard to newspapers, which are most vulnerable.

It is important to note that the mere fact that these newspapers are handled and used daily demands that librarians find ways to effectively preserve them, if they must continually be in use. If well preserved, the life expectancy of newspapers can be as high as twenty years and higher if reformatted on media other than paper.

Preservation Methods

There are various methods of preserving newspapers. The ones most commonly used are discussed below.

REFORMATTING

This is the process of replacing deteriorating pages of newspapers from their brittle state to other paper/magnetic tape–based bound volume. This preservation technique serves as the best option in cases where pages of newspapers are too weak or brittle to be consulted by users. The various methods used include microfilming and photocopying.

Microfilming

Microfilming has a long history of use. It is the process of photographic reproduction of documents or images from one-eighth (1:8) to one-fiftieth (1:50) of their original size, usually on a 16 or 25 millimeter film (Online Business Dictionary 2010). It serves the dual purpose of reducing storage space and preservation. Microfilm boosts life expectancy to five hundred years (Alegbeleye 2002). Microfilms can enhance access to information that would otherwise be unavailable or vulnerable to damage or loss through handling. They are relatively inexpensive to produce and copy. However, Alegbeleye (2002) reported that library users dislike this medium because it is not easy to use and copy. This attitude does not negate the fact that microfilms remain very useful for newspaper preservation. Perhaps it is the advent of better digitization methods that is gradually making the use of microfilm unpopular in libraries.

Photocopying

Photocopying is suitable for heavily used newspapers. It helps to check deterioration. Photocopying with durable paper is an often-adopted option. The process must be carefully carried out since it could cause damage to fragile items. Photocopies occupy as much space as originals, so there is no gain in storage space. It is the cheapest preservation method because the cost per unit is the lowest. One of its disadvantages is that it could be tedious if the number of pages to be photocopied is many.

DIGITIZATION

In our context, digitization is the process of documenting information in electronic format and making it accessible through media such as compact discs (CDs), the Internet, and so on. Digitization in libraries in Africa is relatively recent, having started in the past decade. It began with scanning, and other technologies have recently emerged. Newspaper publishers now sell electronic versions in CD format. Libraries buy these CDs and store them in databases that are made accessible to users. Digitization is very expensive. Apart from the high cost of purchasing software and hardware, trained personnel are needed to run the systems. These are not easy to come by in libraries in developing countries. Nevertheless, this preservation method is very effective, as electronic formats last longer than paper. Predictably, very few libraries in developing economies, especially in Africa, adopt this method due to lack of funds, shortage of trained personnel who are willing to work in the library, and inadequate power supply. Efforts are underway to reduce the cost of digitizing newspapers. Some national libraries take advantage of the legal deposit laws to obtain electronic copies of newspapers, which they make available at very cheap prices to libraries. In Nigeria, the national library sells a whole month's issues of any given title of newspaper on CDs for less than ten dollars ($10).

BINDING

This is the most popular method of newspaper preservation in Africa. Binding helps to store original copies on a permanent basis. Binding has been a frequently used method for organizing and storing newspaper. Whole copies or clips of newspapers are bound on a monthly basis. The bound volumes are provided with thick covers that are labeled appropriately to aid organization and access. The binding of newspapers must be done by a professional binder. The bound papers are arranged on specially designed shelves under favorable atmospheric conditions. Apart from the cost, newspaper binding must be done with care so as not to damage the text. It also creates unwieldy volumes that are difficult to handle properly.

HOUSING

This involves storing frequently used newspapers in boxes. The boxes are custom-made to suit the size of each newspaper. The newspapers are stacked neatly and organized in chronological sequence, and an index created for easy reference.

WRAPPING

Here, newspapers that are not frequently used are tied in bundles and wrapped in a sturdy alkaline paper. The procedure is considered cumbersome because the bundles must be reassembled and tied after each use.

DIGITAL PRESERVATION

As earlier stated, newspapers exist in digital formats that also need to be preserved. Digital preservation refers to the series of managed activities necessary to ensure continued access to digital materials indefinitely. It entails basic handling, storage, and environmental control. Newspapers on CDs need to be stored in special cases made for them and kept in closed access under good environmental conditions. Information professionals must also take proper care of computer systems housing newspaper databases. The systems must be protected from virus attacks. Digital preservation is generally categorized into the following divisions:

Long-term preservation: continued access to digital materials or at least to the
   information in them, stored indefinitely

Medium-term preservation: continued access to digital materials beyond changes in technology for a defined period of time, but not indefinitely

Short-term preservation: access to digital materials either for a defined period of time while use is predicted but that does not extend beyond the foreseeable future and/or until they become inaccessible because of changes in technology.

Enhancing Better Newspaper Preservation Practice

One of the problems of newspaper preservation in most developing nations is either lack of preservation policies or inability of appropriate agencies to monitor compliance where such policies exist. Preservation policy entails drawing guidelines and underlying principles that must be meticulously followed by libraries. Such policies are usually formulated by national bodies (e.g., national libraries) rather than individual libraries. Libraries may only formulate theirs based on national policies. The process of developing policy, or periodic review of an established policy, allows a library to establish and shape an institution's specific mission (Morrow 2000). Newspaper preservation policy will guide both librarians and users in the handling and storage of newspapers. Furthermore, preservation policies will help to outline and sustain standards. Standards play important roles in ensuring widespread accessibility, and in defining formats and methods capable of surviving future technological changes. A typical library preservation policy should include (but not be limited to) the following elements: a statement of need, definition of concepts and terms, preservation principles and practices, institutional preservation priorities, selection strategy, program outline, and cooperative relationships (if any).

Libraries could take advantage of consortia in the area of preservation in a bid to cut down on cost and maximize the use of limited funds. A consortium is an association of libraries set up for a common purpose that would be beyond the capabilities of any of the libraries in the group. This is a popular practice in developed countries. The United States Newspaper Program is a good example in this regard. Shenton (2001) opined that libraries have historically worked together to develop effective methodologies and common standards for effective transfer of information. Libraries with particular strength in a collection could share preservation of specific titles of newspapers among themselves. This option needs to be explored as a survival strategy by libraries on very tight budget. National libraries in these nations must take the lead in bringing about consortia initiatives. The efforts of the British Library in the United Kingdom and the Library of Congress in the United States are worthy examples to emulate. Shenton

(2001) reported that funding is available for library consortia through charity and other nongovernmental organizations.

There is also the need to train and retrain professional and paraprofessional library staff on proper handling of library materials, especially newspapers. Preservation is a specialized field that requires professionals who understand the physical and chemical nature of materials in their custody. Librarians need to be exposed to the theory and practice of preservation. Preservation training can be taught through workshops, seminars, apprenticeships, and internships. Each form offers a different level of education and training over a period of time. Training through workshops and seminars is an excellent way to raise awareness of challenges in preservation and identifying general areas of concentration. Training courses may include general preservation issues such as disaster-response planning, care of newspapers, building design, environmental control, preservation methods, and long-term planning. Special workshops on new methods are helpful in keeping abreast of recent developments. Practical work experience in the library is also very important. Alegbeleye (1993) notes the practical work experience at the Kenya National Archives and documentation services, where new staff members are first sent to the preservation unit before being assigned to duty posts. Other libraries need to emulate this worthy example.

Library users contribute to the deterioration of newspapers. They need to be informed and instructed on how to handle newspapers in the least damaging way. Such instructions could be passed on during library orientations. Appropriate illustrative posters (on proper ways to handle newspapers) could be placed at strategic locations, especially at the point of use. Library users are often unaware of the consequences of their actions, and with the cost of subscriptions escalating and budgets shrinking every year, newspaper management becomes even more critical. Library users will better understand the challenges faced by libraries when they view a display of newspaper pages damaged through careless behavior and realize the effects of pests attracted to the library through their food and drinks. They should be made to see the tedious efforts of preserving papers through live demonstrations. These efforts would help reduce the rate of poor handling of newspaper pages by users.

Disaster planning is part of preservation. Libraries should have a disaster plan. Surprisingly, most institutions are not prepared to handle disaster situations. The absence of a disaster plan implies that in the event of one, the library would not be able to respond to the disaster with the urgency it demands. Alegbeleye (1993) observed that libraries in Africa are prone to disasters that can be classified as natural and man-made. They include fire outbreak, flooding, and earthquakes.

Conclusion

Newspapers are important media of vital information needed for the educational, economic, scientific, and technological transformation of nations. The need to preserve them for current and future use cannot be overemphasized. The fact that newspapers contain important information for current and future use makes their preservation a necessity in every library. Libraries in developing countries have evolved and adopted various preservation methods, but their efforts are limited due to economic and technological factors. National libraries in these countries must liaise at this point with other libraries to develop and monitor newspaper preservation policies. They should also initiate and seek funding for consortia programs with regard to newspaper preservation. Individual libraries must strive to put necessary policies in place and meet high standards.

In an era of information and communications technology (ICT), libraries need to look in the direction of ICT application in the preservation of library resources, especially newspapers. This should begin with the acquisition of digitized copies of newspapers. As earlier stated, these are available from some national libraries at a subsidized rate.

References

Aguolu, I. "Nigerian University Libraries: What Future?" *The International Information and Library Review* 28, no. 3 (1996): 261.

Alegbeleye, B. *Disaster Control Planning for Libraries, Archives and Electronic Data Processing Centers in Africa* (Ibadan: Options Books and Information Services, 1993), 107.

———. "Preservation and Conservation: Rationale, Procedure, Trends and Benefits for Research and Scholarship" (paper presented at the Seminar on Preservation for Posterity, organized by the National Library of Nigeria and UNESCO, June 4–5, 2002), 10–11.

Joseph, P. "Newspaper Circulation Falls Nearly 9%." *New York Times*, April 26, 2010.

Mohammed, Yakubu. "A Long Walk from a Step." *Newswatch*, September 4, 1989, 56.

Morrow, C. *Defining the Library Preservation Program: Policies and Organizations in Preservation Issues and Planning* (Chicago: American Library Association, 2000), 1–27.

Ola, C. *Technology for Information Management and Service* (Ibadan: Evi-Coleman Publications, 2004), 189–200.

Olorunsola, R. "Nigeria Newsmagazines and Their Importance: A Review of Recent Literature." *World Libraries* 7, no. 2 (Spring 1997). www.worlib.org/vol07no2/olorunsolavo7n2.s html (accessed September 3, 2010).

Online Business Dictionary. "Microfilming." www.businessdictionary.com/definition/microfilming.html (accessed September 6, 2010).

O'Sullivan, Arthur, and S. Sheffrin. *Economics: Principles in Action* (Upper Saddle River, N.J.: Pearson Prentice Hall, 2003), 471.

Ritzenthaler, M. L. *Preserving Archives and Manuscripts* (Chicago: Society of American Archivists, 1993).

Shenton, H. "Partnership and Co-operation in Preservation at the British Library" (paper presented at a conference on preservation of library stock: partnership and cooperation held at the Russian State Library, Moscow, November 20–23, 2001). http://www.bl.uk/aboutus/stratpolprog/ccare/pubs/archivepubs/partnership.pdf (accessed September 8, 2010).

Wikipedia. "Newspapers." en.wikipedia.org/wiki/Newspaper (accessed September 6, 2010).

PART III

SCRAPBOOKS

CHAPTER 8

How to Get Scrapbooks into the Hands of Users

Anastasia S. Weigle

Scrapbooks are bits and pieces of memories put together to tell us a story about someone, something, or someplace. Our role as the historian, archivist, curator, and/or preservationist is to protect the story without taking away the intent of the creator.

Scrapbooks are challenging because of the nature of the materials being used to create them. The high acid content of scrapbook paper deteriorates rapidly regardless of if it is black construction paper or buff-colored manila paper. The equally acidic contents, such as old photographs, letters, and cards, make matters worse. Now include the varied adhesives used in scrapbooks, such as paste, glue, rubber cement, masking tape, Scotch tape, and yes, even duct tape, and you have a mess. The acidic nature of the scrapbook page with the various pH properties of photographs, cards, fabric, hair, glues, tapes, and pins causes rapid deterioration. Ah, yes, the formidable scrapbook—we love them, we hate them, what shall we do with them?

Informational or Artifactual?

When I evaluate a scrapbook for preservation, I have to determine if I am preserving the information inside the scrapbook (informational) or the scrapbook itself (artifactual). An informational scrapbook solely contains news clippings with enclosures (covers) not unique or connected to the information inside the scrapbook in any way. I am not interested in preserving the acidic paper the article is printed on, only the words themselves—the information. The newsprint does not have high intrinsic value and, therefore, is not necessary to preserve. I am not a proponent of massive de-acidification of newsprint articles in scrapbooks. The only de-acidification I would recommend is for newspapers that have a high intrinsic value, such as rare and early publications specific to your community. The most realistic and cost-effective method of preserving your newsprint scrapbooks would be preservation photocopying of the articles.

An artifactual scrapbook is one that contains photographs, letters, and postcards and includes handwritten annotations on the pages (social commentary). The enclosures are quite decorative and relate to the content inside. It may also have the creator's name and date on the front. A scrapbook like this requires a much gentler touch when preserving so as not to alter the feel of the scrapbook.

However, if this same scrapbook had plain covers and pages with no annotations, then the items themselves in the scrapbook are the artifacts, not the scrapbook enclosure. This requires the preservation of each item before rehousing them into an archivally sound scrapbook or placing in folders.

The last type of scrapbook is my favorite because it reminds me of altered books. These are old ledgers, cashbooks, dictionaries, or encyclopedias repurposed as scrapbooks. These are signature-bound books in cloth, quarter leather, or full leather with their inside pages covered with articles, photographs, cards, and other ephemeral items.

Now that I have explained the differences between types of scrapbooks, let's review:

1. the informational value scrapbook
2. the scrapbook that houses artifactual items
3. the scrapbook as an artifact
4. the refurbished ledger

I will walk you through the process of preserving and making your scrapbooks accessible based on type of scrapbook.

The Informational Value Scrapbook

As stated previously, the informational value scrapbook is one filled with newsprint of various sizes and adhered on the scrapbook page with Scotch tape or rubber cement. These scrapbooks are common in historical societies and museums and offer a glimpse into local history or a particular family. They may contain articles on births, marriages, obituaries, local business news, or political news. These primary resources are invaluable to genealogists and historians. The newsprint inside these scrapbooks is highly acidic and fragile, making them deteriorate rapidly. The tape or rubber cement used will lose its adhesive properties and eventually fall away, leaving stains behind. The scrapbook enclosure is not unique in any way other than having the word "Scrapbook" embossed on the cover. Due to its brittle nature, these are the scrapbooks that create the largest mess when opening up.

The simplest way to preserve this type of scrapbook is to make preservation photocopies of all the news clippings onto acid-/lignin-free archival paper. For institutions with limited funds, copying the scrapbook in-house using their own copy machine is the easiest. The task of making copies can be cumbersome because not all of the newsprint is fit to size, so before you begin copying, you must unbind the scrapbook to separate the cover from the pages. Most if not all of the clippings may be too brittle or difficult to remove due to the nature of the adhesive. In this case, you will copy the entire scrapbook page. You may also come across a page where a newsprint article is quite large and has been folded to fit on the page. Depending on the size of the platen glass on your in-house copier, you may have to copy the article in two or three parts. If you can make your preservation copies 8 1/2 x 11 inches, you can place each page in a three-holed archival Mylar sleeve. The preservation copies are placed in a binder in the exact order as they were in the scrapbook and identified as such by giving them the same page numbers. If a patron needs to see the original article for whatever reason, you know which page in the scrapbook it can be found.

If the scrapbook is oversized, you can outsource the project to a local copy center that can accommodate the larger page size and have the copies perfect bound. Make sure that the copies are done on acid- and lignin-free 80 lb. text weight paper.

Acid and Lignin Free

There can be confusion between the terms acid-free and lignin-free. Acid-free paper has a pH value of 7.0 or higher (neutral to slightly alkaline). This is created when acid is removed from the wood pulp during the paper-making process. In time, acid-free paper can become acidic again. Not all acid-free paper is lignin free. Lignin is in wood pulp and can be removed in the paper-making process as well. Acid is what makes paper brittle and lignin is what causes paper to become discolored. Although expensive, acid- and lignin-free paper is the preferable choice.

I have come across, from time to time, an ephemeral item in a scrapbook filled with newsprint. I remove the item and place it in an archival Mylar sleeve before adding it to the binder. If you are going to keep the original scrapbook, make sure to place a notation on the scrapbook page indicating where you removed the ephemeral item from and where you placed it in the binder.

The decision to keep or discard the original scrapbook is dependent upon the institution's policies. Some have no aversion to discarding a newsprint scrapbook once the preservation copies have been made. For those who still want to hold onto the old scrapbook for sentimental reasons (and have the space), make sure to remove all pins, staples, and/or paper clips. Using a soft brush, gently remove any loose dirt or particles, and remove any desiccated tape. Finally, any loose newsprint can be hinged in place using document repair tape. The scrapbook pages can be put back together with their original cord and enclosures. For extra measure, you can tie the scrapbook together with cotton string and place it in an archival box. Keep in mind the informational scrapbook, as a whole, is not an artifact and we are not losing any evidential or intrinsic value by reformatting through duplication of newsprint.

The next challenge is indexing these scrapbooks. This is a time-consuming project but not difficult to do if you have a core of volunteers in your museum or historical society. A spreadsheet can be created using Microsoft Excel software. Important information would include the scrapbook page number, date or date range of article or item, subject or topic, and any pertinent names of people or businesses. Once you finish your spreadsheet, you can sort by date, subject, or name.

The volunteer would go page by page and identify important dates, names, and events and notate them in the spreadsheet with the scrapbook page number. Once the entire scrapbook is completed, the spreadsheet file can be printed out and placed at the front of the binder for that particular scrapbook. The Excel file can also be saved on a flash drive or CD-ROM. Because Excel has a simple finding tool, the historian, docent, or researcher can search any topic, person, or event by just typing in the word. If a particular word is indexed in the spreadsheet, Excel will find it and direct you to the appropriate page in your binder. Your scrapbook index is only as good as the person who inputted the information, so creating clear guidelines for indexing is very important.

The Scrapbook That Houses Artifacts

This scrapbook is a bit more challenging because the individual items inside the scrapbook are considered artifacts. The scrapbook itself—cover and pages—is not. This type of scrapbook will have a nondescript cover or enclosure and manila or black scrapbook pages. The enclosure has no information that ties it to the contents. Pages can be held together with cord, ribbon, or metal posts and like all scrapbooks from the nineteenth and twentieth centuries, the pages are brittle. Inside the scrapbook, we find various items such as photographs, letters,

Figure 8.1. Scrapbook pages showing deterioration. Captain Harry M. Jones Scrapbook Collection, Courtesy of Harmon Museum, Old Orchard Beach, Maine.

documents, ribbons, and cards. The adhesives used to attach these items can be rubber cement, paper clips, pins, or pressure-sensitive tape.

The items inside are artifacts, not the enclosure, cord, or pages. Preservation for the scrapbook that houses artifacts requires the removal of the items and

Figure 8.2. Items cleaned and rehoused onto new archival safe scrapbook pages. Captain Harry M. Jones Scrapbook Collection, Courtesy of Harmon Museum, Old Orchard Beach, Maine.

rehousing them. Starting with page 1 of your scrapbook, remove all the items, taking care to clean or repair any tears if necessary. If there is difficulty in removing an item, I find that sliding a Casella knife under the item while gently lifting will do the trick. Items can be placed in Mylar sleeves or envelopes, depending on the size. These items are then hinged onto a new sheet of scrapbook paper in the same order and layout as the original including the page number. This preserves the intent of the creator.

The artifacts are hinged in place using thin Japanese tissue tape because it is reversible and does not add bulk to the pages. I place acid-free buffered tissue paper between every sheet to prevent acid from migrating onto the preceding page. Once the project is completed, I tie all the pages together with cotton cord and place them in a large archival manuscript box.

Another option would require removing the items and placing them in archival folders.

1. Remove items from scrapbook page.
2. Gently remove dust or dirt with soft brush and gently remove any loose tape.

3. Place in an appropriately sized archival Mylar sleeve.
4. Number items accordingly. Place a small piece of document repair tape on the top right of the Mylar sleeve and pencil in the item and page number (example: 1.1 represents item 1 on page 1).
5. Place these items in an archival folder with a description on the tab (example: John Smith Scrapbook, Page 1/six items). Each folder represents a scrapbook page.
6. Place folders in an archival document box.

This is an acceptable method of preserving artifactual items. If a scrapbook had fifty pages, then you would end up with fifty folders. The old scrapbook, page and enclosures, is discarded. The process of indexing these scrapbooks is similar to the informational scrapbook, with each artifact itemized on a list with the appropriate item and page number. Again, by using Microsoft Excel, you can create a spreadsheet and an itemized list, taking advantage of the finding tool when searching for a particular item.

Figure 8.3. A scrapbook with annotations from the creator. Captain Harry M. Jones Scrapbook Collection, Courtesy of Harmon Museum, Old Orchard Beach, Maine.

The Scrapbook as an Artifact

This type of scrapbook has both a distinctive enclosure and pages where you can clearly see the creator took time to put together a unique story. The covers may be adorned with a photograph or an illustration with the creator's name and date. The items inside may be annotated with information about events or family members.

It is important that we honor the creator's intent by keeping the scrapbook as original as possible, only removing and repairing items as necessary.

When it comes to preserving and making this scrapbook accessible, you want to create a digital preservation file of each scrapbook page. By doing so, you help increase the value of these historically significant visual materials via the Internet. This can be said of all visual materials in your institution.

When digitizing scrapbooks, I follow the digital scanning methods of the Maine Historical Society and Maine Memory Network, Maine's premier online digital museum site.

Maine Memory Online Digital Museum

Maine Memory Network was developed and is managed by the Maine Historical Society. The site is free and currently has more than twenty thousand historical items online from more than two hundred organizations across the state of Maine. An ongoing collaborative project, MMN provides museums, historical societies, and libraries with the skills to scan, upload, catalog, and manage digital copies of their historical items. www.mainememory.net.

Each scrapbook page is scanned at 300 dpi (resolution), with a maximum 40 MB (document size) at a bit depth of 24. I also select RGB color mode regardless of whether the image is in color or in black and white. This will ensure a printable output up to 11 x 14 inches of the highest quality. This file should be saved as a TIFF and be regarded as an unedited, information-rich file. This can be saved on your computer's hard drive, an external drive, or on the museum or library server. If you decide to save these files on a CD-ROM, keep in mind that technology changes and migrating these files onto new formats is something you must do every two years. An external hard drive with 1 terabyte (1024 gigabytes) is very affordable and allows for maintaining large amounts of digital files. From these TIFF files you can create smaller JPG files to be used for online digital exhibitions.

Once the scanning project is completed, I make sure to add acid-free buffered tissue paper between each scrapbook page before rehousing in a manuscript box. The original items are safe while the users have access to digital files. Indexing follows the same procedures described earlier in this chapter.

Repurposed Ledgers as Scrapbooks

An old-time ledger or cashbook refurbished as a scrapbook is a real find. If the old ledger is blank, then the ephemeral items and newsprint are all you really need to worry about preserving. Certainly, copying or scanning each page is a way to make it accessible to users while preserving the original. But what if the scrapbook items adhered to the old ledger pages are obscuring information beneath? Better yet, what if the old ledger is from a manufacturing company in your community that is now defunct? What is more important—the ledger or the scrapbook? The answer is the ledger. Clearly, the information beneath the scrapbook has greater value. The challenge now is separating these two distinct items—the ledger from the scrapbook.

There are a couple of ways to preserve this type of scrapbook. First, the ephemeral items adhered to the ledger pages add thickness to the book, causing the binding to crack or break. It is best to cut the signatures and unbind the ledger in order to separate the pages. This shouldn't be too difficult, as the binding will already be quite loose due to the added stress. Once you separate the pages, you will be able to work on removing the adhered items from the pages. If they are taped on, you should be able to dissolve the adhesive with water using a Q-tip. This is a slow process, but one that works well.

If the items are pasted or glued down, the pages must be soaked in warm water to loosen the adhesive. Only do this if the ledger annotations are in pencil, as ink may bleed out. Once the ephemeral items loosen and come off, place the newly removed item between paper towels and sandwich between Plexiglas. The ledger pages will be treated in a similar fashion.

The ephemeral items that you removed and dried may require flattening, as water expands and contracts the paper fibers, causing a rippling effect. You may be able to smooth some of that out with a low-heat tacking iron. Place the item in an archival Mylar sleeve and store in folders. As for the ledger pages, once they dry and you gently flatten with a tacking iron on low heat, you can have the book professionally bound.

Table 8.1. Sample of a Scrapbook Collection Policy

Harmon Museum and Old Orchard Beach Historical Society
Scrapbook Collection Policy

MISSION STATEMENT	The mission of the Harmon Museum/Old Orchard Beach Historical Society is to identify, acquire, organize, preserve, and make available historical documents, photographs, and artifacts pertaining to the history and culture of Old Orchard Beach, Maine.
APPRAISAL POLICY	The scrapbook collection policy was developed for the sole purpose of saving from destruction historical artifacts, documents, and photographs that form a record of Old Orchard Beach's past. Harmon Museum/ OOBHS will collect scrapbooks that pertain only to Old Orchard Beach History and its environs, including local families and important themes or episodes in Old Orchard Beach's past.
PRESERVATION POLICIES AND PROCEDURES	• A preservation survey will be done to help identify scrapbooks with the greatest need of repair. • Scrapbooks housing artifacts will be dismantled and items cleaned and placed in individual archival Mylar sleeves fit to size before placing into folders or new archival scrapbooks. • Scrapbooks recognized as artifacts as a whole will be carefully separated from their enclosures. Pages will be gently brushed to remove surface dirt. Buffered tissue paper will be placed between pages and tied together with cotton cord. Decorative covers with cords will be wrapped in buffered tissue paper. Pages and covers are placed in an archival manuscript box. • Repurposed scrapbooks should be carefully evaluated to determine if there is any hidden valuable historical information underneath the ephemeral items. Any findings will be noted. Book will be unbound before placing buffered tissue pages between pages. Pages will be tied with cotton cord. Book covers can be wrapped in buffered tissue paper and placed in acid-/ lignin-free enclosure before placing with papers in archival box. • Note: Any separation of ephemeral items from ledger pages should be outsourced to a conservator. This is to be done if the information hidden is extremely valuable.
REFORMATTING AND DIGITIZATION	• Information scrapbooks: preservation copies and indexed • Scrapbooks that house artifacts: each item scanned using Maine Historical Society benchmark standards with large TIFF for preservation and small JPG saved for online digital exhibition; itemized list for items to be used as an index • Scrapbooks as whole artifacts: pages of scrapbook scanned using benchmark standards and creating online exhibition • Repurposed scrapbooks: preservation photocopies with index

Final Thoughts

Because scrapbooks vary in size, content, and style, and have their own unique problems, it would be beneficial for your institution to develop scrapbook collection policies. These should at least include a mission and purpose statement, an appraisal policy, and preservation and access policies. Policies help your institution deal with the day-to-day challenges met when dealing with archival materials and should be reviewed once a year.

The more you work with scrapbooks, the less fearful you will be of them. You may even develop new preservation and reformatting methods. Preserving a scrapbook is saving a small piece of history and making it accessible by sharing the stories in it that would otherwise be lost.

Additional Resources

Childs-Helton, Sally. "Evaluating Scrapbooks for Preservation and Access: Information or Artifact?" *MAC Newsletter* 37, no. 1 (July 2009): 30–35. *Library, Information Science & Technology Abstracts*, EBSCO*host* (accessed May 21, 2011).

Helfand, Jessica. "What We Save: Pictures and Ephemera in the Twentieth-Century Scrapbook." *Aperture* 183 (Summer 2006): 40–45. *Art Full Text*, WilsonWeb (accessed May 27, 2011).

Hughston, Milan. "Preserving the Ephemeral: New Access to Artists' Files, Vertical Files and Scrapbooks." *Art Documentation* (Winter 1990): 179–81.

Kuipers, Juliana M. "Scrapbooks: Intrinsic Value and Material Culture." *Journal of Archival Organization* 2, no. 3 (2004): 83–91. *Academic Search Premier*, EBSCO*host* (accessed May 20, 2011).

Ogden, Sherelyn. "Preservation Options for Scrapbooks and Album Formats." *Book and Paper Group Annual* 10 (1991): 149–63. cool.conservation-us.org/coolaic/sg/bpg/annual/v10/bp10-14.html (accessed June 15, 2011).

Teper, Jennifer Hain. "An Introduction to Preservation Challenges and Potential Solutions for Scrapbooks in Archival Collections." *Journal of Archival Organizations*, 5, no. 3 (2008): 47–64. *Academic Search Premier*, EBSCO*host* (accessed May 21, 2011).

Wadley, Carma. "Scraps of Time: Old Scrapbooks Present Preservation Challenges." *Deseret News*, October 5, 2007. www.deseretnews.com/article/695215752/Scraps-of-time-Old-scrapbooks-present-preservation-challenges.html?pg=2 (accessed May 30, 2011).

CHAPTER 9

Keeping Scrapbooks Secure and Available

Erin Foley

Scrapbooks are the most wonderful and the most horrible items in a local history collection. Any page may contain a valuable item: a ticket stub to a lecture by Mark Twain, an image of a building long gone—or a horror: photos defaced with brown glue smudges, a pressed flower with mold. This complicated mixture of problems is why scrapbooks are the last items to be processed.

Scrapbooks are difficult to classify. Each one is unique. The contents resemble an archival collection, but they are stored in something that looks like a book.

So what's a librarian to do? Here is one technique you can use to make the scrapbook contents available, while protecting the original items.

Basic Principles

The most important thing to remember when working on a scrapbook is to preserve a record of the scrapbook's original page order and contents. The items on each page were placed there for a reason. The reason may not be obvious, but nothing should be removed from a scrapbook as irrelevant.

When an item is removed from the scrapbook—usually done for preservation reasons—its association with the other items on the page can be lost. For example, a scrapbook might contain photos and documents from a family business. An unlabeled photo of a pharmacy glued next to an advertisement of the grand opening of the Thompson Bros. Pharmacy allows a researcher to conclude that the photo shows the Thompson Bros. Pharmacy. If the photo is removed from the page, that association is lost—it becomes just another picture of an unknown pharmacy. Items removed from the scrapbook must be documented and identified so that association is retained.

Another basic principle of working with scrapbooks is that the pages probably are in chronological order. There may be some other order as well, but a rule of thumb is that the first pages of the scrapbook hold the oldest items, and the age of the items becomes younger as the page numbers get larger. This rule can help a researcher estimate a date for a specific item. If an undated document is on the page before a clipping from 1892, then the document probably dates no later than 1892.

Getting Started

Before starting a scrapbook project, make sure of three things.

1. Does your library own the item? Don't waste time working on it until you are sure that the library's investment in time and supplies will not be lost due to the item being claimed by its rightful owner. Check for records of how the library obtained the item and how long it has been held. Check your state's abandoned property laws—the length of time an item has been held by an agency may give your library ownership automatically. Check with library administration or legal counsel if you have any doubts about the library's ownership of the scrapbook.
2. Is your library administration committed to supporting the work and providing the funds needed to do the project? Many projects take more time and resources than is estimated.
3. Do you have a workspace where the project will not be disturbed? The work needs a space used for only this one project, and that will not be needed for another project until this one is finished.

Step 1. Quick Inventory

Once the project is clear to proceed, open the scrapbook on a large flat surface. Turn pages gently—large items may be pasted across facing pages and will rip if opened too vigorously. If the scrapbook is tightly bound, open it as far as possible, providing support for each cover from underneath. There are professional book cradles, but two empty three-ring binders are much cheaper. Place the binders with their spines to the far left and right. Put the spine of the scrapbook in between the binders and use the sloping binder covers to support the open scrapbook covers. A clean white cloth may be spread over the binders to protect the scrapbook covers. If a weight is needed to hold the pages open, a small cloth beanbag may be carefully placed on each side.

While paging through the scrapbook, think about the subjects covered in the book. Is it a record of someone's entire life, or the diary of a short trip? Does it document a specific event, or hold a broad selection of local news clippings? How old are the items in the book? The scrapbook may hold only photos, or it may be stuffed with everything from pressed leaves to clippings. Also note problems with the scrapbook and its contents. Keep written notes of what is observed.

This first step is truly a quick survey. There is no need to spend more than twenty minutes unless the book has many pages or the problems require a lot of notes. Here are items to consider:

- What sort of paper was used? Is it strong enough to allow repeated use of the original? Because the pages will be numbered in Step 2, consider whether pencil marks on the paper will be visible.
- If anything falls out of the scrapbook, keep it in its correct spot or insert a place marker with a note about what item belongs on that page. Loose items will be detailed in Step 2.
- Items from unknown pages in the scrapbook should be spread out on the table during this survey. It is possible the correct page for a loose item may be discovered during this pass through the book.
- Is the binding secure? Can it be taken apart? This decision will not be made until Step 3, but it is useful to start thinking about it now.

Step 2. Thorough Inventory

This step is critical and time-consuming. It requires careful handling and the knowledge gained from the first look through the book.

A. NUMBER THE PAGES

All pages must be correctly numbered. The numbers must be dark enough to be readable on the photocopy to be made in Step 4. The numbers must also be removable—it is against archival principles to permanently alter the original documents by using a permanent marker or pen to write on the original.

If the scrapbook is on white paper, it will be simple to write a page number in the margin of each page with a soft lead pencil. Numbers should be applied to the same part of each page. They should be written only on the page itself, not on items glued into the scrapbook. Every page should be numbered, even blank pages. The only exceptions are the covers; these will be labeled on the photocopies.

If the scrapbook has black or colored pages, or if the scrapbook has pages with no margins, you will need to figure out another way to number them. Here are the options:

- Art supply stores contain colored marking pencils that will write on many surfaces. The white pencils will mark on the black paper often used in photo albums. Other colors are available. The marks are removable.
- Post-it notes are not recommended because they leave a bit of adhesive on the page when removed. If absolutely necessary to use Post-it notes, they must not be attached to anything except the scrapbook paper. All the notes must be removed when the project is finished.
- "Magnetic" scrapbooks held items in place on a sticky wax base that was then covered by a clear plastic sleeve. Because the sheets will damage scrapbook contents, these plastic cover sheets should be removed. Before that is done, the sheets can be used to hold page numbers by using a grease pencil to write on the plastic, or by allowing Post-it notes, stickers, or tape to hold the numbers.
- Write page numbers on scrap paper or index cards that can be positioned on the photocopier glass as each scrapbook page is copied. This is tedious, but the numbers may be used for work on other scrapbooks.

B. RETURN MISSING ITEMS TO ORIGINAL LOCATIONS

Make a list of all scrapbook pages with loose or missing items. Each loose item should be placed in an enclosure—I recommend folders because they are easy to store and have a tab on which ID information may be written. The folders should be stored in page number order so they will be easy to retrieve. There should be at least one folder for each page that has any loose items.

Any items for which the original page is unknown should be checked during this step. Old tape and glue marks are a great way to match a loose item to its original location. This careful pass through the scrapbook may allow you to link each loose item with its rightful spot in the book. Once the page is identified, place the item in an enclosure with any other loose items from that page.

Multiple items may be placed in the same folder as long as they fit and do not damage each other.

There may be orphan pieces when this step is finished. A folder of loose items is easily stored with the scrapbook for future research.

Step 3. Remove the Cover

Scrapbooks were constructed out of many sorts of items—prayer books with pressed flowers, ledgers with correspondence taped over old accounting records, purchased albums of blank pages. A scrapbook with a solid binding in good condition will be relatively easy to store intact. If this is the case, skip to Step 4.

But many scrapbooks are not intact. Sometimes the paper has weakened at the binding and pages are ripped out. Other types of scrapbooks were constructed using metal rings or strings through holes in the paper. These bindings often rip at the binding holes. In other cases, the bindings have rusted away, leaving only a loose set of pages.

In these cases, consider whether taking the scrapbook apart will make it easier to preserve. Storage of individual items may be improved when the scrapbook pages are loose and stored upright in a folder.

Before removing the binding, plan how to store the loose pages. Will the pages be stored flat in an acid-free box with a lid? Are the pages sturdy enough to stand upright in a series of file folders within an archival document case? Once the binding is removed, the paper may be trimmed, which helps the pages fit into standard folders and boxes. Once the plan is complete, obtain the necessary boxes and folders so that the disbound pages may be placed immediately in their new storage.

Step 4. Make a Master Photocopy

Most libraries have a good photocopy machine with settings that may be adjusted for light or dark originals. Copiers also can copy originals larger than 8 1/2 × 11 inches, by either allowing larger sheets of paper to feed through the machine or reducing the size of the copy to fit a smaller sheet of paper.

Start by making copies of a few pages. Make sure the page numbers show up on the copies. Test a range of originals to see what settings work best for your scrapbook. Most text documents will copy clearly. Newspaper clippings usually have yellowed; these can be copied with the contrast set very light. Conversely, underexposed photos may require the darkest copy setting. When both extremes are on the same page, make two copies of the page, one at each setting.

Once you have figured out the proper settings for your scrapbook, and have undisturbed possession of the photocopier for some length of time, start copying.

- Check each copy to make sure the page is readable. If a copy is not good enough, do it again.
- Position all loose items into their places on each page for the copies. Return these items to their numbered enclosures when the photocopy is done.
- Each copy should be on its own page. Do *not* make back-to-back photocopies.
- Copy every page in the book in order, each side. If a page is blank, it is best to number and photocopy it. A group of empty pages is the only exception to this. A note such as "14 empty pages" should be written on a photocopy of one of the pages.
- Copy the front and back covers of each book and the inside of each cover. Label the copies with that information—cover, inside front cover, back cover, inside back cover.

Step 5. Check Your Work

Once the scrapbook is copied, take the copy and the original back to your worktable and compare the sheets. Make sure the entire scrapbook and all the loose items are copied and that every copy is clear and complete. Make new copies of pages that are not usable. Make multiple copies of pages where needed for maximum readability of the items on the page.

This copy will be the master photocopy. Make sure this copy is the best it can be so that the original never needs to be photocopied again. When finished, the scrapbook can be placed into its chosen storage container and set aside.

Step 6. Duplicate Photocopies

Make two back-to-back copies from the master copy. The copies may be reduced to fit 8 1/2 × 11–inch paper, or they may be copied at the same size as the master copy. These duplicates also should be placed into binders.

One duplicate is for researchers. The research duplicate should be cataloged for patrons to locate.

The other is a copy for staff. This copy should be stored with the original scrapbook. It will be used for notes about any items that have been removed, scanned, or photographed, as well as any changes to the scrapbook since it was cataloged.

Step 7. Catalog

A good catalog record for the scrapbook is important. What the catalog record looks like will vary depending on the library.

If the main access to the collection is through an online catalog, a MARC record may be created. Use professional cataloging staff if available, or ask for help from other local history librarians.

A finding aid is a useful addition to a simple catalog record, or may be used as the starting point for a researcher. Finding aids are summary documents for archival collections that combine information about the item or collection with background information compiled by a librarian or archivist. A finding aid may be bound with the research duplicate copy and stored with the scrapbook.

ID labels and numbers must be placed on the scrapbook's storage container. This container should also contain the master photocopy of the scrapbook, the staff duplicate, and all of the loose items. If items from the scrapbook are placed in separate storage, the location should be noted on the staff duplicate.

Step 8. Scanning

The only way to produce a good reproduction of an item from the scrapbook is to scan the original item. Scanning should be done only by a trained staff member who will make sure the scanning will not damage the item. The library should purchase a flatbed scanner with a removable lid that will allow large items to be laid flat on the scanning glass. An external hard drive should be purchased to store the scans.

No item should be scanned more than once, so any scanning should be saved at its full size. Scan at a high resolution, no lower than 600 ppi, and in color, not grayscale. Useful file names should be created and used consistently for an entire collection. Here are the standard procedures.

- Make a preview scan at 600 ppi.
- Inspect the preview. Set the margins to cover the entire item. Do not scan for details—those may be cropped from the finished scan later. Make sure the image is as straight as possible.
- Do the final scan and inspect it. Straighten the image if necessary. Did the entire image get scanned? Is the image clear and readable? Do not manipulate the scan other than to straighten or crop the image. The image may be fine-tuned at a later time.
- Give the scan a good file name and save the full-size, 600 ppi image to the appropriate file on your computer. Save it in a lossless format—TIFF is one standard format that is usually available with scanning software.

- Reduce the size of the digital image to a standard size—I used 2 inches as the largest dimension for my scans. Save this copy at a lower resolution (perhaps 150 to 300 ppi) and save it in a glossy format such as JPEG. This JPEG file will be small enough to easily send through e-mail or use on a web page.
- If you have image cataloging software, catalog the scan.
- Write the catalog number of the scan on the staff duplicate photocopy. This will serve as a record of what images in the scrapbook have already been scanned. The scanned items may also be marked in the research duplicate if possible.

Scanning entire scrapbook pages rather than single items produces a great deal of stored images that may never be used. It makes sense to scan only the items requested specifically since these are likely to be the most attractive and most historically interesting items in the scrapbook. These are the images that will be useful for library exhibits and for sale to researchers and genealogists.

Summary

Yes, scrapbooks can be challenging, but they are a valuable source of rare pieces of history. Using the procedure outlined above, it is possible to keep the scrapbook safe while making its contents available to researchers in your collection, in your library, and around the world.

CHAPTER 10

Physical Properties of Scrapbooks

Jennifer Hain Teper

Historic scrapbooks are one of the most problematic formats found in many collections due to their complicated and deterioration-prone structures. The following chapter is meant to identify some of their preservation challenges and offer suggestions to assist collection managers in ensuring long-term access to these valuable assets.

Bindings

Most early scrapbooks have hard covers that are covered in either leather or cloth. Most commercially produced covers were covered in linen and have exposed spines, common to the side-laced and post-bound structures they utilize for page attachment, as described below. More expensive styles of scrapbooks bound in leather may have covered spines to emulate the appearance of a more traditional "book." However, these spines are often decorative only and frequently do not attach directly to the pages of the scrapbook inside the cover. Later scrapbook covers (1950s and later) may be found covered in decorative papers and plastics in addition to cloth and leather.

DETERIORATION

In almost all cases, a general, overall deterioration of the binding occurs over time from exposure to the environment. For most scrapbooks bound in cloth covers, this means a fading of the color of the cloth, fraying of edges and corners, and rubbing on the spine. In addition to the overall deterioration and wear on scrapbook covers, many exhibit failure of their joints, resulting in partial or full detachment of one or both boards from the book itself. The reason for this is twofold. First, as the covering materials deteriorate, both cloth and leather become less durable. The first area to fail on a book binding is most commonly the joint (also called the hinge), as this is where the board flexes every time the book is opened. This failure is then exacerbated by the inflexibility of many of the historic scrapbook structures, such as side-laced and post-bound styles, and by the tendency of owners to overfill scrapbooks.

Page Attachment

Scrapbooks that are constructed as such from the outset are almost always created in such a way as to allow for the removal or addition of pages and for some flexibility in the spacing between pages. Thus, familiar structures such as three-ring binders are often used for modern scrapbooks; however, other methods of page attachment were much more popular before the 1950s. Side-laced bindings were the most popular in scrapbooks in the early 1900s and are still available today. A side-laced binding, in which pages and covers have holes along the spine edge through which a leather lace, silk cord, or other material can be threaded, was a relatively simple binding structure that endured as the most popular method of page attachment for decades. By the mid-twentieth century, however, other options gained in popularity, such as the aforementioned three-ring binder and spiral bindings. Other, less familiar page attachment methods commonly found in scrapbooks include post bindings, in which pages have holes punched through the spine edge similar to side-laced or three-ring binder pages, but are held together by a multipiece metal post which screws together to tighten or loosen its hold on the pages of the book.

In very recent scrapbooks a format called "strap-hinges" has also appeared. In this format, pages are reinforced along the gutter edge of the page with a strip of plastic or metal which runs the length of the page. Held within this strip are two or three metal "hinges" which look a bit like loosely fitting staples. A plastic strap is then laced through these metal hinges, allowing the pages to shift up and down the flexible plastic strap.

DETERIORATION: BINDING STYLES

In the most common scrapbook binding styles (side-laced and post-bound formats), the page attachment results in a very stiff spine that, when combined with increasingly fragile paper, results in pages breaking at the gutter edge, while the construction that holds the pages in place remains intact. In some cases, the lacing used in a side-laced binding may deteriorate and break, resulting in an unintentionally disbound scrapbook. Most metal hardware used to hold scrapbook pages together is quite robust and lasts considerably longer than the paper it is meant to hold. Due to the relative newness of the strap-hinges, it has yet to be seen how these will hold up over time. However, given their reliance on flexible plastic straps, it is very likely that the plastic will not age well over time as it deteriorates and loses plasticizers, thus becoming less flexible and eventually fracturing.

Pages

The papers used in scrapbooks are almost always of a heavy stock due to the work they have to perform—that of supporting multiple documents or photos, which can be quite heavy. The type and quality of paper used for scrapbook pages vary, depending upon the format of the book and the method of page attachment.

For most side-laced bindings and most other pages that have no other surface treatments or overlays, a reasonably low-grade mechanical wood pulp mixed with some percentage of chemically pulped paper fibers (commonly called "sulfited" pulps) was likely used. This paper, which is similar in appearance and feel to construction paper used in crafts, was left off-white or dyed black. The paper had a slightly rough surface texture that took adhesives and writing materials well.

More modern scrapbooks introduced different ways to hold items to a page or to protect items attached to a page. "Magnetic" pages, which were very popular in the late twentieth century, are made of heavy-weight cardstock paper with a thin layer of a tacky wax-based substance covered by a thin sheet of plastic, which allows the user to place objects on the page and have them held in place with no additional method of attachment. To withstand the stress of pulling the plastic off the sticky wax repeatedly, these pages were often constructed of a heavier and harder paper stock and were found mostly in three-ring binder or spiral bindings.

Page protectors also gained popularity in about the same time period and are still popular with scrapbookers today. In this format, paper pages slide in and out of flexible plastic sleeves. This allows for protection of the surface of the pages themselves while the plastic sleeve can then be attached via three-ring binders, post binders, hinge and straps, spiral bindings, or side-laced bindings.

The weight and quality of the paper used in page protectors varies and could easily be replaced by the user if the materials purchased with the scrapbook were found to be unsuitable for their desired purpose. The page protectors themselves are created out of a variety of plastics including, but not limited to, PVC (polyvinylchloride), cellulose diacetate, polypropylene, and polyester.

DETERIORATION: CHEMISTRY

As scrapbooks age, the paper chemistry reacts with the environmental storage conditions, creating acids that attack the paper structure. Over time, this process results in increasingly acidic paper, leading to discoloration and eventual embrittlement. For historic scrapbook pages laden with layers of papers and photographs, this results in the fracturing of pages, either on the edges from the stress of people turning the pages or along the gutter edge from inflexibility of the paper as pages are turned. Magnetic scrapbook pages deteriorate most notably through the chemical decomposition of the sticky wax used to hold materials in place. As the wax deteriorates, it first turns stickier, then hardens and discolors. This results in a firm bond being formed between the object, the wax, and the cardstock base that can be very difficult to separate. Plastics in more modern scrapbooks come in direct contact with the objects held within them and their deterioration can affect the objects they are meant to protect. PVC is a soft, stretchy plastic that is still used widely in school and office supplies such as three-ring binder covers. As it ages, tiny molecules called plasticizers leach out of the plastic and render it less flexible over time. In addition, these plasticizers can speed up the natural aging rate of the materials they are in contact with, leaving items disproportionately discolored and sometimes even sticky from exposure. Cellulose diacetate film is found as an early lamination film, and also in early sheet protectors. As cellulose diacetate deteriorates, the plastic discolors, shrinks, and breaks down to release acetic acid (vinegar), which hastens the deterioration of materials adjacent to it.

Attachment of Materials

Materials enclosed in scrapbooks were attached to the page supports in a variety of ways. Some scrapbooks were purchased with a particular method of attachment already encompassed in or on the pages themselves. These included water-activated glue dots and precut slits in pages meant to hold the corners of photographs in place.

Much more variety in attachment methods is found when the method of attachment was left up to the scrapbook creator. While some mass-produced items, such as photo corners, were used in many scrapbooks for holding photographs, other materials, such as letters, cards, and realia, were often attached using a wide variety of available pressure-sensitive tapes with both rubber and synthetic adhesives, as well as various adhesives including mucilage, flour paste, rubber cement, and acrylic adhesives such as Elmer's Glue.

DETERIORATION: ADHESIVES

Adhesives failures are by far the most common problem in the loss of attachment of materials in scrapbooks. In all cases, the gradual and oftentimes visually dramatic deterioration of these adhesives leaves the aged adhesive yellowed and dry over time. As an adhesive degrades, it frequently goes through several stages of deterioration. It is well documented that natural rubber or animal protein–based adhesives go through three stages of deterioration that grow increasingly discolored and damaging to materials as the tape ages. The last stage of deterioration, where the adhesive dries out, often results in the physical detachment of the adhesive, and of the objects it holds. This applies both to pressure-sensitive tapes as well as commonly used glues such as mucilage and rubber cement. Water-activated adhesives, such as those found on pages of mass-produced scrapbooks and on the back of photo corners, most commonly dry out and lose adhesion to the pages. Acrylic adhesives used in many modern pressure-sensitive tapes and glues do not go through these distinct stages of deterioration, nor do they discolor and dry out in the same fashion. They do, however, become more acidic as they age, resulting in damage to the materials they are attached to and in gradual deterioration of the glue itself. Last, metal fasteners, such as pins, staples, and paper clips, are all subject to oxidation (rusting) when exposed to environments with high humidity. Rusting can lead to discoloration and severe weakening of the affected paper.

Materials Kept in Scrapbooks

While the preservation of many of the materials enclosed in scrapbooks (e.g., paper documents and photographs) is reasonably well understood, it is the variety of other materials such as balloons, felt, plastics, and metals that may be held in their pages that make them simultaneously fascinating and incredibly challenging to preserve.

By far, the most common materials found inside scrapbooks are paper-based materials and photographs. While there is a significant amount of variability among these materials, they also have many similarities. Almost all are on a paper base and have some sort of media, most commonly various kinds of inks, placed on top of them. Mass-produced materials, such as newspaper clippings, cards, printed documents, and printed illustrations, are typically composed of paper and printing inks, but differ in physical format, ranging from single sheets to folio-folded cards and booklets. Inks may vary from traditional black printing ink (the most common) to color printing inks, historic reprographic processes, and modern computer printing processes, such as ink jet prints. Manuscript materials, such as letters and notes, are also ink on paper, but the variety of inks used is much wider.

Photographs are very common in scrapbooks. The most frequently found format is the silver gelatin print (black-and-white photography); however, earlier photographic formats including tintypes, albumen prints, matte and glossy collodion prints, and cyanotypes and modern chromogenic color photographs are also common.

As if the variety of paper and photographic materials enclosed in scrapbooks were not enough, many nontraditional materials are also frequently found. Balloons, pressed flowers, silk ribbons, wool yarns and felts, feathers, leather, metals, celluloid plastics, and modern extruded plastics are all commonly found in scrapbooks. The inclusion of a particular artifact in a scrapbook was really only hindered by the creator's ability to adhere it to a page and have it fit into a book.

DETERIORATION: TYPES

In most cases, deterioration of paper materials due to increased acidity (either from the materials themselves in the case of newsprint, or from the acidic paper of the scrapbook pages) results in discoloration (yellowing) and embrittlement over time. The heavier and better-quality papers used in some stationery and cards tend to withstand acid deterioration the longest, while poor-quality or thin papers such as newsprint, crepe paper, and tissues tend to deteriorate more rapidly.

While deterioration of the photographs themselves may occur, the acid paper on which they are housed is more frequently the biggest preservation challenge. Silver gelatin photographs can yellow and the darkest image areas are often subject to mirroring, a process by which the silver that forms the images changes from a bound color-producing molecule to a reflective elemental form of the metal on the surface of the photograph. Color photographs are made of unstable dyes, which fade over time. While the acidic environment of scrapbooks can hasten this deterioration, closed scrapbooks do limit light exposure on the photographs, light exposure being the main reason color photographs fade. Though less commonly found in scrapbooks, other photographic formats, such as cyanotypes, albumen photographs, and tintypes, are usually reasonably stable, though again the acid levels found in scrapbooks can, with time, lead to discoloration and embrittlement of paper and board supports.

Plastics and rubbers are unstable by their very nature and tend to embrittle and discolor over time, frequently harming materials placed next to them. Plant- and animal-based materials such as wool felt, natural silks, pressed flowers, tobacco products, and feathers can become fragile over time and can attract pests such as dermestid beetles and moths, which can quickly cause substantial damage.

The Preservation Environment

First and foremost, a proper preservation environment is critical. Due to the chemical instability of many of the components that make up a scrapbook, a cool, dry, and dark environment will do a great deal to extend an item's life. By decreasing temperature to a stable level below 65 degrees (the cooler the better), limiting light exposure (especially in the UV spectrum), and keeping relative humidity fluctuations between 30 and 55 percent with daily fluctuations of less than 5 percent, the rate of deterioration for all of the processes mentioned above will be dramatically slowed.

Physical Storage

Due to their fragile nature, scrapbooks should be stored flat to reduce stress on the bindings and attachment of materials. To facilitate flat storage, as well as to create a beneficial "microclimate" that can reduce light and the effects of daily fluctuations in temperature and relative humidity, scrapbooks should be stored in some sort of box or enclosure. A microclimate is created around an object by the environmental buffering created by an enclosure. Lightweight enclosures such as a paper wrapper have a limited effect, but more substantial enclosures such as sealed boxes have a significant buffering capability. Lignin-free, buffered, metal-edged archival boxes are ideal storage, especially when empty space in the box is loosely packed with wadded buffered tissue or cardboard spacers to reduce the shifting of materials inside the box when the box is pulled. Although not as durable as metal-edged boxes, scrapbooks can also be wrapped in heavy, buffered wrapping paper and tied with cotton twill tie to help block out light and dust, as well as contain loose pages and "bits."

Protecting Endangered Materials from Decay

Acid migration from poor-quality papers and unstable materials is a serious threat. While removing items from a scrapbook may not be an ideal solution, it may be the best preservation option for endangered artifacts. If items are to be removed from a scrapbook, be sure to document exactly where they came from and what the page layout looked like so that no secondary information is lost. If items cannot be removed or circumstances require that the scrapbook should remain intact for artifactual value and evidence, interleaving with alkaline buffered paper or tissue between the scrapbook pages will help to absorb a great deal of free acids, acting as a sacrificial "sponge" for acids and keeping them from reacting with the artifacts.

Handling Fragile Scrapbooks

Fragile scrapbooks are a challenge for patrons to handle, and usage often results in damage. Set up policies to reduce unnecessary handling. Some owners may choose to have patrons wear white gloves while handling scrapbooks, as finger oils can damage fragile photographic emulsions. This is recommended for photographic albums and sturdy scrapbooks with many photographs, but is discouraged for scrapbooks with already damaged pages or with few photographs, since gloves reduce the dexterity of the user and can actually increase unintentional damage. Instead, insist on freshly washed hands when fragility is a factor.

Turning embrittled pages that have many heavy items attached to them often results in damage. To reduce this risk, offer users a sheet of clean, stiff, buffered cardstock (20 to 40 point in weight) and instruct them to place the sheet over the front of the right-hand page about to be turned. The weight of the page then shifts to the cardstock while the page is turned, resulting in better weight distribution for the attachments, as well as keeping any floppy pamphlets or other realia in place, and less chance of dropping unwieldy realia.

Conclusion

Although scrapbooks present perhaps the most complex preservation challenges, knowledge of the types of deterioration to expect and the implementation of simple preservation strategies can greatly extend their useful life.

PART IV

LOCAL HISTORY

CHAPTER 11

Creating Local History Collection Development Guidelines

William Helling

It would be ideal if a local history collection could retain every item or artifact that came its way. Most organizations, however, do not enjoy the unlimited space, staff, or budgets that would make indiscriminate expansion possible. Collecting without guidelines can lead to problems that actually make it difficult to maintain a collection and to keep it viable for the future. A local history collection development policy is well worth the effort because it provides a vision as well as a road map for how you want to control and validate what may be a small but very important part of your library.

Why It Is Important to Have a Collection Development Policy

The work spent in creating a local history collection development policy is easier to justify when you outline how you can gain by your policy. An adequate policy helps you:

- achieve your mission
- maintain your organizational system
- deal with donors

- deal with staff
- explain your activities
- assure the collection's future

ACHIEVE YOUR MISSION

A collection development policy can help you address your collection efforts and help you be aware of what you have—and what areas you need to fill. A local history collection falls within the broad grasp of the library's mission, but it will need to be more narrowly defined because of its special nature.

MAINTAIN YOUR ORGANIZATIONAL SYSTEM

A collection development policy prevents unorganized growth that, like weeds, choke out needed items and take up valuable space. Using the policy to describe the collection is also instrumental in getting the collection properly cataloged. If an item is not cataloged sufficiently well, it is often as good as lost—unless memory or serendipity leads a user to it. You do not want to depend on such luck.

DEAL WITH DONORS

Donors expect you to be thrilled with everything they drop on your desk. Sometimes you are pleased with a donation and do not hesitate to show it—but sometimes a potential donation leaves you in an awkward position. It is never easy explaining to a potential donor why Grandpa Joe's business receipts may not be what you want. With a clearly defined policy, it is easier to refuse donations that do not fit your scope. Using a policy removes the personal aspect of a final decision, whether pro or con.

DEAL WITH STAFF

Staff members of the library need to be reminded of the collection's purpose and its future. The local history collection is a special part of the library, but it is still simply a part of a larger collection. All staff should feel some ownership of it. Also, if a few staff members work solely on the local history collection, they risk losing focus on the collection's role in the library. If the same few staff members monopolize the collection and treat it as their own, it may eventually be marginalized in the eyes of the others.

EXPLAIN YOUR ACTIVITIES

You are going to be spending time and money on collecting. If you need to describe your activities to governing bodies (board of trustees) or supervisors (library director), you need to be able to point to your plan.

ASSURE THE COLLECTION'S FUTURE

You and your present staff will not always be around to advise those who take over the collection as you phase out or move on. To provide some sort of continuity to the collection, you can greatly aid your successors by providing them with your well-established plan.

Steps toward Creating a Policy

Before you begin to create a local history collection development policy, you need to ask yourself a series of questions. These questions force you to come to terms with your collection and how you want to handle it.

- What is your library's mission?
- What do you have in your local history collection?
- What are your priorities?
- What subject areas do you collect?
- What geographical and chronological periods do you collect?
- What materials can you reasonably collect?
- Who are your users and how will they access the collection?
- Who will handle original items?
- How do you obtain items for your collection?
- How do you handle donations?
- Under which conditions can users reproduce your materials?
- Will you weed your collection?
- Who maintains the policy and reviews it?

Turn these questions into actionable goals to help you write a successful local history collection development policy.

EXAMINE YOUR LIBRARY'S EXISTING MISSION STATEMENT AND COLLECTION DEVELOPMENT POLICY

The local history collection development policy will be a subset of your library's broader mission. Your local history policy will have variations, of course, but it will not contradict the library's policy.

INVENTORY THE EXISTING COLLECTION TO GET A GRASP ON ITS SCOPE AND WHERE IT IS LACKING

You may be surprised at what you really have and what you are missing. A thorough inventory is tedious but always fruitful. Every collection has strengths and weaknesses, and this is the time to identify these areas. If you have not done so already, make an effort to discover what other local organizations own so that you do not duplicate efforts.

IDENTIFY YOUR PRIORITIES FOR YOUR COLLECTION

Know what is most important to you in spite of the global statements you may make about your collection. For example, you may want to say that you collect everything about schools in your town or city. However, you may want to qualify some statements. Is your library located near a college or university that has its own archives and fully documents its own history? Collecting items on such an institution may not be one of your priorities, even if it easily falls within several of the guidelines you have established in your collection development policy. This would be a good time to develop cooperative agreements with other organizations whose collection scope may overlap yours. Competing local history organizations (whether libraries, historical societies, clubs, etc.) do not serve a community well. Cooperation can be as simple as more openly reporting what you have and announcing what you acquire so that at least other organizations can be aware of your collection, if not actively cooperating with you.

Local Authors

Your area will certainly have residents whose creations (books, photographs, and so on) you collect as a matter of course. You may need to define what a "local author" is, however. The Crawfordsville District Public Library, for example, is located near Wabash College. The library has decided that out-of-state authors who merely resided in the town as students of Wabash do not qualify. Temporary faculty members of Wabash are also excluded unless they have become part of the community.

ESTABLISH THE SUBJECT AREAS COLLECTED

You should know which subject areas you collect as well as which you will not collect. In Crawfordsville, the Montgomery County Historical Society already collects artifacts dealing with Henry S. Lane, a Civil War–era senator and friend of Abraham Lincoln, and also maintains his former home as a museum. Although we have obtained Henry S. Lane items, we do not actively seek them because there is a more appropriate repository for them.

ESTABLISH THE GEOGRAPHIC AREAS AND THE CHRONOLOGICAL PERIODS COLLECTED

Your reach may be well defined, perhaps just your town or city, if you have no other organizations (libraries or other) covering the same general area. On the other hand, your reach may be countywide or even wider if you are the sole entity for a particular region. Do not simply consider the geographic areas, however. It may be possible that another organization is collecting for certain time periods, perhaps focusing on early settlement. Will you need to limit your reach? The Crawfordsville District Public Library is located in Montgomery County along with four other libraries—but none of these libraries has the resources to maintain an extensive local history collection. In addition, several of our surrounding counties do not enjoy libraries that spend much time on local history concerns. We have thus determined that we cover primarily Montgomery County but also manage items of our contiguous counties (with a few exceptions).

ESTABLISH THE TYPES OF MATERIALS COLLECTED—AND NOT COLLECTED

Many types of formats exist, and each one has unique requirements for providing access as well as requirements for preservation. The formats you collect are determined mainly by the physical limitations of your archives as well as the skill of the staff. Some common formats include:

- manuscripts
- monographs
- drawings
- photographs
- CDs/DVDs
- brochures
- three-dimensional objects, etc.

You may not be able to create a list of every possible format that you collect: you can't anticipate all that will be donated, and new formats appear regularly. You can determine what you will never be able to collect because of your storage situation or because another entity handles that format better (such as a local museum that manages three-dimensional objects). For example, we have the good fortune to also operate a county museum as part of the library, in a different location. We can use our museum to display and store items that we cannot physically handle, and the museum can use the library local history collection to house paper-based items that it often receives.

Remember that electronic resources make up an increasing part of many local history collections. These resources include not only what you offer on a website but also what you digitize and what products you subscribe to (for example, web-based databases). The Crawfordsville District Public Library creates a lot of digital resources, including databases that serve as an index to most of the local newspapers that were published throughout the years. Our electronic data is not in print form but is just as valuable to us as other items.

IDENTIFY THE USERS AND WHAT LEVEL OF ACCESS YOU WILL GRANT

Understanding your users can help determine what you digitize, what you shelve, and where you shelve it. Are your users mainly from the immediate area or does your collection attract a much wider audience that seeks access? When is it necessary to give on-site users access to original documents and when should you provide only reproductions shelved on open stacks? If you digitize items, will you allow access only through your local network, or will you provide a web portal to the digitized collection?

DESIGNATE WHICH STAFF MEMBERS CAN HANDLE ORIGINAL DOCUMENTS

Library staff members who handle documents do not always have archival training, but such experience is not difficult to obtain. Of course, some training is necessary, for those who come into direct contact with old and fragile items. Training is also necessary for those who are involved in document storage and safekeeping.

DETERMINE HOW YOU BUILD YOUR COLLECTION

Your collection will often grow through a combination of active and passive collecting. If you have funds to purchase materials, establish where, when, how, and by whom this activity is accomplished. For example, which staff person can pick something up at a local antique shop under which procedure? Some organizations refuse to purchase local history items because of budgetary concerns or philosophical objections. Other organizations take advantage of every avenue to compete for resources (for example, monitoring eBay for items of interest).

DECIDE HOW YOU WILL HANDLE DONATIONS

When someone donates items to your collection, legal ramifications arise. Transfer of ownership is the most common problem. Political concerns are also an issue. How do you refuse a gift? Your deed of gift is a necessary document to legally transfer ownership of a donation to your institution, and you must mention this fact in your policy. Refusing a gift is sometimes even more difficult unless you have stated that you cannot accept materials in risky condition (damaged, moldy, worn, etc.), materials that are duplicates of existing items (unless duplicates are desirable), and so on. Also consider how you will deal with donated materials that come with restrictions. Donors often attempt to set conditions that you may be unwilling to satisfy (including restricted access, perpetual retention, etc.).

The Deed of Gift

Although the signed deed of gift exists mainly to establish that you now have legal ownership of a donation, this document serves other purposes. In addition, the deed of gift is a brief inventory of the donated materials and proof of provenance that you may need in the future. It is used to register the date of the transaction as well as the donor contact information for your records. A signed deed of gift not only provides a transfer of private property to your library, it is also a record for the donor. This record outlines your commitment to care for the donation as specified and contains any conditions, if allowed, to which you have agreed.

ESTABLISH REPRODUCTION RIGHTS

If your local history collection owns an item (such as an item that has been deeded to you or an item you created), you enjoy copyright protection and can do whatever you want with that item. Even if you do not control the copyright of an item (such as a book you simply purchased), you can still allow copies to be made of materials for personal use. If a user wishes to reproduce a copyrighted item controlled by your institution for publication or commercial use, the institution needs to establish the procedure for obtaining permission and how credit will be specified. For copyrighted items that you do not control, the user is responsible for obtaining permission. The copyright law of the United States (Title 17, United States Code) governs reproduction of copyrighted materials, including fair use.

DECIDE HOW, IF EVER, YOU MAY
NEED TO WEED YOUR COLLECTION

If you have a solid collection development policy in place, you can lessen the chances that you will ever have to weed your local history collection. However, in reality, your collection was probably begun before it came under the control of a policy—and the existence of a policy does not guarantee that this policy will always be followed. In the interests of maintaining your collection as well as ensuring a positive experience for prospective donors, you may find it advisable to include statements that address weeding. There will certainly come a time when you need to make some decisions about de-accessioning materials. Few topics in libraries are more controversial, so you need to anticipate this procedure.

A local history collection is not weeded in the same way as a regular collection whose weeding is often based on age and usage statistics. The local history collection development policy will not be concerned with these factors and can say so. You will often deal with duplicate items, damaged items (mold, insects, etc.), incomplete materials, and irrelevant items that patrons donate or which you find already in your collection. Your collection development policy can remind donors and staff that any item "accepted" into the collection can be given to a more appropriate institution or disposed of in different ways later. The Crawfordsville District Public Library, for example, has a Friends of the Library organization with a monthly book sale to which we contribute items from all our collections. Finally, realize that one of your biggest factors for weeding may stem from lack of suitable storage space. You can mention in your policy that limited space does not allow the promise of permanent display or shelving.

DETERMINE WHO WILL MAINTAIN THE POLICY
AND HOW IT WILL BE REVIEWED

In a library setting, the library director may nominally be in charge of maintaining all policies, including the collection development policy. The director works at the discretion of the board of trustees, however, which may need to annually review and reapprove the policy, even if changes are not proposed.

A Sample Policy Outline

A collection development policy can be as long or as short as you want, depending on what it takes to describe your position and make your effort understood. The order is not always important, although it is best to begin with the broader statement of purpose and your collection priorities as a general introduction. What follows is a sample policy outline of My Library for My Town located in My County, with some generic text that gives you an idea of how to elaborate. Be sure to examine the policies of other libraries, too; you will soon notice that many attempt to say the same things often in the same ways.

My Library Local History Collection Development Policy

Statement of Purpose

The purpose of the local history collection is to preserve the materials that document the history and heritage of My Town and to provide access to the community, to the general public, and to researchers. In order that this material be maintained for future generations, all local history items are noncirculating.

Collection Priorities

The emphasis of the collection is on significant local historical information as well as genealogical resources. The local history collection focuses on materials documenting the town of My Town, including the surrounding communities in My County. Secondary emphasis includes the adjacent counties of My County.

Subject areas include materials by and about the residents of My County including politics, economics, education, clubs, entertainment, [and so on]. The local history collection does not limit itself to any chronological periods but rather emphasizes the years after the founding of My County.

The library director and the board of trustees may add to the collection at their discretion any materials regardless of whether these materials meet the collection descriptions. Certain factors may prevent the library from meeting its collection priorities, whether items are donated or purchased. These factors include but are not limited to space considerations, the ability of the library to preserve the materials, the potential usefulness of the materials, the accuracy or inauthenticity of the materials, and the condition of the materials.

Duplicate copies of local history items will be made available for reference and/or circulating collections depending on the material types.

Materials/Formats

The collection acquires materials in most formats including but not limited to books, atlases, manuscripts, maps, photographs, postcards, pamphlets, prints, brochures, yearbooks, videotapes, CDs/DVDs, scrapbooks, minutes, music scores, ephemera, [and so on]. The collection does not house three-dimensional objects including artifacts and sculptures. Three-dimensional materials may be referred to My Museum for proper storage and/or display.

The library subscribes to online databases for the use of local history users. Depending on the database, some access is only on-site. The library produces its own online databases that are available from any location via the web. The library also produces some information in electronic format that is available only on designated library computers.

Public and Staff Access

Original or fragile materials are in closed storage and cannot be accessed directly without the permission of the head of the department. Only designated librarians are permitted to access, handle, or process items of significant historical value. Most original or fragile items exist in facsimile, however, and can be accessed on local history open shelves along with other reference works in this collection. Digitized photos and documents from the local history collection are also available from several of the library-owned databases.

Acquisitions

Donations are accepted on condition of a signed deed of gift that legally transfers ownership to the library. Library staff cannot provide an appraisal of donated materials. Items for short-term storage will be accepted only in the case of temporary exhibits. Items donated with restrictions may not be accepted. Authority to acquire items rests with the head of the department in consultation with the library director, who can override acquisition guidelines.

Besides preexisting historical and genealogical information, the library collects material that may someday be of historical or genealogical value as it is published, as funding is available.

Copyright

Copies of materials to which the library owns the copyright are permissible under the auspices of fair use (private study, research, scholarship). If a user obtains a photocopy under the auspices of fair use and later exceeds fair use, that user may be liable for copyright infringement. Reproduction of materials does not constitute permission for publication or display. This permission must be sought from the head of department, who will indicate the conditions of use and methods for providing credit.

Weeding and Retention

Materials are not weeded from the local history collection according to the guidelines used for the library in general. Items of permanent intrinsic value (first editions, works by local authors, original documents and photographs, [and so on]) are rarely weeded. Items of permanent informational value may be weeded on occasion. Weeding can occur in special cases including but not restricted to unnecessary duplication, irreparable damage, and space considerations. Items of temporary informational value may be weeded at the discretion of the head of the department. Every effort will be made to preserve materials or pass them on to suitable organizations if they are withdrawn.

Policy Maintenance

The board of trustees reserves the right to amend this policy at its discretion. The library director shall review this policy annually and seek approval from the board of trustees. It is the responsibility of the director and the board to update this policy if priorities for the collection are adjusted.

Without active management, your local history collection can quickly become disorganized. With a weak or nonexistent collection development policy, your collection may still grow, but it will eventually become less of a resource and more of a burden for your library to maintain. Remember that your local history collection is of great value to your community—as well as to historical or genealogical researchers everywhere. Don't let this responsibility become overwhelming, however. Your careful approach to your collection development policy will determine the effectiveness and the survival of your local history collection for many years to come.

CHAPTER 12

Keeping a Past: Preservation Issues in Local History

Nancy Richey

Thomas "Tip" O'Neill, a longtime speaker of the house in the U.S. Congress, once opined that "all politics is local." This idea can be applied to the concept of historical preservation. For a community, all history is local and the preservation also starts locally. By its accessibility, history invites the nonprofessional as a participant in its collecting and recording, since the past belongs to us all. What is local history? First of all, it is not "national history writ small" but "the study of past events, or of people or groups in a geographical area based on a wide variety of documentary evidence and placed in a comparative context that should be both regional and national."[1] However, though its focus may have a limited geographical area, its study must still follow the accepted rules of all historical inquiry: honesty, accountability, accuracy, and intellectual freedom. By preserving and studying local materials, a more complete political, religious, economic, and social picture will be available. Local libraries, archives, and historical societies are also places for the underrepresented, as their stories may have been thought too small to tell or to be given copy in the local newspaper. Saving local history then becomes "a duty which we of the present generation owe to the memory of the pioneers of civilization in the region of the country where we dwell, to gather up with care, whatever records of the times there are left and [by] studying them well, transmit them in the most enduring form to successive ages."[2]

This "gathering up" is the hardest process. Communities are plagued by the disappearance of materials that are needed to preserve the knowledge of our past. Losses have come through major catastrophes such as courthouse fires but to an even greater extent through individual neglect. Mice have nibbled away at carelessly stored family letters, documents, and photographs, and rare volumes of books have been discarded. With the passage of time, the task of preserving our local history becomes more urgent and falls within the purview of the local information professional.

Preserving Local History

- gather
- organize
- catalog
- preserve
- present

In a local community, the library or historical society will usually be the first place an individual goes to ask questions about materials that they own. They may simply be seeking an appraisal as to the worth of an object or collection. Others want to know: What is this? Is it worth saving? It is a very difficult question, for everything that people have made, written upon, or used, regardless of condition, may have pertinent value to local history. However, everything cannot be saved and preserved, so how does an institution decide what to collect, keep, and preserve? There should always be a written collection policy that takes into account the following questions:

- What will be the focus and mission of the collection?
- What is the archival appraisal of items? Age and rarity?
- Will you accept donations? Who else is collecting?
- Do other libraries, historical societies, genealogical societies, private collectors have this?
- Is there sufficient staff and budget for processing, maintaining, and providing bibliographic and physical access to the collections?
- Are there going to be privacy or time restrictions on the material?
- What range of services will be provided in relation to the collection?
- What formats and languages are to be collected?
- What materials will not be considered due to preservation and other issues?
- Is there a separate and unique space needed?
- Will there be a web presence for the materials?
- Is the present space secure and environmentally suited for such collections?
- Will there be a special access policy with limitations on use?

- Will the collection be related to the functions of the local historical society? If so, what is the nature of the relationship?
- Will special equipment be needed for use of the materials?
- Are there written de-accessioning policies and prepared "deed of gift" statements and forms?

The answers to these questions are very important for both the donor and the institution. "The deed of gift is a formal legal agreement that transfers ownership of, and legal rights in, the materials to be donated. Executing a deed is in the best interests of both donor and repository. After discussion and review of the various elements of the deed, it is signed by both the donor or donor's authorized agent, and an authorized representative of the repository. The signed deed of gift establishes and governs the legal relationship between donor and repository and the legal status of the materials."[3] Additionally, a written collection policy offers other advantages:

- Declining unwanted materials is easier ("I'm sorry, our policy states that we do not collect or accept . . ."), thus eliminating the appearance of personal rejection.
- Donors, supervisors, and library boards are protected with clear guidelines.
- Continuity can be maintained through changes of staff or boards.

Yesterday's News, Tomorrow's History

After deciding what to keep, the task of preservation becomes paramount. Many local organizations are the benefactors of very fragile donations such as collections of newspapers and other paper materials. Newspapers are unsurpassed for local history as they are a wonderful mix of opinion, gossip, lurid detail, criticism, and of course, some facts! Preservation polices must be integrated into the decision of accession. Preservation is not a onetime commitment but an ongoing process. For any type of collection, the setting of preservation priorities can aid in assessing what should be handled first and what can be handled in-house or by outside agencies or not accepted at all. If the materials cannot be properly cared for, the institution should be able to provide information about alternative sites.

The phrase "preservation process" describes all of the activities that minimize chemical or physical deterioration and damage to informational content. Thus, "the primary goal of preservation is to prolong the existence of library and archival material for use, either in their original physical form or in other ways."[4] For newspapers, preservation is a matter of minimizing further deterioration as most newspapers were and are produced from untreated, low-quality wood

Preservation/Conservation Checklist

- Importance of item to local community?
- Bibliographically complete?
- Loss of access?
- Heavily used?
- Copyright protection constraints?
- High theft item?
- Permanent research value?
- Storage issues?

fibers with many impurities such as resins, lignins, and tannins. These compounds produce acidic reactions when exposed to heat, high humidity, or light. The newsprint or other materials produced from this type of paper will quickly become brittle and rapidly begin deteriorating. In preserving the papers, consider the following options.

To preserve the content of clippings or the physical clipping, you may photocopy the piece on buffered, acid-free paper. If the clipping is rare or has artifactual value, you may also want to save it as an artifact. In this case, spray the clipping with a de-acidification spray such as Bookkeeper and then place the clipping in a polyester film sleeve with a piece of acid-free paper for support and stabilization. Never store newspapers or newspaper clippings with any other documents. These sleeves of clippings can then be stored in file folders in archival boxes. However, traditional clippings files are now considered a "low-tech tool in a high-tech world," and are very vulnerable to theft. Increasingly, institutions are going toward green research techniques (using current and emerging digital imaging technologies) where the clippings are digitized and then the newsprint is recycled. This creates a copy for surrogate use. These textual forms are being replaced by new digital forms, but these formats also have their own evanescence that creates special preservation issues.

What My Heart Wants to Tell: Managing Manuscript and Book Collections of Local Authors

One of the joys in trying to preserve local history collections comes in the form of collecting the scholarship and research of local authors. These intellectual properties can be the building blocks of any collection, as they often contain the collective memory of a community. Researchers use them to understand the contemporary state of the community and what it meant to be a member of that society. The works of local authors are present in the form of manuscript records, self-published items, and professionally published books. They will have different storage and cataloging needs, according to their rarity or physical condition.

What Makes a Controlled Environment?

- stable temperatures
- controlled humidity
- UV filtration of indoor and outdoor lighting
- fire detection and suppression
- leak detection
- security
- disaster response planning
- adequate HVAC systems
- compliance with safety codes
- adequate infrastructure support for digital repository
- rodent and insect control
- food and drink limitations
- air quality

Manuscript records such as letters, diaries, remembrances, and hand-drawn maps are one-of-a-kind items that cannot be replaced. They also present cataloging challenges; the dates of creation, authors, subjects, and even titles can be difficult to determine. Special storage and filing considerations may be present, as these materials will exist in a variety of shapes and sizes and may be in very fragile condition due to previous improper storage, mishandling, or simple age.

History Caught on Camera

Photography collections present "the past as culture, as ways of thinking and feeling, as experience."[5] This makes local photography collections very important resources in preserving a locale's history and evolutionary change over time. Photographs of the community show details of everyday life and the context in which events occurred in the community. Just as with book and manuscript collections, written polices with selection criteria must be produced to deal with existing photograph collections and future acquisitions.

Threats to Images

- humidity
- housing material contaminants
- temperature fluctuations
- airborne pollutants
- light

Important parts of any policy will include:

- condition and clarity of the image
- ownership/copyright clearance
- scope/pertinence to the current collection
- identification of subjects
- feasibility of creating a digital image for archival use

Collections of photographs may contain examples from the evolution of the photographic process. Examples of the types of images found in many collections include:

- Daguerreotype (1839–1855; note: all dates are circa): highly reflective photographs produced on silver-coated copper plates; often found in ornate cases.
- Ambrotype (1854–1870): sharply detailed one-of-a-kind nonreflective photographs produced by collodion on glass negatives that are viewed against a dark background.
- Tintypes (1854–1900): durable, inexpensive images produced on sheets of iron coated with dark enamel.
- Salted paper prints (1830–1855): earliest photographic prints on paper.
- Albumen prints (1850–1895): most common type of photograph from the nineteenth century; finely detailed. Sample sizes of mounts: carte de visite (4 1/4 x 2 1/2), cabinet (4 1/2 x 6 1/2), promenade (4 x 7), boudoir (5 1/4 x 8 1/2), stereograph (various).
- Cyanotype prints (1885–1910): blue tinted on uncoated paper.
- Gelatin silver print (1895–): dominant black-and-white photographic process of the twentieth century.
- Kodachrome prints (1935–): the first commercially successful color film for the novice.

By using this timeline, dating a photograph becomes easier. After determining a type and age for a photograph, storage and preservation issues can be addressed. The next steps involve handling and housing of the images. Handling of the images should be limited, and there should be a supply of clean white cotton gloves for both the professional and the patron. For housing the image, choose appropriate enclosures for storage such as envelopes or "Hollinger" boxes, PVC-free sleeves, plastic bags, and acid-free paper, mats, and backboards. Check for the actual composition of the enclosures to make sure that they are well constructed and acid-, lignin-, and sulfur-free. These types of materials limit damaging light and dust. All paper clips, rubber bands, pressure-sensitive tapes, labels, rubber cements, and glues should be removed from the original image and never used again. Lamination is never used. There are paper enclosures, sold as buffered, that contain an alkaline material that can neutralize acids as they form. These types of buffered enclosures last longer than nonbuffered and will offer more protection to photographs that may have been previously mounted or stored with poor-quality mat or board.

Additionally, the types of acceptable plastics that you choose for the storage of photographs should be uncoated polyester (often sold as Mylar), polypropylene, and polyethylene. Do not use polyvinylchloride (PVC) plastics. These are never recommended; they are chemically unstable and can cause further damage to a vulnerable image. Many individuals still have the self-adhesive or "magnetic" albums in their possession; these will come in as donations. If possible, remove the images from these types of albums and rehouse. If you receive fragile historic albums and scrapbooks, keep these intact and stored horizontally in a high-quality acid-free box or wrapped with quality paper. All materials that come in contact with images should pass the Photographic Activity Test (PAT), and this designation should be on all purchased materials. The PAT was developed by the American National Standards Institute. Further information can be found at www.ansi.org and www.archives.gov/preservation.

After choosing correct enclosure for the images, label and identify them. Correctly identifying the subject(s) of photographs enhances their enjoyment, value, and use. Labeling with a soft graphite pencil is recommended because it is considered harmless to the photograph and fade-resistant. Other archival-quality marking pens or blue photo pencils can be used on other types of contemporary color prints that may be resin-coated and difficult to mark with a pencil.

The creation of a digital library of photographs also involves care, management, and use issues and will require additional consideration and planning. The main reasons to digitize are to improve access and enhance preservation. Just as everything is not worth saving for a library or manuscript collection, everything is not worth scanning; scan only what will be most valuable to the end user. Some questions to ask before beginning a scanning or digitization project include:

• Do you have enough information about photographs/materials to create a valuable online resource?

- Amount to be scanned?
- Format type (4 × 5 negatives, 35 mm slides, scrapbooks)?
- Condition (fragile, deteriorating, faded)?
- What is the staff and budget availability?
- Impact of digitization (how will handling affect the original?)

Scanning and digitization can be very time consuming and costly. However, the process is unparalleled in the preservation and presentation of local material for current and future generations. Choosing a digital imaging storage or management system is an extremely important decision. According to the Northeast Document Conservation Center (NDCC), "the technology for optical disks [and systems] is still in flux. Professionals estimate that innovations in disks and computer hardware and the design of new software to use them necessitate replacement of systems every three to five years. Therefore, institutional budgets must include funds to continually upgrade the systems with new software and hardware. Also, no standards have yet been developed to insure the translation of information from one generation to another."[6]

Saving Air: Preserving Oral and Written Interviews

Historians are worried not only about the past but also about the availability of primary resource materials for study in the future. Sadly, not many people are leaving behind written records in the form of long letters, journals, or diaries. But "the use of oral sources as original historic information, weighed carefully, is potentially the most valuable and yet, up to now, the least exploited in local history research. Without the use of orally communicated materials, the task of researching [many] topics can never be successfully undertaken."[7] The careful and select use of written and oral histories can provide a fuller historical record for any community because they will include local place-names, landmarks, events, heroes, and villains. Many individuals who will never leave a written record have very rich memories that they would be willing to share and have shared through the oral interview process. The challenge to librarians and others who will be entrusted with preserving oral interviews for posterity will be to determine which, and how much, of the many of hours of interview recordings to save and how to save them. A most important question for a smaller institution will be: can they be deposited in a central location with better facilities for housing these invaluable resources?

For over fifty years, the preferred preservation medium was quarter-inch analog magnetic tape on ten-inch open reels. How quickly this has changed, and with it the realization that there is no permanent storage for these and many other formats. It should be noted that, as of this writing, only two major companies still produce tape stock, and only a few companies still manufacture the machines that are capable of playing open-reel tapes. The digital migration of these magnetic tape audio recordings and cassette tapes, which have a life span of about thirty-five years, must be a consideration. It should be noted that all audio preservation is expensive. Collaborative help can be sought as well as grant monies that are available specifically for this type of preservation. Conversely, if the collections are small and the information is in danger of being lost, they can be transcribed and cataloged with other manuscript materials.

A Private Past: Overcoming Liability and Invasion of Privacy Issues

Most patrons assume that their privacy is protected by law. To highlight this concept, we can educate our patrons by making available a written privacy statement for them. Such a statement proactively provided will emphasize our role as a trusted resource as they seek and share information. This type of practical measure also decreases our risk of liability if privacy is compromised. The detailed donor agreements mentioned previously also help to eliminate liability risks.

For libraries and archives, professional standards and codes such as the Archivist's Code provide an example that all can use as a template for producing privacy polices. Their code of ethics includes the following: "Archivists protect the privacy rights of donors and individuals or groups who are the subject of records. They respect all users' right to privacy by maintaining the confidentiality of their research and protecting any personal information collected about them in accordance with the institution's security procedures."[8]

Additional considerations for liability and privacy issues include:

- Are physical structures, websites, and written materials compliant with ADA accessibility requirements?
- Do you have copyright for digitizing material?
- Are there guidelines for the reproduction of documents? Signs posted for fair use and copyright?
- Are the documents in the public domain?

Last, for specialized and one-of-a-kind materials that may be housed in local collections, be careful when dealing with patrons who may be more interested in the financial value of your materials than in the informational value. Be sure that you know the local laws regarding issues such as defacement, theft, and trespassing.

Lighting the Way: A Librarian's Role

Librarians can aid local communities in interpreting and understanding the past so that it becomes relevant to our present and future condition. By preserving materials and other resources, we not only explain the causes but the "why" of the past. Information professionals are also among the first to establish dialogue with individual and local institutions by offering advice and assistance in the basics of collection and preservation issues.

Archival Resource Suppliers

Light Impressions
PO Box 22708
Rochester, NY 14692
800-828-6216
www.lightimpressionsdirect.com

University Products
PO Box 101
Holyoke, MA 01041-0101
800-628-1912
www.universityproducts.com

Gaylord Bros.
PO Box 4901
Syracuse, NY 13221
800-448-6160
www.gaylord.com

Hollinger Corporation
PO Box 8360
Fredericksburg, VA 22404
800-634-0491
www.hollingercorp.com

Conservation Resources International, Inc.
8000 - H Forbes Place
Springfield, VA 22151
800-634-6932
www.conservationresources.com

For the librarian and information professional, preserving the heritage of the community can be our most important community role. When one looks at successful historic preservation, connections have been made and relationships formed with people at the local level. Librarians can never take for granted that someone will care about the past; instead, they can be on the forefront of saving a local culture's history. The push now is to preserve all history, not just a local collection of upper-class materials, and to collect materials that will democratize interpretation. Historian Robert Archibald says that everyone "must be a practicing historian because our species is defined by its ability to remember, learn, and interpret. Without historical reasoning, we would not have identities and we would be incapable of any action that required the use of precedent."[9] Preservation issues will constantly be transforming as the materials preserved change. Collecting, maintaining, and providing access to historical records entails significant expense with staffing, space, and funding issues. State-of-the-art conditions will be beyond the limits of most library budgets, but a minimal level of best practices can be accomplished by an informed librarian or archivist. Local history, well kept, then becomes our national heritage, and a lasting legacy.

Notes

1. Carol Kammen. *On Doing Local History* (Walnut Creek, Calif.: AltaMira Press, 2003), 5.

2. Ibid., 14.

3. Society of American Archivists, "A Guide to Deeds of Gift," www.archivists.org/publications/deed_of_gift.asp (accessed October 1, 2010).

4. Kenneth E. Harris and Susan E. Schur, "A Brief History of Preservation and Conservation at the Library of Congress," Library of Congress, www.loc.gov/preserv/history/careamer.html (accessed September 21, 2010).

5. Alan Trachtenberg. *Reading American Photographs: Images as History, Mathew Brady to Walker Evans* (New York: Hill and Wang, 1989), 3.

6. Northeast Document Conservation Center, "Preservation Leaflets," NDCC, www.nedcc.org/resources/leaflets/6Reformatting/02HistoricalNegatives.php (accessed October 5, 2010).

7. Barbara Allen Borart and William Lynwood Montell, *From Memory to History: Using Oral Sources in Local Historical Research*. (Nashville, Tenn.: American Association for State and Local History, 1981), 7.

8. Wayne C. Grover. "The Archivist's Code," www.archives.gov/preservation/professionals/archivist-code.html (accessed October 3, 2010).

9. Robert Archibald, *A Place to Remember* (Walnut Creek, Calif.: AltaMira Press, 1999), 31.

CHAPTER 13

Minimizing Privacy and Copyright Concerns with Online Local History Collections

David Gwynn

Local history collections often present a variety of materials and formats that might include photographs, oral histories, scrapbooks, or newspaper clippings. Each presents a specific set of copyright or ethical challenges for librarians and archivists, and these challenges are compounded if the material is to be made freely available on the Internet. A snapshot or letter that poses no problem when browsed by a researcher in an archives or a museum may prove very problematic when reproduced online. It is essential that librarians, archivists, and curators understand both the potential risks that might limit exposure and the rights and loopholes that may allow them to make more material legally available.

At the University Libraries of the University of North Carolina at Greensboro (UNCG), we have completed numerous digitization projects involving materials related to both the history of the institution and of the wider community. This chapter offers an overview of some potential legal issues related to local history projects and tips for making as much material as possible available to users with particular attention to providing online access. We will first discuss some of the major issues involved, and then consider options used by UNCG for one specific project.

Copyright and Intellectual Property Concerns

Most copyright issues come down to four basic questions:

1. WHAT IS THE PLANNED USE FOR THE MATERIAL TO BE REPRODUCED?

Unless you are planning to republish it (and this includes publication on the Internet), to create a derivative work, to perform it publicly, or to reproduce it in some way, the copyright status of the material may not be an issue at all. U.S. copyright law gives the copyright holder exclusive rights to conduct these activities, within certain limits. Therefore, if you plan to do nothing with the materials other than keep the originals within your institution and make these originals available for research, your copyright worries are minimal.

2. IS THE MATERIAL SUBJECT TO COPYRIGHT?

The short answer is that a work is considered to be in the public domain if any of the following criteria are met:

- The work was never subject to copyright protection to begin with (e.g., U.S. government publications, works that were published before the advent of copyright laws).
- The copyright has expired.
- The copyright was forfeited due to lack of legal compliance, such as failure to publish with required notice or to renew copyright when so required.

U.S. copyright law is largely clear on works published before 1923, which are almost indisputably in the public domain. There is also relatively little disagreement on those works published after 1978: Most remain under copyright for 70 years after the death of the author, 95 years after first publication, or 120 years after creation. Less clear is the status of works published in the intervening years. Works from this period are subject to a variety of registration renewal and copyright notice requirements. A common estimate is that some 85 percent of material published between 1923 and 1963 has fallen into the public domain through lack of copyright renewal.

Even murkier is the status of material that has not been published or was published sometime after it was created. Unfortunately, most of the photographs, correspondence, and other personal artifacts that are the bulk of so many local history collections are unpublished materials. Just as for published material, the current copyright term ranges from the life of the author plus 70 years to 120 years past the creation of the material. However, these dates are not retroactive and the 1923 cutoff does not apply as it does for published material.

What Is in the Public Domain as of 2011?

- material that was never subject to copyright
- material published before 1923
- material published between 1923 and 1963 if copyright was not renewed
- material published between 1923 and 1977 if published without copyright notice
- material published between 1978 and 1989 if published without notice and not registered within five years
- unpublished material created by an individual who died before 1941
- unpublished anonymous and corporate works created before 1891

Different rules apply to works created or published outside the United States and to sound recordings.

---

3. JUST WHO IS THE COPYRIGHT HOLDER, ANYWAY?

This question is not as easy to answer as you might think. In the case of most unpublished personal materials, the copyright holder is the creator of the work—that is, the person who wrote the letter, took the photograph, or kept the diary. For published materials, it is generally either the author or the publishing company. While the latter may be easy to determine, the former may be less so.

Mixed-format items such as scrapbooks, which might contain anything from newspaper clippings to pressed flowers, can be a bit trickier. Is it necessary to obtain permission to reproduce each small item glued into a scrapbook? Perhaps not; OCLC's "well-intentioned practice" guidelines (2010) suggest that copyright assessments be made at the collection or series level, which is also consistent with the archival theory of "more progress, less process" (Greene 2010). It is also possible to make a case that placing items into a scrapbook qualifies as a transformative use that may be permissible as "fair use."

Oral histories are another special case. Most experts seem to agree that the interviewee is the party most responsible for the intellectual content of an oral history interview, although there is some suggestion that the interviewer might be considered a co-author and therefore might share copyright with the interviewee. This is significant because the law generally requires consent from only one of the two parties in the case of a work of joint authorship. However, it is advisable to secure written permission from both parties before publishing an oral history recording or transcript.

4. WHEN AND HOW CAN I SAFELY PUBLISH MATERIAL THAT MAY BE SUBJECT TO COPYRIGHT?

The safest way, of course, is to obtain permission from the copyright holder, assuming this entity is known and can be contacted. With archival collections, copyright specifics should be spelled out in the deed of gift when the collection is accessioned. Unfortunately this step was often ignored, particularly in the years before digitization projects were common.

Deed of Gift

This donation has been received by [institution] as a gift for use in the [library or archives], and the owner or his agent with full authority, desiring to absolutely transfer full title by signing below, hereby gives, assigns, and conveys finally and completely, and without any limitation or reservation, full and complete ownership of the property described below to [institution] for use in [library or archives] and its successors and assigns permanently and forever, together with any copyrights therein and the right to copyright the same. . . .

It is understood that the donated materials may be reprinted in whole or in part in an academic publication, and may be used in whole or in part for exhibit display, electronic reproduction, and distribution via the Internet or by other means, as serves the [institution] educational mission. If the donor is the owner of the donated material's copyright, he/she hereby grants to the [institution] a paid-up, perpetual, royalty-free, nonexclusive license to use the materials to support its educational mission.

Interview Agreement

The [collection name] is an oral history project of the [institution]. Recordings and transcripts resulting from interviews conducted for the collection are deposited in the [institution] where they are made available for historical and other academic research and public dissemination, regulated according to any written restrictions placed on their use by the interviewee and/or interviewer. Participation in the project is entirely voluntary.

We, the undersigned interviewer and interviewee, have read the above and hereby grant [institution] a perpetual nonexclusive license for full use of the information contained on recordings and in transcripts of the interview(s) identified below—including but not limited to academic publication, exhibit display, and distribution via the Internet. We waive any claim to privacy in the information contained within the recordings and transcripts. Interviewee will have at least thirty days to review and edit the transcript. If the transcript is not returned within sixty days, it shall be considered approved and complete.

Section 107 of U.S. copyright law permits "fair use" reproduction of copyrighted material under some very specific provisions related to nonprofit educational and research use, among others. Our sister institutions in the Triangle Research Libraries Network have devised an intellectual property strategy (Brown, Ruttenberg, and Smith 2011) that offers the following justifications for their digitization of manuscript collections:

1. Use of the collections is noncommercial and transformative in nature; aggregating and organizing the collections completely changes their character and purpose. This addresses both the "purpose and character" and "nature of the copyrighted works" aspect of fair use.
2. The educational purpose of the work makes it necessary to provide documents in their entirety, thus satisfying the "amount and sustainability" factor.
3. These documents generally have no real commercial market and even those that do will be presented at a noncommercial-quality level, so there is essentially no effect on the market value.

U.S. Copyright Law Section 107 (Fair Use)

The fair use of a copyrighted work . . . for purposes such as criticism, comment, news reporting, teaching (including multiple copies for classroom use), scholarship, or research, is not an infringement of copyright. In determining whether the use made of a work in any particular case is a fair use the factors to be considered shall include—

1. the purpose and character of the use, including whether such use is of a commercial nature or is for nonprofit educational purposes;
2. the nature of the copyrighted work;
3. the amount and substantiality of the portion used in relation to the copyrighted work as a whole; and
4. the effect of the use upon the potential market for or value of the copyrighted work.

Under Section 108, libraries and archives also have the option of producing preservation and replacement copies under certain conditions, including digital surrogates. While this provision is very helpful in terms of providing access to on-site researchers, it cannot be used as a justification to make these digital copies available online if they would otherwise be subject to copyright restrictions; the law permits these copies to be used only within the physical confines of the library or archives. One major exception is that Section 108(h) does permit publication of digital copies of works that are in their final twenty years of copyright protection.

Possible risk management strategies for digitization projects that may or may not qualify under other specific provisions of copyright law stress selecting collections carefully, documenting all relevant activities such as attempts to locate and contact the copyright holders (due diligence), working closely with legal advisers before claiming "fair use," and posting a very proactive "takedown policy" stating that the institution will remove upon request any potentially infringing material while an investigation is conducted (Hirtle, Hudson, and Kenyon 2009; OCLC 2010).

Copyright Resources Online

Cornell University's Copyright Information Center
copyright.cornell.edu

Stanford Copyright Renewal Database
collections.stanford.edu/copyrightrenewals

Copyright and Cultural Institutions
ecommons.cornell.edu/bitstream/1813/14142/2/Hirtle-Copyright_final_RGB_lowres-cover1.pdf

The Catalog of Copyright Entries at Google Books
books.google.com/googlebooks/copyrightsearch.html

Ethical and Privacy Issues

ORAL HISTORY

Aside from copyright, oral histories also present some unique issues of privacy and disclosure of potentially sensitive material. Defamation complaints are a significant threat for which publishers of oral history transcripts are potentially liable. John Neuenschwander (2009) identifies three specific privacy-related torts that should be recognized by oral historians:

1. False light: the publication of false or widely offensive information.
2. Public disclosure of private facts: the publication of private information that is not of some legitimate or newsworthy concern to the public.

3. Right of publicity: the use of someone else's name or likeness for one's own benefit or commercial gain.

It's noteworthy that material need not always be untrue or unsubstantiated to pose a threat. Under the "public disclosure" provision, it may simply be an embarrassing fact or one not meant for publication, such as a medical issue or intimate facts regarding a sexual relationship.

Other potentially sensitive materials that might be found in oral histories could include:

- trade secrets
- classified military or intelligence information
- confidential human resources information
- allegations of misconduct
- sealed testimony
- medical or education information subject to privacy legislation (e.g., HIPAA, the Health Information Privacy and Accountability Act of 1996)

A successful oral history program, particularly one that will result in online presentation of interviews, should address these issues in advance and have a strategy in place, starting with the interview process. It is also important to remember that one's right to privacy and the ability to be defamed ends at death; unlike intellectual property rights, these cannot be assigned to one's heirs.

CORRESPONDENCE AND OTHER DOCUMENTS

As local history materials also may include correspondence or records, it is wise to consider that these materials may also include sensitive material and disclosures even beyond those found in oral history interviews, including:

- Social Security numbers
- bank account and credit card numbers
- addresses and other identifying information
- sensitive interpersonal issues never intended for publication

While the age of materials in local history collections may minimize concerns about this type of material, they still must be considered. As with oral history interviews, there may also be privacy concerns that fall under various legislation, particularly if the documents come from an educational institution or if they contain human resources or medical information.

Civil Rights Greensboro: A Case Study

UNCG's *Civil Rights Greensboro* digitization project included materials from many different formats and sources and presented numerous copyright and privacy issues—primarily centered on oral history, correspondence, and newspaper clippings.

Of particular concern were the three oral history collections that made up a significant proportion of the project. The Chafe collection, oldest of the three, was a group of interviews conducted in the late 1970s under the supervision of Dr. William Chafe as part of his research for the book *Civilities and Civil Rights*. There were no release forms for these interviews since they were not originally intended for publication. In addition, the project incorporated material from another project, *Greensboro VOICES*, which consisted of oral histories from two other collections that were already available online—and for which copyright research had already been completed.

Based on advice from university counsel, we were satisfied that our legal requirements on the Chafe interviews were likely satisfied as long as permission was obtained from one of the two participants in the interview. We based this assumption on the theory of joint copyright. Permission was relatively easy to obtain as we were in contact with Dr. Chafe and an assistant who had conducted the interviews. However, we felt an ethical need to perform due diligence and make an attempt to contact the interviewees or their next of kin. We also believed that this process would strengthen our legal standing.

Many of the Chafe interviewees had also participated in the *Greensboro VOICES* project, so a database of contact information was already available to us. We augmented this with a variety of strategies to locate interviewees, including the use of search engines, LexisNexis queries, and local newspaper databases. We documented all of our search and contact attempts in a spreadsheet and retained letters that were returned as undeliverable. In the end, we were able to obtain full permission to use fifteen of the sixty-seven interviews in the collection and we felt that we had sufficiently documented due diligence for the remainder. Only two interviews were not used as part of the project, both of them because the interviewee had specifically mentioned during the interview that it was "off the record."

Correspondence was handled in a similar fashion. Since UNCG is a unit of the state university system, much of the correspondence contributed from our own archives was already a part of the public record. University counsel advised us that letters both to and from state employees pursuant to their employment were within the public domain under this provision. For other correspondence, we followed and documented the same due diligence procedures we had employed for oral history interviews. Success in obtaining permission was much more limited in this case, and we relied on due diligence for most of the letters that were not already in the public domain.

Civil Rights Greensboro also included a number of newspaper clippings found in scrapbooks, personal files, and library vertical files. Most of these were articles from the campus newspapers of the participating institution (which posed no problem) and from the local newspaper and its predecessor publications. By contacting the librarian for the newspaper, we were able to secure blanket permission to use any articles provided they were part of an existing archival collection. Our attempts to secure permission to use materials from other publications were considerably less successful; in fact, most of our requests were simply ignored. Since there were very few of these clippings and they were not crucial to the project, we did not include the ones for which we could not obtain permission.

While *Civil Rights Greensboro* was a curated digitization project that involved very specific and labor-intensive criteria for item selection, the current trend is more toward mass digitization of entire collections. When dealing with thousands of documents, there is simply no time for agonizing deliberations about the fate of each individual item. At UNCG, we are still formulating our approach to this issue. It seems obvious that at some point our digitization priorities—including copyright and privacy assessments—will have to be assessed at the collection rather than item level.

Conclusion

Local history materials are a significant area of interest for many of our users, and they increasingly expect to be able to find these materials online. Understanding the legal, ethical, and privacy issues that can hinder this process—and finding ways to minimize these issues—is essential to our profession as we try to meet the needs of our users. Barring significant changes to the copyright law, a risk management plan may prove the best option to archivists and librarians as we pursue our goal to make as much relevant material available to as many users as possible.

Works Cited

Brown, Laura Clark, Judy Ruttenberg, and Kevin L. Smith. *The Triangle Research Libraries Network's Intellectual Property Rights Strategy for Digitization of Modern Manuscript Collections and Archival Record Groups.* 2011. www.trln.org/IPRights.pdf (accessed August 3, 2011).

Greene, Mark. "MPLP: It's Not Just for Processing Anymore." *The American Archivist* 73 (2010): 175–203.

Hirtle, Peter B., Emily Hudson, and Andrew T. Kenyon. *Copyright and Cultural Institutions: Guidelines for Digitization for U.S, Libraries, Archives, and Museums.* Ithaca: Cornell University Library, 2009.

Neuenschwander, John A. *A Guide to Oral History and the Law.* Oxford: Oxford University Press, 2009.

OCLC. *Well-Intentioned Practice for Putting Digitized Collections of Unpublished Materials Online.* 2010. www.oclc.org/research/activities/rights/practice.pdf (accessed August 3, 2011).

CHAPTER 14

Lavaca County Records Retention Project

Brenda Lincke Fisseler

This chapter tells how a small group of volunteers in a rural county in Texas, joined by a county official and an Amigos Library Services preservation field services officer, decided to establish a records retention project from the ground floor.

The Project

While every records retention project has its own needs, answers, and tempo, the project in Lavaca County illustrates some of the basic steps that are inherent in a retention project. Literally hundreds of minor decisions and actions regarding this project have taken place in the past five years, so this section will focus on the defining moments in the project and how those decisions molded and directed our journey.

The records retention movement in Lavaca County began in May of 2004, when the Lavaca County Historical Commission requested that the Lavaca County Commissioners Court transfer to the Regional Historical Depository at the University of Houston/Victoria College Library the remaining Lavaca County school superintendent's records. Prior to 2004, some of the records had been transferred to the library by a previous county administration. The remaining records were being stored in unstable conditions, so to ensure their safety the decision was made to transfer the remaining records. The library was equipped to store them in stable environmental conditions, and the collection would remain intact. After this move, several individuals realized that immediate action was needed to prevent further physical deterioration or the loss of local ownership of the collection.

In October 2004, the Lavaca County Commissioners established a Records Management Committee made up of county officials and volunteers. In December 2004, County Clerk Kouba received a $3,500 preservation assistance grant from the National Endowment for the Humanities for a site survey of the county clerk's records and a training workshop. The following March, the Records Management Committee requested that the professional consultant be retained by the county to do a records assessment plan for all the Lavaca County records. This additional work was paid for out of the courthouse records management fund.

Originally, the plan was to build a separate records retention facility. However, in April 2006, the commissioners court voted to integrate the records retention project with a newly established courthouse annex project. The new plan involved allotting space in the courthouse annex for records retention and storage.

While the county officials were debating exactly where the records retention project would be housed, the volunteers were being trained and work began on identifying the scope of the project. In May 2005, Rebecca Elder of Amigos Library Services conducted a preservation site survey and presented a one-day workshop on preserving historical records, a general overview and understanding of preserving and storing historical documents. Since that day, Rebecca and Amigos have been our constant companions. Attendees at the workshop became records retention volunteers (aka the Press Gang). In February 2007, Rebecca returned to Hallettsville for a two-day workshop for more advanced training on handling and storage, mold removal, environmental concerns, and the correct use of a HEPA vacuum.

The Press Gang immediately began a complete inventory of the historic records of Lavaca County. During 2005 and 2006, the volunteers spent hundreds of hours creating a list of the county's historical records, their location, the type of records, and the amount of damage. Measurements of the bound volumes and boxes were taken to ensure that when the collection was rehoused, adequate shelving would be available.

Our biggest challenge was the infamous "boxcar." In April 2006, the members of the Press Gang began inventorying the contents of a large metal railroad boxcar that was the home of thousands of pages of county history. Over the next several months, the volunteers would begin working at the boxcar at 6 a.m. so that they could put in several hours of work before the Texas sun heated the interior to a point where it was uninhabitable. The records in the boxcar were in abysmal condition. After years of being stored in what was basically an oven in the summer and a freezer in the winter, the records were dirty, moldy, and a source of food and shelter for rodents, insects, and snakes. To add insult to injury, after a major flood in the 1980s, records were unceremoniously dumped in the boxcar while they were still soaked with floodwater.

After several months of work, the volunteers were able to present to the county an inventory of what was stored at the boxcar. County officials were then asked to visit the box car and, using their records retention schedules, inform the volunteers as to which records would need to be retained. The volunteers also requested that certain record groups be kept for their historic value. In June 2006, the volunteers were granted permission to remove records from the box car for cleaning and re-housing.

The records were ready to move, but to where? In July 2006, the Commissioners Court appointed a committee to gather information on leasing a temporary facility for records retention. In August, the court accepted the recommendation of the committee that a lease be signed with a local resident who owned a building that had previously housed a cotton commodities business. The building, called the Cotton Row Building, became the records retention facility from September 2006 to October 2010. After some delays, the box car records were moved to the Cotton Row Building by the volunteers in April of 2007. After the initial move, a report was presented to the court detailing the completion of the move. The committee also suggested to the court that a second review of the remaining records be conducted by the county officials and a possible means of record disposal be discussed and selected.

What followed was months of discussion as to how the records could be destroyed correctly and legally. Eventually, in January 2010, the remaining records at the box car were destroyed by a reputable firm.

While the volunteers had been working with the county records since late 2005, it was decided that a schedule was necessary. Beginning in May 2006, the Press Gang began official work days on the third Monday of each month. Over five years later, this schedule is still in force.

Because the volunteers were not receiving any funding from the county outside of the rental expense, alternative funds were necessary in order for the program to continue. In December 2005, the then Raymond Dickson Foundation, a local granting entity, awarded the fledging project a grant of $10,000 for equipment and a feasibility study for a records retention building. In November 2006, the volunteers received an additional grant of $5,000 from what was now the Dickson Allen Foundation for supplies and equipment. In December 2010, a third grant was awarded to the project by the foundation. This grant will enable the volunteers to purchase computer equipment and software to begin inventorying and scanning documents and networking with other county offices.

Everyone involved knew that the Cotton Row Building was, at best, a temporary fix. The records retention facility had become part of the courthouse annex project back in 2006. During 2006 and 2007, plans were being set forth by the county to build a new courthouse annex to alleviate courthouse overcrowding and provide space for a permanent records retention facility. In May 2007 the general bond election for the annex was defeated.

In October 2007, Lavaca County purchased a grocery store building in Hallettsville, which was remodeled and now serves as the courthouse annex. The annex was used to house all county offices during the restoration of the over one-hundred-year-old Lavaca County Courthouse from June 2009 to October 2010. After county offices were returned to the courthouse, the records retention project was moved from its home at the Cotton Row Building to the annex in October 2010.

Lessons We Have Learned

RALLY THE TROOPS

Throughout your project, actively pursue and involve anyone who understands your goal and the reasons behind it. These are the individuals who don't need to be educated about the importance of your mission. For whatever reason, they have an innate understanding of the importance of preserving and using historical documents. Consider approaching people such as librarians, historians of all kinds, genealogists, writers, members of historical commissions, and museum staff as potential victims/volunteers.

UNDERSTAND THE COMMITMENT INVOLVED

Everyone involved should realize that this is a long-term (emphasis on *long*) project. Remember to celebrate your small successes along the path to your ultimate goal. Your membership will ebb and flow; do not let that unduly upset you. It is important, however, to keep a core group of individuals who have long-term commitment to the project to provide stability and to mentor new members.

ESTABLISH AND MAINTAIN A SCHEDULE

By establishing and maintaining a schedule, working on the project becomes part of everyone's routine. Make one of the volunteers responsible for sending out monthly reminders about upcoming work days either by e-mail or phone. For example, with the Press Gang our monthly work day is the third Monday of the month and the group receives a reminder e-mail. E-mails are also a great way to keep everyone up to date with special work days and upcoming events or workshops.

INJECT SOME FUN WHENEVER YOU CAN

While everyone involved already personally enjoys the work, it builds camaraderie and good interpersonal relationships when some fun can be added. For example in Lavaca County, the volunteers are jokingly referred to as the "Press Gang," referencing the days when pirates would "impress" or basically hijack people into service. The volunteers have T-shirts designed by a local artist that they wear to each work day and other events. As a public service, the group decorates the courthouse Christmas tree. The Gang also privately paid to have a copy of the 1852 Tax Roll Book reproduced for public use. If and when you can, put a little money where your mouth is: that is, show a personal commitment to the community and its history.

GRANTS: APPLY AND APPLY AGAIN

As with any project, funding is always going to be an issue. For most governmental agencies and other institutions, records retention is not a high priority in their budget. In most cases, you will receive little if any financial support for the project. This is why applying for grants is paramount. The records retention project in Lavaca County would not be where it is today without the grant monies received from our local foundation and from the National Endowment for the Humanities.

Grants, especially federal grants, are very competitive, complicated, and not for the faint of heart. Be not discouraged; for those who commit the time and resources to grant writing, the return can be tremendous. At first, you might not succeed, for there is a learning curve when it comes to grant applications. The more grants you apply for, the easier the process becomes. While we have been successful with our grant writing, we have also received our share of rejections and we learn from each of them. My best advice is this: never accept a no as your final answer.

LEGISLATION IS YOUR ALLY

In Texas, the State Library and Archives Commission is responsible for creating and updating record retention schedules, which provide state and local

governments with the legal responsibilities they have concerning records retention. Every state has rules for records retention. Find out what these are and use
the information to remind your governmental agency that they have records
that must be maintained permanently and records that must be maintained for
differing lengths of time. By doing so, you are making your governmental body
aware of the fact that you have educated yourself and you know what your state
requires. Also, you can use this information as an opportunity to present yourself
as part of the solution, not part of the problem. Not only do you and your group
want to help your agency maintain these records and meet their legal responsibilities, but you're actually "volunteering" to do so.

Another example of legislative support occurred when in May of 2003, the
seventy-eighth Texas legislature passed Senate Bill 1731, which allowed commissioners courts to adopt a record archive fee. This fee was imposed for the
purpose of preserving, restoring, and managing county records. The beauty of
this legislation is that when a record archive fee is adopted and collected, the
money from this fee can only be used for historic records and can be a vital
first step toward promoting and paying for an efficient and comprehensive
preservation program. In such a case, your potential fund for preservation is
protected by the law.

EDUCATION

First educate yourself, then educate the public. To educate yourself, read everything you can on records retention and preservation. Study other successes and
failures. Always ask questions. Talk to and correspond with individuals who
have already walked the path before you. Attend every workshop you can on the
subject. In Texas, the State Library and Archives Commission provides a series of
workshops for training record retention officials. Amigos Library Services Imaging and Preservation Service is an outstanding source of workshops on a variety
of preservation issues.

Educating the general public and the people who actually own the records
is one of the most time-consuming yet essential parts of your project. First make
every attempt to have a positive working relationship with the governing body
to which the records belong. Without their support, it will be almost impossible
to even have the physical access you require to the records.

Your government officials do not want to be publicly called "on the carpet"
about the condition of their records. In the beginning, concentrate on private
meetings and conversations to air your concerns about the condition of their
records; this will be a more productive way to gain their ear. The meetings will
also reveal the lay of the land; that is, you can determine what members of the

governing body are willing to listen to you and support your endeavor. If at all possible save any airing of your concerns in a public fashion as a last resort (or, as I like to call it, a veiled threat).

On the other hand, every success should be put on public display. Share the glory; lavish praise on your volunteers and give them the credit due. Also, share the limelight with your governing body. Frankly, they are more likely to support projects that make them look good in the public eye than those that do not. This idea of a positive public image is especially important in election years. Also, when appropriate, make quarterly or yearly reports to your governing body outlining what the group has accomplished since your last report.

To educate the public, take a multiprong approach. Someone in your group should be comfortable with public speaking because they will be doing a lot of it. Accept any offer to talk about your project, whether it is for the local Rotary Club or a state or national venue. In your program, talk about how the movement is not only helping the governing body meet state requirements, but is also ensuring that vital documents, such as birth, death, marriage, deed, and lease records will be retained properly so that they can be accessed and used by the public whenever needed.

For your programs, pictures are essential. A picture of a badly damaged, moldy, insect-riddled book is worth a thousand words. The pictures you use in your program and exhibits should be as graphic as possible. If possible, use an actual object instead of a photograph. Pick a small book or document that is damaged beyond repair and show it as an example. The ever-so-slight essence of mold can really get people's attention. Also encourage interested parties to visit your facility.

THERE IS NO SUCH THING AS BAD PUBLICITY (IF YOU USE IT TO YOUR ADVANTAGE)

Do not underestimate the power of the press. Make sure to contact the local press when you have any major event, exhibit, or presentation about your project. If your newspaper is diligent about publicizing local events, your project will be a novelty. In the newspaper world, volunteers make for good press. For example, in September 2010, due to prior publicity, an adjoining county contacted us when an 1874–1877 Lavaca County Justice of the Peace book was located in their courthouse holdings. The book was given to the volunteers, who presented it back to the county via the commissioners court. The local press gave us excellent coverage.

Do not shy away from letters to the editor. Twice over the course of our project, someone has publicly questioned the validity of our project and how it is being funded via letters to the editor. Do not let these challenges go unanswered.

Always base your responses on facts, never on emotions. While you hope that education is enough, be prepared to defend your project.

If you are lucky, your project will draw attention from outside parties. In Lavaca County, our project has come to the attention of Amigos Library Services and the state library. Both agencies used our project as an example of how to successfully begin and maintain a fledgling records management project.

In closing, we offer our best advice. Lead by example. Surround yourself with dedicated people who share your vision. Use all available resources. Make it fun whenever possible, and realize that education is one of your primary objectives. Be realistic: some folks will never buy into your idea. Remember this quote: "Those of you who say it can't be done, stop bothering those of us who are doing it."

The People

Bottom line: the success of any project rests with the individuals involved. In the case of the Lavaca County records retention project a unique group of people have and continue to pool their talents together to create a great team.

REBECCA ELDER

Rebecca Elder is adjunct preservation field services officer for Amigos Library Services Imaging and Preservation Service. She received her MSIS and a certificate of advanced studies for conservation of library and archival materials from the University of Texas at Austin. She is also an adjunct instructor at the University of Texas at Austin, where she teaches preservation management. Rebecca is a member of the American Institute for Conservation of Historic and Artistic Works and the Society of American Archivists.

Rebecca has been the mentor of the project. The volunteers have received preservation training in workshops presented by Rebecca. Rebecca also prepared the extensive on-site study of current storage conditions and provided the county with written guidance on making needed improvements. She has offered, and continues to offer, professional advice, encouragement, guidance, and friendship during the entire process.

ELIZABETH KOUBA

Elizabeth Kouba is the county clerk and records management officer for Lavaca County, Texas. She is the custodian of records and responsible for recording documents pertaining to the county courts, real property, commissioners court, probate, and vital records. Her professional activities include training from the Texas State Library in records management and from Amigos Library in preserving historical records. Elizabeth is a member of the Lavaca County Historical Commission. The Lavaca County Clerk's Office is a member of Amigos Library Services, Inc.

Elizabeth is the local go-to person. She is the liaison between the volunteers and the county. As the county's records management official, she handles all of the budget requests and purchases for the program and assists other offices with their records retention issues. She is the vital link between the two groups that makes the project run efficiently and effectively.

LAVACA COUNTY RECORDS RETENTION VOLUNTEERS (THE "PRESS GANG")

The "Press Gang" consists of a group of individuals who have committed time and money to the records retention project. Two of the members can be considered "Founding Mothers" as they were instrumental in setting up the program six years ago. Other individuals have come and gone as happens with many volunteer organizations. The current members include Janice Saunders, the curator of the local museum; Irene Szwarc, a part-time library/museum employee; Holly Heinsohn, a history teacher/writer; and two members of the local historical commission, Margaret Dornak and Theresa Volkel. They are the reason this project is successful.

CHAPTER 15

Managing Archives in Local History Collections

Sarah Welland

Archives play a key part in documenting memory. They ensure accountability by recording decisions and events as they happened. When they are appropriately managed, archives are the closest thing to unbiased evidence of what actually happened in the past. They allow the user to make their own interpretations, rather than having an author make interpretations for them.

This chapter gives an introduction to what an archive is and how it is selected. It explains how archives should be organized, stored, and accessed so that they retain their meaning.

Meaning for archives is not just about content but also about context—that is, where they came from; who created them; when, how, and why they were created; and what else was created for the same purpose. For most archives, this information is not within them, making it important to use methods of organizing and cataloging that enable a user to understand the full picture behind an archive's content, creation, and use. Archives management is a distinct profession from librarianship, with different core principles. It is strongly recommended that further research is carried out before accessioning any archives and that relevant professional standards, codes, policies, and guidelines are located and applied.

What Is, and Isn't, an Archive?

It is important to understand the term "archive" in order to identify the material that will need to be correctly managed and stored as archives.

- Archives are original. There is only one copy of each item (for example, annotations can make an archive unique), and it doesn't exist anywhere else.
- Archives document what people do in their daily lives. In other words, they originally began life as records.
- Archives were not created with the general public in mind, as published materials usually are. They were not made for any purpose beyond that of providing evidence of what the creator did or decided to do. For example, businesses create records of their company formation, and artists write letters to friends about their work. These records have the potential to become archives.
- Archives have value even after their creator(s) have finished with them. They have been carefully reviewed and a decision has been made that they have evidential or informational value that lasts beyond their original purpose. On average, less than 10 percent of all records become archives.
- Archives rely on context to give them meaning. Information about how an item was created is as important as the item itself.
- Archives are kept for the long term and usually forever. The standard rule should be: once an archive, always an archive.
- Archives can be in just about any format, from handwritten letters and bound ledgers to photographs, sound recordings, databases, and websites.

   Archives are not:

- books, serials, or newspapers, regardless of their age
- information copied from another source for reference purposes (for example, genealogical information sourced from another library)

   Keeping the above characteristics in mind, an archive can be distinguished from other material when aspects are considered such as:

- where it came from,
- who the creator was,
- what it was used for,
- the reasons why it was (or should be) collected, and
- what (if anything) makes it original.

For example:

- If draft chapters of a book written by a local author were donated to the local history collection, these would be considered archives because they are a record of the work that the author actually did. The published copy of that book would not be an archive.
- If a local family donated their family research, and the papers included copies of material from other collections and newspaper clippings, these items would be listed and kept with the archival collection in the same order in which they were donated. This is because even though the information is not original and exists elsewhere, the research in its entirety is an archive and all parts of that must be kept together to give context and meaning to it.

What Archives to Collect

The range of material that could potentially end up in a local history collection is extremely wide and varied. There are two key steps to acquiring material that is suitable for an archival collection.

DEVELOP AND FOLLOW AN ARCHIVES ACQUISITION POLICY

An archives acquisition policy may be part of a library's collection development policy or a separate document. The important thing is that it explicitly covers archives and their unique requirements and what will and will not be accepted. If it doesn't, it becomes difficult to validate any archival decisions and processes or maintain consistent practice.

There are many good examples on the web. Most include information such as:

- the aim(s) of the local history collection;
- who has ultimate authority (and therefore responsibility) for the collection;
- how the archives will be acquired and managed professionally and ethically;
- the sorts of materials that are accepted and not accepted as archives (this is usually done by outlining collection "boundaries" such as geography, date or topic);
- the types of formats (e.g., paper, film, electronic) that will be accepted or not accepted;
- how restrictions will be applied and managed (for example, personal papers may not be able to be viewed until the creator has died);

- an outline of the de-accessioning policy (if this is practiced);
- definitions of key terms (for example, archives, records, donation, restriction). These should be provided to avoid misunderstanding.

This policy will make it easier to identify likely inclusions for the local history archive. Once material has been identified, a second step is necessary: appraisal.

ARCHIVAL APPRAISAL

Archival appraisal refers to the process of deciding whether an item or group of items should be kept as archives. Once they have been appraised, they can be called archives. Up until then they are still records.

Archival appraisal ensures that only key or significant records that correctly represent a time, event, place, or decision are kept. Appraisal keeps collections to a manageable size and ensures that precious space and money is not wasted storing low-value information that is too fragile or expensive to maintain.

Appraisal involves a careful and detailed review of a variety of aspects. It is a job for a professional librarian, archivist, or records manager. It should not be carried out by students or volunteers, unless they are fully trained and have archival experience.

There are six key steps to the archival appraisal process.

Scoping the Potential Donation

It is important to determine early on in the process whether the offered material fits the requirements of the archives acquisition policy and, if it does, whether the local history collection is willing to bear the cost of storing it. Some materials, such as electronic, fragile, or large-format items, will have higher maintenance and storage costs.

It is also important to check that the donors have the right to transfer the records; for example, that their family is happy for the family documents to be deposited, that they have the sign-off of the general manager or chief executive of the company, and so on. If they do not have this right, then any agreements with them about the records will not stand up legally.

Obtaining a List of the Material

A list of the material in the order it was originally used needs to be supplied by the donor or created in-house. This provides a good overview of what is offered and also provides examples to back up later appraisal decisions. At a minimum a list should have:

- original item references if they exist (e.g., original file classification numbers)
- title of each group of related items (e.g., "Inwards Correspondence")
- title of each individual item (e.g., "Letter from R. L. Bolger to E. M. Marriott")
- date range of each item (e.g., the dates of the oldest and most recent documents within a file)

It is important to check a sample of the list to make sure that it gives the required information. Check any item(s) with vague or nonsensical titles, such as "General Miscellaneous," and write further explanation on the list in square brackets as necessary; for example: "General Miscellaneous [Collection of loose papers outlining establishment of T. Smith and Company]."

Finding Out about the Material

Information on the individual, business, group, or organization that created and used the material plays an essential part in determining key or significant records.

This will include:

- where and when the items were created and used (for example, research on school records would need to cover the school, the dates it operated, its past curriculum and staff, and so on)
- the purpose of the records; that is, why and how the records were created and used. This information can be gained through questions like:
  - Who created it?
  - What was it used for?
  - Why was the range of material created?
  - How are the items organized (e.g., numerically, chronologically, in no order)?
  - Do the original item codes exist? Can they show us how the items used to be organized?

Reviewing the Material

Once the background research is done, the material needs to be looked at in more detail. If a small number of items are offered, each could be looked at individually. If a larger collection is offered (for example, business records divided into policy, human resources, and client files), each group of related records would need to be reviewed, with individual records checked as required.

Determining the Value of the Material

Value is another key concept when it comes to appraisal. It is used to establish whether an item will become an archive or not. The following values are commonly applied:

- Evidential value: Regardless of whether a local history collection acquires material from one major donor or from multiple sources, each item should demonstrate some form of evidential value. Evidential value provides evidence that an item was created by a source that is significant in some way to the local history collection and documents a significant decision, activity, idea, or transaction. Evidential value can be demonstrated either through the different types of legal, fiscal, or administrative information held within the record, or through the record showing how the creator is held accountable in some way.

  Evidential value can only be applied if there is awareness of the circumstances surrounding the creation of an item—something that is not known until appropriate background research is carried out. For example, an e-mail from Mary to Bob saying simply "yes" may not be interesting on its own, but if the information associated with that e-mail demonstrated that Mary was giving Bob permission to illegally dump used oil in a local river, it takes on new meaning, and new value.
- Informational value: This is value based on the information contained within the record. This value is useful but needs to be applied carefully, as just about any item (rail tickets, check-out dockets, etc.) can have some form of informational value. It is best to think of informational value as something that gives an item its "intrinsic value," which may not be evidential in nature but may provide insight into key or significant aspects of social, cultural, artistic, and historical lifestyles and/or heritage within the local area.

Documenting Decisions

Once the value of the material has been determined, documentation on the decisions that were made needs to be written and signed off by the donor and by management. This is unlike a library's treatment of donations and is done to explain to future generations of staff and users why the decisions made were considered to be the most appropriate ones at the time.

At a minimum documentation should cover:

- how the material offered for donation fits the archives acquisition policy;
- what material is recommended for transfer and why;
- which material requires special equipment, software, or storage or handling, and why it is justified.

How Should Archives Be Transferred to the Local History Collections?

Once the decisions are made on what is going to be transferred, a formal transfer agreement with the donor needs to be drawn up and signed by all parties.

Good examples of transfer agreements can be found on the web and in archival publications. Most include information on:

- the right of the donor to transfer and make access decisions
- the length of the custody arrangement, if it is not permanent
- who holds ownership (this sometimes remains with the donor or their nominated representative)
- who owns copyright
- the moral right of the creator(s)
- "cultural copyright" for information created by or about indigenous peoples
- reproduction of items

The signed agreement and all related information must be filed safely within the local history collection's records management system.

How Should Archives Be Organized?

There are two key archival principles that affect how archives are organized and described.

PROVENANCE

The principle of provenance states that collections from different donors should be kept separate to maintain the context of their creation and use. For example, the photographic collections of two local photographers should never be integrated, even if the subject matter is the same. (Indexes or catalogs would provide subject headings or links to both sets of images.)

ORIGINAL ORDER

The principle of original order states that all items should be described (cataloged or indexed) and kept in the same way as they were when they were created and used (or when they were given to the local history collection).

These principles (original order and provenance) may not always seem to make sense, especially when archives are transferred in an order that makes it difficult for users to access the information within them. However, removing an archive from its original arrangement takes it out of context, reducing its value (and the user's ability to understand the full picture) because its ability to provide evidence of what happened is compromised.

ARTIFICIAL ORDER

Occasionally a collection may be offered for donation that is in no discernable order whatsoever. If this happens, an artificial order needs to be established and documented. Because context is so important for archives, it is best to decide on a form of artificial order that relates to the original purpose of the items rather than the needs of the researcher or the collection itself.

For example:

- Dated information is best arranged by date, as this follows the natural progression of events.
- A group of personnel records from the same donor can be organized alphabetically by surname, as this would most probably be the way they were originally arranged.

A group of disparate objects that have no discernable relationship to one another should be listed and cataloged separately.

How Should Archives Be Cataloged?

Archives need to be cataloged in ways that include content-based and contextual information, and reflect the archival principles of provenance and original order.

This information needs to be provided so that meaning (and therefore value) is not lost.

While there are a large variety of systems available that catalog archives, there are some key aspects that must be included. These are described below.

DESCRIPTIVE ELEMENTS

The best way of describing an archive is by using a number of descriptive elements. These describe the content and the context of each archive from the most general to the most specific. (This is often called multilevel description.)

Essential descriptive elements are:

- Donor information (also called agency information, biographical information, or group information): describes the donor of the material. Information may include reference code, name, biography, relevant dates, list of all archival accessions transferred by the donor, and relevant deed of gift/restriction information. Similar information will need to be entered for the creator of the items if this is different from the donor.
- Accession information: describes the entire donated collection. Information may include reference code, title description, dates, scope, and content notes.
- Item description: describes the item itself. Usually in the form of item lists, this may include information such as reference number, title, format, dimensions, location, and restriction details.

If a MARC system is used and records are included within a library's catalog, new fields may need to be added, or else existing ones creatively changed, in order to document each item adequately.

If the local history collection has a number of larger collections that are divided into subcategories, the addition of a series description element (one that describes related groups of items) is recommended.

CODE LINKAGES

In many systems the relationships between the descriptive elements described above are made through archives classification codes. These codes also aid physical and electronic location and retrieval in the same way as library classification schemes do.

A simple example is:

ABCD 1111 /2 5/8   Policy on Roading Changes   1965–1968 R
Looking up

- ABCD would provide information about the creator(s);
- ABCD 1111 would provide information on the entire donated archival group;
- ABCD 1111 /2 would provide an item description and location information;
- 5/8 would provide the reference code under which the item was originally organized; and
- R would show that the material is restricted and direct the user to check restriction information under ABCD.

Coding varies significantly, depending on the rules that are followed and the systems that are used. It's possible to use DDC or LCC to code the creator and archival group, if the organization wishes. The key thing is that levels of archival description exist, and that they are linked to each other.

Describing archives through archival description tools or within a catalog takes time and experience. The cataloger must have an in-depth understanding of the principles of provenance and original order, and how to apply them, before beginning their work.

How Should Archives Be Stored?

Correct storage conditions and techniques are vital. There are a variety of archives storage standards on the web, as well as some excellent books and websites on this topic.

The important themes are:

- A preservation program should be established for planning and resourcing purposes.
- Archives should be stored separately from other material, as they have different access and storage requirements.
- Each format has its unique storage needs.
- Storage areas, shelving, and containers need to meet archival standards. (These are significantly higher than most library standards, because the archives are irreplaceable, unique items. Considerations include temperature, humidity, light, pest control, and acid-free containers.)
- A disaster management plan specifically for archives should be in place.

How Should Archives Be Accessed?

Archives should only be accessible by staff. User access should take into account the following:

- staff availability to supervise use
- restrictions put in place by the donor
- the fragility of the items
- the possibility of intentional or unintentional damage
- the inherent value of the items (that is, whether they are a temptation to thieves)

Measures to manage public access to archives can usually build on existing procedures. They include:

- use of suitable policies and procedures (e.g., research area rules) to ensure compliance and consistency of approach by staff and users
- user registration (this is very important, and picture ID should be required)
- finding aids (for example, descriptive elements within the catalog, "how to" guides, and indexes)
- a suitably arranged research area that minimizes opportunistic (or planned) theft;
- building security
- reproduction (e.g., through photocopying or digitization) of heavily used archives to reduce use of originals
- information on restrictions

There will always be circumstances that are not covered by existing rules or guidelines. In these cases, it is best to be guided by professional ethics and consult others in the industry.

Conclusion

Archives need to be managed differently from other reference materials. This is because:

- Archives are unique and irreplaceable; there is usually no other copy of them anywhere.
- Archives need to be viewed and used within the context of their creation and use, as without this information, the content of an archive becomes valueless.
- Properly established processes and knowledgeable management will ensure that these treasures within local history collections will continue to serve as a key source of community memory.

PART V

GENEALOGY

CHAPTER 16

Partnering with Local Genealogical Societies

Lisa Fraser

Partnerships between public libraries and genealogical societies provide opportunities for both organizations to increase their reach and better serve the growing population of family history researchers. For more than a decade, King County Library System has partnered with Eastside Genealogical Society (EGS) and South King County Genealogical Society (SKCGS), two local organizations that provide materials, volunteers, and educational programs that enhance the library system's offerings. This chapter will provide tips for establishing successful partnerships, ideas for joint programs and services, and real-world examples.

Establishing a Partnership

Partnerships have both benefits and drawbacks. They often allow each organization to accomplish more than it would be able to do on its own. However, developing partnerships requires attention to detail in the formation stage and regular maintenance thereafter. Successful partnerships rely on positive relationships, open communication, and a well-thought-out partnership agreement.

When forging any kind of partnership, it is important to assess how well the partnering organizations' missions and values align and what resources each brings to the table. Generally speaking, libraries and genealogical societies have similar goals—to provide guidance and access to information that meets the needs of the family history researcher. This basic compatibility is a good foundation, but both organizations should be able to express a more detailed image of their values and goals. Before entering into any agreement, start by understanding what your library is looking for in a partnership. Then meet with the genealogical society to determine what they are hoping to gain from the relationship. It is not necessary that the two parties be identical in their desires for the partnership, but having values and goals that are widely disparate may be an indication of potential future problems. Once you determine that the values and goals are compatible, it will be easier to move forward with planning the partnership.

As you make decisions about how the partnership will look, record them in a letter of agreement (LOA) that will be signed by representatives of both organizations. Be sure that the signers have the authority to enter into agreements on behalf of their organizations. At a minimum, the LOA should include the names or titles of any individuals who have specifically designated roles in the partnership, information about any use of resources, the time frame for reviewing the arrangement, and the process for ending the partnership. A sample LOA is provided at the end of this chapter.

General Guidelines for Partnerships

- Involve the people who are authorized to make the decisions.
- Get input from those who will be affected, such as cataloging or programming staff.
- Keep in mind any policies or laws that govern the activities of either organization.
- Put all decisions in writing.
- Set a time frame for revisiting the agreement.

Resources

Genealogical societies and libraries often bring complementary resources to a partnership. Libraries' greatest strengths usually include trained staff, space for people and materials, and access to the larger community. Genealogical societies may have specialized materials, knowledgeable members, and access to a targeted segment of the community.

Examples of organizational resources include:

Genealogical Societies

- members who are experts on genealogy-specific sources, specialized resources, and information repositories outside the library
- specialized materials

- access to targeted segments of the community
- access to other genealogical societies, conference materials, and trainings
- funding for genealogy-specific materials

Libraries

- staff who are experts on information sources, searching techniques, and library resources
- materials on a wide variety of topics
- space
- access to larger community
- funding for general-purpose materials
- infrastructure for programs and classes

EGS President Judy Meredith sums up the benefits of sharing resources, saying, "I think EGS/KCLS is a good partnership because it gives the society somewhere to meet and a place for any books we acquire. Meeting in the library means we don't have to purchase things like projectors and gives us a space for classes that includes computers. It also gives the society more exposure to the general public. It's good for the library, too, because our meetings, classes and books bring in people who might not otherwise use the facility."

Collections

One natural connection between libraries and genealogical societies lies in the area of collections. Most libraries will come to the partnership table with at least a basic collection of books and magazines on genealogy topics. However, the collection may lack depth due to limited resources or difficulties in selecting more specialized items. The society and its membership may also own materials, including specialized genealogy and family history topics. The challenge for many societies is providing access to the collections that they have. One solution provided by a partnership is housing the society's collection in the library, where it will be more easily accessible.

There are several important issues to be considered when proposing to house the materials of a genealogical society in the public library. State and local laws as well as the policies of each organization will shape the arrangement. Laws and policies can be open to interpretation; be sure to involve all key decision makers in the process to avoid misunderstandings and future problems.

The first issue is the ownership of the materials. This may fall under the laws that govern use of public funds and property, so be sure that those are clearly understood. The main determination to be made is whether materials become the property of the library or remain the property of the society. If they become the property of the library, then they will be subject to the same collection development guidelines and processes as the rest of the collection. It is critical that the genealogy society board understand and agree to those processes before the partnership is finalized.

If the society intends to continue adding materials to the collection, there should be clear parameters in place for selecting materials, in accordance with the regular collection development policies of the library. This may include criteria for subject, material type, age, or other attributes. In addition, the individuals who have the authority and responsibility to select and discard materials for the

Genealogy Reference Collections at KCLS

A key feature of the partnerships between KCLS and the two genealogical societies are the genealogy reference collections located at the library branches in Bellevue and Auburn. Prior to partnership, the genealogical societies owned reference books and other materials, but they were not easily accessible to the membership. The library system had space for the collections, which would increase access for the members as well as the general public. After considering the relevant laws, it was determined that the materials must be considered donations and become the property of the library system in order to be housed in the libraries. Both societies donated their collections to the library system and continue to purchase new materials. These are governed by the same laws and collection development policies as any other part of the collection. New books are selected by a committee that includes several members from the society and a KCLS librarian. The society purchases the books, affixes a bookplate, and delivers them to the librarian, who adds them to the collection through the regular process for donations. When the genealogy librarian identifies materials to weed, the committee is given the opportunity to weigh in on that decision. In addition to the donated items, the library system also continues to purchase materials for the genealogy collections. The entire collection is searchable in the KCLS catalog, and the societies also maintain lists of the materials that they have donated. Access to the list for the SKCGS collection at Auburn Library is available at www.rootsweb.ancestry.com/~waskcgs/library.html.

Sarah Fleming, EGS acquisitions committee chair, expressed some of the benefits that she observes from the Bellevue Library/EGS partnership. She finds the participation of the genealogy librarian in the acquisitions committee to be mutually beneficial. In addition, other staff members at KCLS provide insight. "The interlibrary loan librarian is a valuable resource for determining which books need to be added to the genealogy collection to best serve patron interests," Fleming says. ILL staff are able to provide information on frequently requested genealogy titles that may be worthwhile additions to the collection. Fleming added, "We appreciate that the society's book acquisition committee is allowed to provide input to the weeding process."

collection should be specified. If processing the materials for use requires special handling, that procedure should be determined at the outset of the partnership. Likewise, the process and responsibility for weeding materials from the collection should be clearly communicated.

Programs

Depending on the agreement and the level of partnership desired, the society and the library may consider all genealogy-related activities as jointly held, or they may continue to provide mostly separate programs. Joint programs benefit from the publicity of both organizations, while offering separate programs requires less coordination between the two organizations.

SOCIETY MEETINGS

Most genealogical societies have quarterly or monthly general meetings for the membership, and finding a meeting space can be a challenge. The ability to meet at the library is a powerful incentive for partnership, yet it is often one of the easiest benefits for a library to provide. The library offers a consistent venue that is usually conveniently located and easy to access. Facilities differ, but the library may have one or more meeting rooms or other spaces where library events are held. When negotiating a partnership that will include use of space for meetings, keep in mind these issues:

- Will the society be held to the same rules as the general public, or will the arrangements be different? For example, if the usual policy is for an organization to be able to use the library's meeting room once per quarter, but the society meets monthly, will the library make an exception to the policy as a result of the partnership?
- Will the exceptions be allowed only for specific meetings, or will they apply to all meetings of the society? Some societies have a general meeting, meetings of the board and/or subcommittees, and meetings of special interest groups. It should be decided in advance which of these are part of the use exceptions and which are not.
- Does the use of space include staffing, equipment, or supplies?
- Will the meetings be promoted on the library's website or event calendar?

WORKSHOPS

Educational workshops are one of the most valuable services that genealogical societies and libraries offer. As genealogy grows in popularity, the need for individuals to learn about best practices, research techniques, and resources will also increase. By working together, genealogical societies and libraries can enjoy the benefits of combined resources. Workshops can take several forms.

- A librarian may provide a demonstration of library resources at a general meeting of the genealogical society. This can introduce a large number of people to library offerings at one time. It also provides an opportunity for those attending to see the "face" of the library, which is particularly helpful if there is a designated genealogy librarian.
- Another way to showcase library offerings is to have a librarian teach a hands-on workshop on a single resource. This approach can allow time for more individualized instruction.
- A society expert may teach a workshop as a library program. The list of possible topics for library-sponsored programs is limited only by the expertise of society members who want to teach. A good place to start is a basic genealogy workshop for beginners.

Successful Genealogy Program Series

Bellevue Library and Eastside Genealogical Society offered a workshop series every other Sunday afternoon in fall 2010 that introduced patrons to many of the most widely used genealogy resources. Each workshop was two hours in length. Library staff taught Genealogy @ KCLS, an overview of the resources available at Bellevue Library and through the KCLS website. All other workshops were taught by EGS volunteers. A selection of books and other materials relevant to the workshop topic was selected by the librarian and displayed at the workshop, along with book lists and handouts. Two weeks after the final workshop, library staff taught a smaller, hands-on class on using Ancestry Library Edition and Heritage Quest at KCLS in the same time slot. The workshops covered the following topics:

- Introduction to Genealogy
- Genealogy @ KCLS
- Genealogy Research on the Internet
- Finding and Using Census Records
- Finding and Using County Histories, Maps, and Land Records
- Finding and Using Newspapers and City Directories
- Documenting Milestones and Daily Life: Church Records, Taxes, and Military Records

Between fifteen and thirty people attended each workshop, with Internet research drawing the largest crowd.

Outreach in the Community

Whether your library is focused on providing services in the library or is expanding its reach into the community and online, taking advantage of opportunities to promote the library in the community is one important way to build support and inform patrons of the resources available. Partnerships with genealogical societies provide many opportunities for librarians to reach beyond the library building.

- Many genealogical societies have websites or newsletters and would be happy to have contributions from the local librarian. Reviews of genealogy books, information about online resources, and tips on research techniques would all make good topics. As for frequency, a regularly occurring column provides another public face for the library, while the occasional article on a special topic can be flexible and timely.
- If your local genealogical society has special interest groups, such as those for researching specific countries, their meetings provide an excellent opportunity to introduce members to the resources the library has on that topic.
- Larger cities are often the site of genealogy and local history events, conferences, and trainings that can be both a source of valuable information and a place to promote library services. Attending these events is great for professional development, and opportunities to present may also be available.
- Smaller cities have local events that provide a way to interact with community members outside the library. Libraries and genealogical societies often have booths at city celebrations, farmers' markets, and fairs—why not attend together? Ask for the library and society tables to be placed near each other, and referrals between organizations can increase the traffic for both.

Volunteers

Volunteers from the society can provide many services at the library. Before engaging volunteers, make sure that training and background checks meet the expectations of both the library and the society. Be sure to work out any administrative details, such as how recruitment of volunteers or registration for workshops will be handled, in the partnership agreement. There are many ways that volunteers can enhance the services already provided by library staff.

- Research help: It can be difficult for the library to provide one-on-one help for individual researchers, and often that level of assistance is exactly what beginning genealogists need. Volunteers from the genealogical society are a valuable resource to address this need. Depending on the preferences of volunteers, staff, and patrons, research help could be offered at specific times on a drop-in basis or by appointment.

- Hands-on workshops: Many topics lend themselves well to hands-on practice, and society volunteers are likely to have a wide variety of knowledge and skills. Some examples of possible workshops include instruction for new users of a genealogy software program (with attendees bringing their own laptops loaded with the software), using a specific genealogy website, or care and preservation of photographs.

- Orientation to library materials for specific groups: Library staff may love to provide orientations and tours in the library, but it can be helpful to have additional guides, particularly for specialized resources. If your society has an expert in Civil War–era resources or researching German ancestors, offering a tour of the related materials in the collection is a service that benefits everyone.

Volunteer Research Help

Volunteers from Eastside Genealogical Society are available for drop-in research assistance two days per week at Bellevue Library. Usually working in pairs, volunteers are supplied with a laptop computer in a room near the genealogy collection. They field a wide variety of questions, from general information on getting started with research to pinpointing facts about a particular ancestor.

Finalizing and Maintaining the Partnership

The finished and signed letter of agreement lays out the expectations for the partnership, but periodic maintenance is needed to keep things running smoothly. A representative from the library should meet regularly with the board of the genealogical society to discuss successes and concerns and to generate new ideas for programs and services. Keeping the society up-to-date on changes within the library system that may affect genealogists, and soliciting input from board members, when possible, also contributes to a good working relationship. By establishing clear expectations at the outset and keeping communication open, the public library and genealogical society can work together to provide valuable and innovative support to the growing community of family historians.

Sample Letter of Agreement

LETTER OF AGREEMENT BETWEEN THE
GENEALOGICAL SOCIETY AND THE LIBRARY SYSTEM

The Genealogical Society agrees:

1. To donate a collection of books and research materials to the Library System, to be shelved in a special area of the library to be identified as the Genealogy Collection. Donations to the collection become the property of the Library System and are subject to the library's current policies for disposal. The Library System will notify the Genealogical Society of titles selected for disposal. The Genealogy Collection may also include material purchased by the Library System. The Genealogical Society and the Library System agree that the collection will be housed on open shelves as a non-circulating reference collection and that it will be cataloged under the existing library cataloging system.

2. To provide an appropriate bookplate or label, identifying each book and all research materials as donated to the Library System by the Genealogical Society.

3. To provide a contact person from the Genealogical Society to act as a liaison between the Genealogical Society and the Library System, to provide guidance on the status and condition of the collection, to offer suggestions about the removal and addition of materials to the collection, to work with the library to facilitate growth of the collection, and in general, to facilitate the usefulness of the Genealogy Collection. The liaison from the Genealogical Society will be the Acquisitions Committee Chair.

4. To provide occasional educational opportunities in the field of genealogical research to library patrons, such as genealogy classes, seminars or appointments.

5. To add to the collection as funding becomes available and as library space permits, through donations and purchases.

6. To maintain newsletters, quarterlies and bulletins on a rotating basis, keeping the most current issues on file and removing those that are outdated or no longer deemed useful.

The Library System agrees:

1. To house a collection in the Main Library branch of the Library System in a special section to be identified as the Genealogy Collection; this area may contain materials purchased by the Library System as well as those items donated by the Genealogical Society. The Library System will provide space and shelving for the collection at no cost to the Genealogical Society.

2. To enter the collection into its cataloging system, at its own expense. The collection should be cataloged and shelved under a system compatible with that used in other areas of the Library (Dewey Decimal System). The Library

System will be responsible for keeping the collection in good condition, and will weed the collection as necessary.

3. To provide a contact person from the Library System to act as a liaison between the Genealogical Society and the library.

4. That library staff members will help researchers to locate books and materials and will provide general information about the collection as requested by library patrons.

5. To accept donated items from the Genealogical Society which meet Library System criteria for content and condition. Preference will be given to those works which relate directly to people who lived in the local geographic area and to those which strongly support the genealogy interests of those living in the Library System's service area. In addition, preference will be given to materials covering regions or states. Books covering longer time periods and larger numbers of people are preferable to those covering a more limited area.

Use of the Collection:

Since the Library System has multiple locations, it is agreed that the collection may be circulated between the Main Library Branch and other branches of the Library System on intra-library loan to meet the needs of its patrons, but research materials and books may NOT be made available for Interlibrary Loan outside the Library System. All materials are to be designated "For Reference Only" and are to be used in the borrowing facility, not checked out. All materials are to be returned to the Main Library System site where they will be maintained.

Use of materials from the Genealogy Collection, by official representatives of the Genealogical Society for seminars, meetings or special programs of the Society will be allowed with one-week advance notice. These materials must be returned to the Main Library within the standard loan period.

Term of Agreement

The term of this agreement will be for a ten-year period beginning on the date listed below. During this ten-year period, the agreement may be amended only with a mutual written agreement between the Genealogical Society and the Library System. If one or the other of the parties wishes to cancel the agreement that party must give 90 days written notice to the other.

At the end of the ten-year period, the Agreement will be reviewed and resubmitted for approval signatures by both parties to the Agreement.

Date of Agreement: _____

By:_____ By:_____

President   Director
Genealogical Society   Library System

CHAPTER 17

Patron-Driven Family History Preservation

Howard C. Bybee

"How can I digitize, preserve, and share my genealogical materials—photos, letters, journals—so they will last forever?" That is one of the most frequent patron inquiries in our library, the Harold B. Lee Library at Brigham Young University. In the family history area of our library in Provo, Utah, we provide advice and technology for scanning transparencies (slides and negatives of various dimensions), photos, books, journals, and documents, along with the means to store them on archival media. We do not have equipment for digitizing movie film; that is best left to commercial conversion companies. VHS to DVD conversion equipment is offered in another area of the library.

Patrons bring many different types of family history documents that require very different treatment. Once these materials are digitized, preservation becomes the main concern. Our vision is to create a system that links all the input devices into an archival preservation mechanism. The digital objects are to be saved in one networked location, then downloaded at a workstation connected to an archival DVD option or another media storage device, portable hard disc, or USB flash drive or uploaded for cloud storage. In this system a patron can come to the library, digitize all their family history supporting documents and also collect results of their library research, and leave with the digital archival result safely preserved in any format they choose. This vision drives our technology and our acquisition policies at the same time, all aiming at customer service from beginning to end in the research process.

Digitize

Digitize has become the preservation buzzword. Libraries do it to provide broad access to unique materials and to preserve rare documents by reducing exposure of the original to adverse environmental conditions and handling. Individuals preserve their materials for the same reasons. All historical documents left in the hands of individuals will inevitably be destroyed or be forever lost through dissemination, environmental conditions, fire, or flood, unless they are protected in archives. The physical object is best preserved in an archive, where a digital surrogate may be offered to researchers, where possible. Family memorabilia will likely be divided among family members, generation after generation, separating important collections from context, destroying their historical research value, or ending up in private collections.

The library will need to provide equipment and expertise to the public. To do this the library must be able to expend funds for equipment and personnel. Personnel must be knowledgeable about scanning methods, provide instruction to the public, evaluate and select the best equipment, maintain equipment, and support the software. While many libraries have a scanning department that digitizes special collections or provides copies for the public, it may be more challenging to dedicate an area to family history or genealogical research and preservation for public use. Operating costs can be partially recouped by charging a fee to use the equipment, though some libraries are prohibited from charging.

Providing a place for digital preservation will attract more patronage and improve the quality of preservation for individuals and may aid the library in discovering important research materials that would otherwise disappear.

DEFINITION

Digitization simply put means to transform from analog to digital, to create a digital surrogate for a physical text, image, or object that can be stored, shared, and edited or manipulated with a computer. The object can become an image in several formats; TIFF, JPG, and PDF are common formats. Enhancements to these formats range from optical character recognition (OCR) that creates a searchable or editable document, to marked-up documents with web links, pop-up notes, and references to related materials in the library. Individuals in images can be identified with mouse-over pop-ups, and all digital files can be made searchable within a large database or collection by tagging them with metadata.

Equipment

There are many equipment brands and configurations for scanning. Flatbed scanners are the most common. A large format book scanner is essential. Family history documents such as certificates, pedigree charts, photos, or portraits vary in size and are often larger than 8 × 11 or 11 × 14. Maps require large formats even to reduce the size of the original. The most affordable large-surface desktop scanners accommodate objects up to about 13 × 17. Larger scanners pull the original through the scanner and scan 36 inches or larger. Scanners that provide a book edge that protects the book and gives an image without gutter shadow are available and affordable. They scan to PDF, TIFF, or JPG and perform OCR. These are used for books, photos, and loose paper. Models are available that scan negative and positive film. Scanners and printers improve and require upgrades as often as possible.

FLATBED SCANNERS

Many modern scanners digitize positive film transparencies and negatives and offer many automatic features. We use different brands and models to serve various needs. Large-format scanners are recommended for scanning slides and negatives as well as opaque photos and documents. These scanners can scan twelve or more slides at a time, in sequence, with very high resolution. As of this writing we are not aware of inexpensive high-speed slide scanners for public use, especially for high-resolution, quality scans.

Several companies sell 35 mm slide and negative scanners for home use. These devices scan using five- to seven-megapixel photo cells to photograph a projected image and store it internally or on a removable memory card. The images can be transferred to a computer via a USB connection or by using the removable flash memory card. These slide copiers are easy to use and self-contained and come with software that automatically enhances the scans, adjusting for brightness and contrast and color enhancement.

Be prepared to learn the details of the software and the care needed to clean and properly orient slide film in order to obtain a good image, correctly oriented, as efficiently as possible. Scan a thousand slides or other media on a new scanner to become thoroughly familiar with the equipment in order to save time in preparing instruction sheets that help patrons through the learning curve.

SHEET-FEED SCANNERS

A sheet-feed scanner differs from a flatbed scanner in several ways. There is no glass bed on which to arrange documents for copying. Instead there are fixed scanning sensors and lamps and feed mechanisms that introduce loose papers or photographs into the scan area, sending the scanned objects out to a second tray. Typically these scanners can scan stacks of hundreds of leaves at relatively high rates of speed. Speed depends on the number of operations performed, such as auto color detection, blank page detection, punch hole removal, simplex or duplex scanning, or degree of resolution. They accept objects of varying size in the same stack from a business card to 12-plus inches wide up to 116 inches long, depending on the make or model.

There are many sheet-feed scanners for quickly scanning loose sheets of paper and photographs. Select the highest-speed model that the budget allows. A good one typically costs from around a thousand to several thousand dollars. There are competing brands designed for production that will stand up to heavy patron use. Speed is important to both the patron and the library so that patrons can scan quickly, allowing more patrons to be served. Select one that scans duplex (both sides) in one pass; offers software that will perform OCR, color, grayscale, and auto detect length; and saves in multiple formats. Some software is capable of detecting staples, digitally removing punch hole shadows, and much more. Word will quickly spread about these services without much advertising.

LARGE-FORMAT SCANNERS

Scanners that scan objects larger than 12 or 14 inches wide are often used for maps or other large, flat objects. These scanners draw the object through the scanner on a horizontal plane and can scan objects of varying thickness. They are great for maps, large portraits, large format documents, long scroll documents, art reproduction, and any number of objects that will not fit on a flatbed or a sheet-feed scanner. They output in most digital format and often come combined with a color printer that allows the scanner to also duplicate the image immediately. Our library offers a 36-inch wide scanner in the maps department that scans to any length, as well as a large-format printer capable of printing up to 60 inches wide, though we only provide paper up to 36 inches wide.

PHOTOGRAPHIC SCANNERS

If you have a big budget and high demand for large-object scanning, consider a photographic scanner. These usually consist of two cameras, a stand, a cradle for books or other objects, software, and a computer. Some employ integrated cameras but are essentially as described. The high-end cameras photograph the pages as fast as the operator can lift a glass cover and turn the pages. Images are sent to a computer, and software captures and then edits the images as defined by a template created by the operator, rotating, cropping, deskewing, converting to PDF, and performing OCR. There are several makes and models—the simpler the better for public use. Usage on ours declined when we acquired high-speed flatbed and sheet-feed scanners, yet they are useful in situations where the object is too large or too fragile to scan on other equipment.

SOFTWARE

Software applications of many kinds come with scanning hardware. These include PDF converters, OCR applications, photo editors, and many more. A good scanning workstation will have a suite of applications for doing these operations. Though the software that comes with the scanner includes some editing functions, independent applications are useful. Consider installing full-featured PDF editor, photo editor, and disc-burning software. Some of these are available as excellent open-source applications.

Data Storage

When the scanning is done, data needs to be stored in a manner that will preserve it "forever." Most storage media is impermanent and subject to degradation or device failure. Everyone, it seems, carries a USB flash drive. The name used to refer to these drives varies: flash drive, jump drive, pen drive, pocket drive, and probably more, but they all refer to the small drives carried in a pocket, on a key chain, or on a lanyard around the neck. I have several of varying capacity reflecting the increased storage capacity and falling price of these devices. USB drives have replaced CD and DVD media in most cases because of their small size and large data storage capacity. Because they are small, our employees gather them, often several a day, from our computers when people forget and leave without them. Because they are easily lost they should be identified on the outside in some manner so they are easily returned when found. We have experienced flash drive failure on some of the cheaper models. Failure can be for many reasons and so they are not to be relied upon for archival data storage. They are, however, very useful for transporting and sharing data instead of CDs or DVDs.

CD/DVD

These discs have a short life span, about three to five years before they begin to fail. Left in the sun they will fail in a very short time. Exposure to heat and humidity causes failure. Usually they fail because the chemical layer used to record the data deteriorates or the surface is damaged. There are discs that use gold or other metals for the burn layer and that purport to last a century. The newest technology employs a ceramic layer and requires a special high-intensity laser that etches the data into the rock-like recording layer. These discs are readable on any CD/DVD player but require a special burner. This very recent technology claims a thousand-year life span and has been tested by the military and by our library's digital preservation librarian. The results of the tests indeed verify the claims that these discs outlast all other discs on the market. Be ready to migrate data when technology changes and discs or file formats become unreadable.

SOLID STATE DRIVE

USB flash drives are really miniature solid state drives (SSDs). The high-capacity SSD devices are very expensive at the moment so we don't see them in large numbers yet. They are appearing in laptops. These may be the best form of "permanent" portable compact storage in the near future, if they replace spinning external hard drives and the price falls.

EXTERNAL HARD DRIVE

External drives are being promoted heavily on the commercial discount Internet websites, and a terabyte sells for very little. We see storage capacity doubling and tripling with little or no increase in price. This is probably because spinning discs are on their way out in favor of solid state storage devices, and the market is trying to reduce inventory before solid state becomes affordable and drives the mechanical spinning discs from the market place. External hard drives of substantial storage capacity plug directly into a USB port and operate without external power. Many patrons bring these with them to store their data instead of a USB flash drive. These can be damaged or may fail because they are mechanical, but they do have very high capacity.

CLOUD STORAGE

Most techno-genealogists advise storing data in the cloud, meaning on servers scattered around the Internet. Limited storage capacity is free at most Internet storage websites. Users can purchase increased or unlimited storage for a modest fee. Patrons who have an online data storage account can upload their data directly from the scanner or from the computer's memory when scanning is complete. Cloud storage provides convenient access from any Internet-connected computer, eliminating the need to carry other storage media and the worry of losing a small flash drive. Data is secure here but should also be archived in one or two other storage solutions such as archival DVDs or portable hard drives. Redundancy is essential.

Digital Preservation

Today's best practices recommend multiple copies, multiple places, along with format migration as technology changes. Think of the process of book reproduction. Early books were handwritten manuscripts on vellum or papyrus and, prior to that technology, clay tablets, tediously reproduced by legions of scribes at very high cost. Hand copying introduced errors and restricted supply. The invention of paper and printing changed the format and technology, causing supply to increase and cost to decline. The old formats migrated to the new technology. Digital is no different. It will increase supply, improve access, and preserve artifacts that otherwise were destined to destruction. When libraries and historical organizations provide technology and instruction to patrons, they will not only preserve information, but also can build collections by collecting otherwise inaccessible materials and make them widely accessible.

We trained one of our patrons, who had volunteered in our area. When he moved to a rural area of the state, he began contacting the local historical societies, cemeteries, and town and city record repositories, which led him to record collections and photographs in public and private locations that he scanned and photographed. He even persuaded individuals to donate important items to our library. He has brought us digital copies of his efforts to preserve these otherwise inaccessible resources, which we will preserve for research.

Another patron spent three hundred hours over several months scanning newspaper images from microfilm. These images document his family's history in the towns in which they lived during the nineteenth century. He donated thirteen DVDs containing the results of his research.

Retrieval

It is not enough to digitize the material. One must be able to retrieve the data and quickly locate specific items within the digital content. This implies indexing and search capability. While files can be named and alphabetically sorted by the computer, finding something is still a difficult process. In addition, if the data is archived on CDs or DVDs, one must know which disc in the archive contains the desired digital object. Software exists that will index and provide search functions, even across multiple disc collections. If documents have undergone OCR, the software can create full text indexes. Handwritten documents and photos will need to be labeled in their file names in sufficient detail to make them readily retrievable. However, software is available that will allow tagging. This means that objects can have associated descriptors, called metadata, manually attached to them and separate from the file names, that will make them easier to find with a search engine. There are online and stand-alone applications that allow photo tagging within images. This creates a pop-up that identifies a person in an image when the cursor passes over the individual in the photo.

Scheduling Usage

Patrons have learned to adjust their schedules to use the equipment when it is most available, and we have not taken on the task of scheduling usage. Remarkably, some patrons with preservation projects that require days, months, even years, have coordinated with others on their own initiative to be here at times that permit them to avoid conflict or to avoid unnecessary trips only to find the equipment occupied. Some call to see if it is in use. In some instances we have purchased multiple scanners to meet demand or specialized equipment to meet a need.

Acquisition

The library may choose to selectively collect digital files from patrons who have created quality digital objects. Concern about copyright and permission to disseminate digital content acquired from individuals will govern acquisition and access of these materials. We will not treat copyright here because it is outside the scope of this article. Many librarians are aware of these considerations, and many institutions support a copyright and permissions office to which librarians may refer when questions arise.

Patron Satisfaction

Preservation services seem to lend themselves to the library environment. Employees and patrons both benefit when the library is able to provide the equipment and expertise, and patron numbers using the facility will rise significantly.

PART VI

PHOTOGRAPHS

CHAPTER 18

Collecting and Preserving Photographic Materials

Amanda Drost

One of the most interesting, valuable, and challenging types of materials an institution can have in its possession is the photograph. A photograph can serve an institution in a variety of ways. First, a photograph can provide a window into the past by accurately representing architectural styles, period fashions, geography, and many other aspects of culture. Second, a photograph can serve an evidentiary purpose by identifying people, places, and events accurately. Where written accounts are wanting, a photograph can fill in many missing and important details. Photographs can be a great asset to a collection if they are well taken care of and organized.

In order to care properly for any photograph collection, an institution must know what kind of process was used in making that particular photograph. Different chemical processes have been used in making different types of photos over the years, and some of those chemicals can break down, causing major problems to a particular photograph and to other photographs that may be stored with it. It can be very costly and time consuming to deal with the chemical breakdown of photographs. In some cases, photographs can be treated and "saved," but in other cases duplicates must be made and the originals disposed of in the appropriate manner.

Collection Management

When accepting photographs as gifts for a collection or when purchasing them, an institution should make sure that it is capable of caring for and storing the photographs properly. It is important to make sure that there is enough staff, space, money, and expertise to support a photograph collection. Here are some questions to consider when deciding whether to keep a photograph:

- Does it fit the scope of the collection? Do you or will you consider collecting photographs on the subject? For example, if the institution is a costume library, it would not collect nature photographs.
- Can you identify the person, place, or occasion of the photograph? If nothing is known about the photograph, it is hard to add metadata to make it findable and it is hard to know if it fits the scope of the collection. If nothing is known about the photograph, it is possible that it will not be very valuable to the institution unless it is kept as an example of a certain type of photographic process or time period.
- Is the photograph in good shape? If a photograph is not in good shape (e.g., moldy, bent, half missing, cracked), the institution should consider whether it is worth keeping. If the photograph is deteriorating, it could ruin other photographs stored with it and be costly to maintain or restore.
- Is it a duplicate? Is the original housed somewhere else or does the institution already own a copy of the photograph? Unless it is a well-used photograph, the institution might not want to take up extra space with a duplicate photograph. If the photograph is a duplicate and the original is housed elsewhere, the institution likely will not hold the rights or the copyright to the photograph.
- Does another institution nearby have a similar collection? If an institution has a collection that duplicates a nearby collection, it may be wise to consider combining collections unless photographs are in great demand at both places. Doing this is often more cost effective.
- Do you own the rights to the photograph? If an institution does not own the rights to the photograph, it might be more trouble than it is worth to keep it. Whenever an institution acquires a photograph, it is best to make sure that the rights come with the photograph. This will allow the institution to sell, duplicate, or display it.
- How much will it cost to preserve and maintain the collection? Does your institution have enough money to buy preservation supplies? Does it have the money to hire and educate the staff to oversee the processing of the collection? Does it have the space?
- Who donated the collection? If a prominent funder of your institution or a person of influence over your institution either donates a collection or insists a collection be accepted, it may be in the institution's best interest to accept the collection. Sometimes if an undesirable item is accepted, other items of more value may be donated in the future. (Ritzenthaler and Vogt-O'Connor 2006)

Considering all these questions will help those in charge of acquiring photographs to more accurately gauge what the presence of photographs will add to their collections. Carefully documenting the process of a questionable purchase or donation will allow others to see the reasons behind accepting the photographs and help to make the institution (especially publicly funded institutions) more transparent in its actions.

Privacy

Sometimes photographs can contain subject material that is confidential in nature. For example, the Robinson Studio Collection at the Grand Rapids Public Library in Michigan contains a photograph of a sick person in a hospital bed. The collection of crime-scene photographs in Western Kentucky University Libraries' Special Collections is another example of confidential materials. The graphic images were part of a collection donated to the university. In order to maintain privacy, there are factors to be considered in order to decide which users of the collection can view a possibly restricted photograph.

First of all, consider who donated or purchased the photograph. Did John Doe donate his photographs with the stipulation that only members of the historical society could view them? Did Jane Doe give her family photographs to the university library so that anyone can use them? If the donor or seller set guidelines or restrictions, the staff of the institution must follow them.

Second, is it ethical for just anyone in the general public to view the photograph? Most institutions (e.g., libraries, archives, museums) that collect photographic materials follow codes of ethics. An example from the American Library Association's code of ethics states that "we . . . resist all efforts to censor library resources." The Society of American Archivists' code of ethics states that "archivists strive to promote open and equitable access to their services and the records in their care without discrimination or preferential treatment." Codes of ethics statements like these can help an institution to decide how restrictive it must be when displaying certain photographs of a private nature.

Ritzenthaler and Vogt-O'Connor (2006, 298) give a good summary of needs to balance regarding privacy:

1. democratic society's need for access to photographs for research
2. the creator's desires to make a profit and need to control how her works are used
3. the donor's need to ensure that what he has donated is cared for and accessible based on his guidelines

4. individual and group needs for privacy and control over how sensitive information is used

  Those in charge of deciding how photographs are used and available to the public should take all these needs into account and try to balance them. In the case of the Grand Rapids Public Library, the photo could be used by the general public for research needs. Western Kentucky University Special Collections decided to restrict the use of their crime-scene photographs. There is no hard-and-fast rule for deciding what to do with photographs that are confidential in nature. Each institution serves a different community and has different needs to balance.

Types of Photographs

The modern photograph traces its origins to the early nineteenth century (Ritzenthaler and Vogt-O'Connor 2006, 1). Diane DeCesare Ross (2001, 40) describes a photograph like a sandwich with four layers: a support material, an interlayer, a binding medium, and an image-forming substance. There are quite a few different types of photographic processes and products. Once an institution knows the kind of photographs it is handling, it is easier to determine the type and cost of care. The purpose of this section is to give an overview of common types of photographs that an institution may come into contact with, not to give an exhaustive list of all the types and processes. The following is a list of some of the types of photographic materials and negatives that an institution might own.

Salted paper prints

- popular around the 1840s to the 1860s
- this type of print was not very common in America
- lack fine detail
- made from paper and glass negatives

Daguerreotype

- most popular between the 1840s and the 1860s
- this is the oldest type of photograph an institution is likely to come across
- it is a positive image on a copper plate covered with a coating of polished silver
- it could not be reproduced at the time it was popular (today, of course, it can be reproduced digitally)

- very fragile; usually presented in a case with glass protecting it

Albumen prints

- popular around 1850–1900
- printouts made of thin paper, usually mounted on cardboard
- often hand-colored
- warm brown or purplish brown in color
- people appeared less stern and rigid in their poses than in other early processes due to the decreased exposure times necessary to produce the photograph
- examples of albumen prints are carte de visites, which are 2 1/4 × 3 1/2–inch photographs attached to a 2 1/2 × 4–inch paper card; stereographs; and cabinet cards

Ambrotype

- most popular between 1855 and 1865
- very similar to a daguerreotype
- almost always appears as a positive image (i.e., no negative is produced)
- the image is sandwiched between glass and backed with a black background (paper, cloth)

Glass plate negatives

- popular from the 1850s to the 1920s
- easy to identify: a light-sensitive emulsion fixed to a glass plate
- very fragile

Cyanotype

- popular in the 1880s
- also called blueprints
- used by professional photographers to proof their negatives
- not widely used as final prints because of their blue tint

Tintype

- late 1800s to early twentieth century
- a positive image on a sheet of thin metal
- very popular with soldiers because they were inexpensive and durable

Platinum print or platinotype

- 1880s to 1930s
- paper prints with images of metallic platinum
- the image could be reproduced

Cellulose nitrate film

- popular from around 1889 to early 1950s
- can be very dangerous since it is highly flammable; gives off a gas when deteriorating, which can be hazardous to human health and materials around it
- sometimes has the term "nitrate" printed on the border
- stages of deterioration: the film turns yellow-brown, the emulsion becomes tacky, it emits nitric acid gas, it gets covered with viscous froth, and eventually it turns into a brownish acid powder

Cellulose acetate/diacetate (safety) film

- introduced around the mid-1930s; replaced all other types of film by 1951
- usually has the word "safety" printed on the edge, but not always
- can shrink and warp as it ages
- can give off a smell like vinegar, and if the smell of vinegar is present, the film is deteriorating and can damage other negatives and prints around it

Platinum print or platinotype

- 1880s to 1930s
- paper prints with images of metallic platinum
- the image could be reproduced

Polyester film

- began use around the mid-1950s
- ester or Estar sometimes printed on the edge
- strong and stable with excellent keeping properties

Digital photographs

- first appeared in the early 1990s
- these are the newest type of photographs
- they are produced in several ways (photo lab, print-at-home, kiosk printing)
- can be black-and-white and color

Preservation or Conservation?

The two terms "conservation" and "preservation" are often used interchangeably, yet they mean different things. The New York State Archives gives the following definitions: preservation is working to *prevent* deterioration while conservation is to *repair* damage already done (www.archives.nysed.gov/a/records/mr_storage.shtml). This section is concerned with preservation. Conservation is costly; practices depend on the type of material. Conservation is best done by a professional and is beyond the scope of this chapter.

The first step in preserving photographs is prevention. Following some simple practices can ensure that your photos will not suffer preventable harm. Make sure staff are educated as to the proper handling of photographs. In turn, staff should teach users how to properly handle photographs. Simple things like wearing archival gloves, not writing on top of photographs, and avoiding food and water while working with them are some minor steps to take toward nondamaging use.

In order to provide the best conditions for preserving them, all types of photographs should be stored in a cool, dark environment; a temperature around 68 degrees Fahrenheit and a humidity level between 35 and 40 percent are ideal. Keep photographs and negatives in a consistent environment. Fluctuations in temperature and humidity can cause them to deteriorate. Exposure to light and ultraviolet light (such as sunlight and some fluorescent lights) should be limited as much as possible. Prints and negatives should be stored separately from each other, as should color and noncolor photographs. Ideally, photographs should be handled only while wearing white cotton gloves (Buchanan and Domer 1995, 2), unless you are handling items where the emulsion can be snagged by the gloves (e.g., glass plate negatives). In that case, use latex gloves (National Archives, www.archives.gov/preservation/storage/glass-plate-negatives.html). Deteriorating film negatives should be stored in a frost-free freezer until they can be dealt with in the appropriate manner.

One of the best ways to preserve photographs and film negatives is to make either physical or digital copies of them for use and to permanently and properly store the originals. Unfortunately, this option can be expensive. However, it should be a priority for heavily used items or items that are in poor condition and should no longer be handled. Before storing items long-term, it is a good idea to write down information from the photograph, case, or accompanying materials, such as any label written on it, including captions, names, dates, and places (Ritzenthaler and Vogt-O'Connor 2006, 238). Doing this will aid in later classification and organization.

Another important preservation practice is the development of a written emergency plan in case of a disaster (Ritzenthaler and Vogt-O'Connor 2006, 268). The most likely types of disaster are fire and flood, but there are others.

The following are care instructions for the various types of photographs.

- Daguerreotypes, ambrotypes, and tintypes: If possible, these should be left in their cases, if available. They should be wrapped individually with acid-free tissue paper and stored in a single layer in a box. Pasting a copy of the photograph on the box will help to reduce handling. If the photograph is not in a case, one can be made to protect it. Tintypes are prone to being bent since they are flexible. One should not try to straighten it because the emulsion could crack (Ritzenthaler and Vogt-O'Connor 2006, 238–42).
- Paper prints (salted paper, albumen, platinum, cyanotypes): These types of photographs can be stored in acid-free envelopes or folders. They should be kept separate from each other and remain flat. If a photograph needs extra support, it can be housed between alkaline buffered boards. Albumen prints are subject to curling, so they require rigid support in storage (Ritzenthaler and Vogt-O'Connor 2006, 243–45).
- Glass plate negatives: These are heavy and fragile and should be handled with care. Intact plates should be stored with like sizes grouped together. The plates should be stored standing vertically like recipe cards in a recipe box. They should be wrapped individually in heavy paper. Do not stack plates on top of each other. Cracked and broken plates can be stabilized by sandwiching them between two other clear glass plates (National Archives website).
- Film negatives: Cellulose nitrate film is very unstable and flammable. Cellulose acetate/diacetate film is prone to vinegar syndrome, which is harmful to human health and other negatives and photographs around it. Both types of film should be copied and/or digitized and discarded appropriately. If duplication is not possible right away, film should be stored at 0 degrees Fahrenheit or below until it can be dealt with properly. Polyester film is stable and can be stored in buffered paper or stable plastic enclosures (Ritzenthaler and Vogt O'Connor 2006, 253–54).
- Digital photographs: Since a few different processes are used to print digital photographs (mentioned above), products of those processes last for different amounts of time. The best thing to do with digital print photographs is to store them away from light sources and to avoid moisture; digital prints are especially vulnerable to water (Ritzenthaler and Vogt-O'Connor 2006, 246). Digital files of images should be transferred to the latest and most reliable media for long-term storage. Periodically, as digital storage improves or changes, the files should be transferred in order to make sure they are still viewable by the latest technology.

If an institution needs to unroll paper prints, fix glass plate negatives, remount daguerreotypes, or use any other advanced restoration techniques, it should employ the services of a professional photograph conservator. Otherwise photographs or negatives could be irreparably damaged by untrained personnel.

Conclusion

Unlike the written word, whose meaning can be derived from a text that does not change over time, a photograph's meaning and usefulness are dependent primarily upon visual forms that may be threatened by deterioration or improper handling. These factors, among others, present a unique challenge to the librarian when a photograph or photographic collection is presented for inclusion into a collection. With proper selection and care, it is possible to have a useful and well-preserved photograph collection.

Resources

There are many good resources available to help an institution manage a photograph collection. However, two resources stand out:

- *Photographs: Archival Care and Management* by Mary Lynn Ritzenthaler and Diane Vogt-O'Connor is a wonderful book that covers all aspects of collecting and preserving photographs, from privacy and copyright issues to description and cataloging.
- The Image Permanence Institute (www.imagepermanenceinstitute.org) has many useful resources for preserving images.

References

Behrnd-Klodt, Menzi L., and Peter J. Wosh, eds. *Privacy and Confidentiality Perspectives: Archives and Archival Records.* Chicago: Society of American Archivists, 2005.

Buchanan, Sally A., and Margaret Domer. "Writing with Light." *Wilson Library Bulletin* 69 (1995): 68+. vnweb.hwwilsonweb.com/hww/results/results_single_fulltext.jhtml;h wwilsonid=L14UVT5M2WQWXQA3DIMCFGGADUNGIIV0 (accessed October 5, 2010).

Davenport, Alma. *The History of Photography: An Overview.* Boston: Focal Press, 1991.

Hirsch, Robert. *Seizing the Light: A History of Photography.* Boston: McGraw-Hill, 2000.

Jimerson, Randall C. "Ethical Concerns for Archivists." *The Public Historian* 28, no. 1 (2006): 87–92.

National Archives. "How Do I House Glass Plate Negatives?" 2010. www.archives.gov/preservation/storage/glass-plate-negatives.html (accessed November 2010).

Ritzenthaler, Mary Lynn, and Diane Vogt-O'Connor. *Photographs: Archival Care and Management.* Chicago: Society of American Archivists, 2006.

Robb, Andrew. "Albums, Photos, Glass Plate Negatives." *Library of Congress Information Bulletin* 60, no. 5 (2001): 118–19.

Ross, Diane DeCesare. "An Overview of the Care of Silver-Based Photographic Prints and Negatives." *Mississippi Libraries* 65, no. 2 (2001): 40–44.

Schwarz, Judith. "The Archivist's Balancing Act: Helping Researchers While Protecting Individual Privacy." *The Journal of American History* 1 (1992): 179–89.

Spuhler, Jaci. "Identification and Preservation of Photographs in a Local History Collection." *Colorado Libraries* 34, no. 1 (2008): 43–44.

Sterling, Rayette. "A Picture's Worth a Thousand Words—Unless It's a Copy." *ALKI* 24, no. 2 (2008): 8.

CHAPTER 19

Organizing and Indexing Photo Collections

Rose Fortier

Historical photo archives or collections can put an organization on the map and make it into a destination for patrons. Conversely, if not well organized and indexed, collections and archives can languish in obscurity and occupy valuable space and resources with no tangible return for the organization.

The Milwaukee Public Library's (MPL) Historic Photo Archives (HPA) contain around thirty thousand historic images; of those images, most are located in the Historic Photo Collection, one of the archives' 45 individual collections. The HPA has evolved over the decades. Various reference librarians have been assigned the archives, and the rotation of responsible parties has left its mark. The challenge created by having many individuals with different backgrounds, priorities, areas of interest, and time to devote to the maintenance of the collection has been mitigated by a strong collection development policy.

Collection Guidelines

The first step in organizing archives is to decide what will be organized. A policy must outline:

- scope of the collection or archives
- how archives fit the institution's stated mission
- types of archival materials that will be included

At MPL, the scope of the photo archives is mostly geographic in nature; the images included in the collections relate to Milwaukee and the immediate surrounding counties. The only exceptions to this rule are found in the smaller, discrete collections in the archives where removing non-Milwaukee images would have meant dismantling individual collections and ruining the context that the collection provides as a whole.

MPL's mission statement, as accessed in February of 2011, states that the library "provides materials, services and facilities for all citizens of Milwaukee and others in order to meet present and future informational needs and raise the level of civilization in Milwaukee." The HPA fits that statement by preserving a visual record of Milwaukee's past and present, ensuring that these images will be around to inform present and future generations of Milwaukeeans about their history. The mission statement ties in directly to the scope of the archives, and it underscores the importance of photo collections to the library and to Milwaukee's citizens.

Another important area of distinction governed by the collection development policy is in the types of materials that are included in the archives. The HPA exists for photographic and visual materials; it seems fairly straightforward that only photographic materials should be included. In practice, that seemingly simple criteria can be easily muddied; only included are original photographs and images in the archives. The types of materials that can be added to the photo archives are:

- photographs of all types: black and white, sepia-toned, rose-toned, cyano-types, tin-types, etc.
- slides and negatives: glass, celluloid
- prints: etchings, woodcuts, lithographs

Types of materials that are not acceptable for the HPA are:

- reproductions of images that have appeared in publications
- photos from calendars
- ephemera: greeting cards, flyers, brochures, pamphlets, etc.

Even with these guidelines in place, there are still items that fall into a gray area; postcards are included in MPL's collections, though greeting cards are not. Copy prints, where a photographic reproduction has been made of another photograph or image, can be a hard call as well. MPL includes copy prints and negatives even though a compelling argument, according to MPL's own criteria, for their exclusion can be made since they are not original images. In these instances the materials have been added to the archives because they speak to the other two parts of the collection development policy: the archives' scope and how the collection fits the mission statement.

Organization of Collections

After determining what should be included in the photo archives, the next step is to organize in such a way that materials are locatable and retrievable. There are two basic ways of organizing collections and MPL uses both.

The easiest way to organize a collection is by arranging the collection according to its original order. This method is most easily applied to small collections consisting of similar subject matter. This arrangement method also depends on having a collection in which it is possible to discern the original order. Photo albums are an excellent example of the application of this method. Even if the album needs to be dismantled to address preservation issues, it is easy to arrange the photos or pages in the order in which they appeared. Similarly, a box of slides that arrives from the original owner and/or photographer can be arranged to preserve the order in which it arrived at the archives even if the box is replaced. From there it is as simple as labeling the item's container with a unique identifier, often using consecutive numbering and a truncated form of the collection's name or a code.

The application of original order preserves the context that the collection's creator established in developing the collection and can bring a better understanding to the collection as a whole. Original order has its advantages, but it also has drawbacks. "Applying original order also offers a practical advantage, retaining existing filing systems and saving the archivist from having to decide upon and apply a new and artificial structure. Of course, original order can be problematic for the researcher" (Millar 2010, 101).

Another main method used by MPL applies functional order to a collection. This application involves breaking a collection down into a certain order based on specific criteria. Those criteria will typically be subject- or chronology-based. This method works best with large collections containing diverse subject matter and for collections made up from multiple sources. The Historic Photo Collection is an artificial collection that is a match for all three of those instances; it has a little more than twenty thousand images from multiple sources that cover many subject areas.

Natural vs. Artificial Collections

Archives are made up of collections that can take a couple of forms. The first is the natural collection that comes into the archives from one source and is made up of multiple archival materials related through that source. The second is an artificial collection made up of like materials that have been gathered together by the archivist over a period of time, from a variety of sources.

The Historic Photo Collection was originally organized by volunteers under direct supervision. It was decided that the collections should be arranged alphabetically by main subject. A list of 235 main subject headings was developed, and over time another 26 subjects were added. From there, all but the smallest subject areas were broken down into more specific subheadings. Larger subheadings were further split by adding additional identifying characteristics. If that sub-subheading was still fairly sizable, a date range was added. The date chosen to act as a dividing line was 1960. Thus, image headings could be listed as pre-1960, post-1960, or pre/post-1960 (if the year could not be determined). Once the photos had been arranged by subject, they were then arranged within the subject alphabetically and were filed in folders. The folders were labeled with a truncated version of the main subject heading and then were numbered consecutively.

As an example, the subject of airports contained seventeen folders labeled AIRP.1 through AIRP.6. A patron looking for an interior view of Milwaukee's Mitchell Field Airport would need to have folders AIRP.5A-AIRP.5E retrieved. The problem with the system is immediately apparent. How can seventeen folders be labeled AIRP.1 through AIRP.6? There are eleven folders missing: where are they?

The system worked well for a while, but eventually a number of flaws emerged. It became obvious that the decision to include multiple photos in each file was unwise. This placement created preservation, security, and organization issues. One preservation issue was that multiple photos on different grades and ages of paper, using different methods of development, and some with more chemical residue than others, were promoting cross-contamination of acid and chemicals in that closed environment. Larger, sturdier photographs were damaging smaller, more fragile ones by being stored together.

It was difficult for reference desk staff to track how many photos were in individual folders. Photos of varying sizes, coupled with a hectic desk environment, meant that determining how many photos came back from a patron versus how many had gone out was no easy task.

Additionally, the consecutive numbering system made it difficult to add new materials to the collection. If new materials did not fall under an already existing subheading, there were two options for adding it. The first was to change the consecutive number by adding decimals or letters to slot something between two numbered folders. Returning to the example using airports, "Curtiss-Wright Airport" was listed as AIRP.1A because it needed to fit alphabetically between "1st Milwaukee County Airport" (AIRP.1) and "Maitland Field" (AIRP.2). This solution was not ideal, as soon combinations of letters *and* decimals were being concocted and the combinations soon proved cumbersome in filing and retrieval. Eventually those types of situations became common.

The second solution was to add the new folders to the end of a run, preserving the consecutive numbering system. This solution proved less than ideal. Within the subheadings of a main subject area, the folders were arranged alphabetically. Adding new subheadings to the end of a run of consecutive numbers broke the alphabetic system of organization and negatively affected filing and retrieval. When Miller Park was added as a subheading to the Business & Industry subject, it ended up being physically filed after Mutual Drug Co.

Because of these issues it was decided that a modified system of organization and identification should be implemented. Volunteers trained by the digital projects librarian were recruited to implement the modified system.

Each item is housed in its own folder, addressing preservation and security issues. Then each folder and corresponding photo has been assigned a unique identifier. The identifier is based on the old system: in fact the bones of the original system are still evident; only the expression of that system on the individual folders has changed.

The new identifying system eliminates the consecutive numbers and it spells out the subheadings, sub-subheadings, and date ranges; so AIRP.5A-5E becomes AIRP.MITCHELL.INTERIOR.POST1960.001-024. While the new system of identifiers is visually more cumbersome, it is more flexible and allows for the addition and alphabetical collocation of new subheadings.

The process of refoldering has been time-consuming and there have been periods of downtime because of a lack of volunteers, but after four years of refoldering, the project is halfway to completion. To this point approximately ten thousand photos have been refoldered. Working on this project has allowed the standardization of some methods of organization. For example, with the new identifiers the pre- and post-1960 date ranges have been added on a regular basis. Adding the date ranges has made it easier for staff to retrieve materials for researchers by enabling them to chronologically eliminate some items. Breaking down the ranges of dates further was contemplated but discarded because of the time and additional oversight that would be required.

"Unknown" and "Miscellaneous" as Headings

Using "Unknown" or "Miscellaneous" as a designation is not a great idea. An item that is identifiable should be clearly labeled, not lumped together with like items. Similarly, unknown items should not be included in artificial collections and de-accessioning of those items should be considered in natural collections. Patrons simply do not use items labeled in those ways; there is not enough information there to inform them that the items may be useful.

This project highlights the importance of thinking through an organizational scheme and really knowing the collection, the audience, and how that audience is going to be using the collections and/or archives. The original organization of the Historic Photo Collection was necessary to make it usable for MPL's patrons, but the lack of flexibility that was endemic in the system and prevented the addition of new materials was its downfall. Modifications were made to the original organizational scheme to allow for that flexibility, and to address the preservation and security flaws that the method of storage revealed about the scheme.

Indexing Collections

When a collection is organized, how is it possible to make sure that patrons and staff can easily find what they are looking for? The easier a collection is to search, the more likely that it will be used. Not that a collection with an opaque method of organization and/or indexing will never get used, but it scares off casual users and creates frustration in those who try to tackle it.

As with organization, some collections require more indexing than others. One advantage that an index affords is the ability to use multiple access points for the same image. While physically organizing a collection, an item can only be placed in one spot. In an index, the same item can be listed multiple times according to different situations portrayed in the photo. A street scene with a view of a streetcar could be indexed both under the name of the street and under streetcars. It would be impossible to have the image stored in both places, but it is discoverable in an index under either heading.

Often the amount of work that goes into an index is inversely proportional to the amount of work that went into the collection's organization. If the original order of a collection is maintained, then the accompanying index should make up for the organizational deficiencies of the original order. Very small collections solely related to one subject are an exception to that rule. On the other hand, the larger the collection, the more important the index becomes.

The secret to crafting great indexes is to be consistent in the application of the index to the collection, yet flexible in index design across collections. Not every collection will have the same indexing requirements; attempting to force every collection to match the same type of index is an exercise in futility and it makes the index much less practical for use.

An index is something that is created for the end user, and in the creation of the index the user's point of view must be considered. It is important to ask how patrons will use the image. Here are some approaches to an index depending on the type of collection:

- alphabetical: good for portraits, place-names
- subject: good for things, places, events
- chronological: good for events and areas that are time-sensitive (e.g., historic costume)
- geographic: good for place-names, addresses

Larger indices can include combinations of those methods. A collection of historic locomotive photographs can be indexed by the type of locomotive (subject) and broken down by the locomotive's year of manufacture (chronological).

One of MPL's collections is indexed in both alphabetical and geographic fashions. It is called the MPS (Milwaukee Public Schools) Album. The album consists of a visual inventory of each building owned by MPS in the late 1960s. Initially, the decision was made to retain the original order of the album, though the photos were removed from the acidic pages to which they had been glued. The original order was based on an internal numbering system that divided up elementary, middle, and secondary schools and was not easily useful.

An index was created with two different aspects. The first lists the schools by their names. This portion of the index makes liberal use of the USE function. USE indicates what the preferred term is in an index; for example, cars USE automobiles (preferred term). USED FOR indicates the nonpreferred terms that are listed in the index; for example, automobiles USED FOR cars, trucks. USE is more frequently used in indexing than its counterpart.

Many schools have changed names or are known colloquially by one name while the official name is somewhat different. For example, what is commonly known as King High School now has the official name Rufus King International School but was once known as Rufus King High School. The decision was made to go with names in common usage, but references to the preferred term were included so that patrons would be led to the index's preferred term.

Garfield Ave

School Name				Date	Image Location
Elm School					
2616	W	Garfield Ave	53205	1968-07	Box 1. No. 9
Garfield Avenue School					
414	W	Garfield Ave	53212	1968-07	Box 3. No. 40
Hi-Mount Boulevard School					
4921	W	Garfield Ave	53208	1968-07	Box 1. No. 36

Figure 19.1.   MPS Album Index sorted by address.

The second aspect of the index is sorted by address, which adds another access point for the user, who can choose either way of searching through the index with equal effectiveness.

Unsurprisingly, portrait collections that are housed in the HPA use an alphabetical index. The Historic Portrait Collection is an artificial collection of general-interest portraits of individuals and groups. The individuals portrayed in this collection have all been identified. However, since the portraits in the collection include group portraits, the index makes liberal use of SEE and SEE ALSO indicators. These indicators lead the user to additional images of people that may be housed elsewhere in the collection. This particular index also goes one step further and lists portraits included in other collections. Thus, the index acts not only as an index to its own collection, but as a master index for other portrait-related materials in the HPA.

SEE and SEE ALSO

SEE refers index users to a different location to find the item they are looking for. SEE ALSO refers users to additional locations to find additional items that relate to the item that is being looked for.

The creation of one or more master indexes should be seriously considered; MPL uses two. One is the aforementioned Historic Portraits index; the other serves a dual purpose as the index to the Historic Photo Collection and as a reference leading to smaller collections. That index is broken down by subject and leads the user directly to image folders in the Historic Photo Collection. However, because it is indexed by subject, the other collections that use subject arrangements are listed as SEE or SEE ALSO references next to the main entry.

F

Farm Equipment				Digitized?
	Pre 1960	FARM.1		No

Federal Buildings				Digitized?
Federal Building & Post Office	Post 1960	FED.B.1	See also Post office	No

Festivals & Celebrations				Digitized?
Bastille Days	Post 1960	FEST.21		No
Brady Street Days	Post 1960	FEST.4; Also OS	See Streets - E. Brady St.	No
Carnival Week	Pre 1960	FEST.41	See also RW 227	No
Christmas Season	Pre 1960	FEST.5	See Also Historic Negatives	No
Christmas Season	Post 1960	FEST.6		No

Figure 19.2. Historic Photo Collection Index showing SEE and SEE ALSO indicators.

The use of these references allows users to check one index instead of many. One thing to remember with a master index is that careful upkeep is imperative; the index is only as accurate as its latest entry.

Technology also allows indexes to be more flexible. MPL's indexes are typically created in Microsoft Excel or Access, though other spreadsheet and database software will suffice. Using these programs allows the same index to be sorted in different ways or by different access points without having to re-enter information. Excel is used for more straightforward indexes.

More complex indexes are done in Access to provide further options in sorting.

The use of technology additionally allows wider dispersal of the index. MPL's indexes are accessible in at least one, but frequently more, of three

1	Keyword	Title	Date	Number
48	A.O. Smith	A.O. Smith made bomb casings?	7/10/1979	1626
49	Aberdeen Hotel	the Aberdeen Hotel graced Wisconsin Ave.	5/15/1968	471
50	Abner Kirby's	Wisconsin and Water was Abner Kirby's Bl	5/30/1978	1511
51	Academy	the Shubert was the Academy?	1/27/1976	1268
52	Accidents	streetcars had accidents?	9/23/1975	1232
53	Adler strike	Milwaukee's first arbitration board settled th	11/4/1967	416
54	Ads	ads marked Milwaukee's riverfront?	11/20/1985	2020
55	Ads	the phone book ran ads like these?	7/19/1991	2211
56	Advertise	children helped companies advertise?	1/16/1973	954
57	Advertised	little charmers advertised Atlas flour?	1/4/1966	329
58	Advertisements	advertisements came printed with song on	2/14/1978	1481
59	African elephant	the African elephant greeted visitors in the	10/30/1982	1876
60	Aggies	the Hilltoppers beat the Aggies?	10/13/1979	1653
61	Air conditioned	streetcars were 'air conditioned'?	7/30/1966	284
62	Air conditioning	air conditioning was blanket in the shade?	6/26/1985	2001

Figure 19.3. Remember When Index created using Excel, sorted by key-word.

formats. The first format is in print; all the indexes are printed out and accessible at the desk that services the HPA. Printing out the indexes allows patrons to peruse them in person. The majority of the print indexes are also available to reference librarians through MPL's network, which allows librarians to use the indexes no matter where they are working or whether the index is already being used. Having access to the index through the network also means that it can be searched with simple keyword searching using the FIND (Ctrl-F) function.

Last, an increasing number of indexes (for various special collections materials, not just photos) are being made available for public use through MPL's website. This format allows users to access certain indexes remotely so they are better prepared when they come in to use the materials. When indexes are available on the Internet, the chances that they and their accompanying collections will be found and used are increased. Most search engines can locate these indexes on the Internet.

Conclusion

Organizing and indexing are two ways of serving a similar purpose: to make archives and collections easily accessible to patrons. All collections and archives shall require some degree of organization and indexing. In order to be successful at both, the needs of the user must be assessed and met. Each collection is different, so organization and/or indexing must be handled differently so that the end user will have the most successful time using the collection.

References

Millar, Laura A. *Archives: Principles and Practices.* New York: Neal-Schuman, 2010.
Milwaukee Public Library. "Library Vision and Mission Statements." mpl.org/file/library_mission.htm (accessed February 12, 2011).

CHAPTER 20

Photograph Selection, Access, and Preservation for the Public Librarian

Rebekah Tabah

Photography has been with us since 1839 and pursued by professionals and amateurs with equal enthusiasm, if not skill. For sheer quantity, photographs, along with newspaper clippings, appear in virtually every local history collection. The librarians providing reference for those collections know that photographs are among the most popular and frequently requested materials.

The value of these images to the library and the community is largely defined by how they are used: for publications, for evidence, for documentation, for exhibits, for publicity, for classroom instruction, and/or for celebrations and tributes, not to mention the pure fun of searching for local people, places, and events. If managed well, photographs can be a significant revenue generator for the library.

> For all their popularity and potential research value, photographs and albums languish in libraries not because of the lack of patron interest, but due to the library staff's lack of confidence and knowledge.

In a recent statewide survey of the major repositories in Arizona, unprocessed photograph collections ranked either first or second on their backlog priority list.[1] There are two major library/archival practices that contribute to backlogs. One is poor collecting. The other is time-consuming, item-level description.

This chapter challenges conventional thinking about collecting, processing, and accessing photographs and offers a way out of the backlog dilemma.

The Special Training Myth

Because most librarians and many archivists have little formal training in photo preservation, they often avoid working with these collections. What they fail to realize is that the vast majority of photographic media found in local history collections does not require advanced training. Over 80 percent of twentieth-century photographs in local history collections are gelatin silver prints on paper. You know them as the standard black-and-white photograph.

Gelatin silver prints are one of the most dominant photographic processes. They have been in popular use for over one hundred years. Almost everyone has seen one, owned one, or created one. Handling this type of photograph is not unusual. Like other photographic processes, they are susceptible to extreme swings in temperature and humidity, but generally speaking are very durable and stable. Because these prints are found on a paper base, as opposed to metal, wood, or glass, they are typically found in good condition. This means that 80 percent of photographic materials, if they are in fair to excellent condition, can be processed by nonspecialists.

By observing some basic guidelines, a nonspecialist can process these collections quickly, stay within budget, and avoid common, costly mistakes. Note that the strategies described here do not apply to art photography collections, collections of a photographer's work, unusual formats, or rare or fragile photographs in poor condition. These types of photographs and collections require another level of skill that is discussed later in this chapter.

Working with photographs is an opportunity to build on existing librarian skills. You will see the connections between collections more quickly. You will develop closer partnerships with patrons and donors. It will add depth and breadth to your reference services. The better you know your photograph collections, the better you can serve your patrons.

Visual Literacy and Reference

Visual literacy is the ability to interpret and critically analyze an image. Photo professionals and researchers use visual literacy to gain knowledge on a subject, event, or person using the visual clues provided. As you become more familiar with photographs, you will improve your ability to examine and evaluate for value, significance, and condition. Photographs are understood and preserved in libraries in different ways and for different reasons. The more you understand the information provided in photographs, the greater your ability to provide reference.

Photographic requests are on the rise. While most research requests are generic in nature, patrons' knowledge and expectations about photographs and photograph collections continue to grow. There are many types of information that can be gleaned from a photograph. Using photographs as historic documents, researchers examine many different details of a photograph to gain knowledge about:

- historic periods (e.g., Depression era, World War II, etc.)
- clothing
- hairstyles
- architecture
- transportation
- social customs
- individuals, both prominent and common
- events of political, historical, or cultural interest
- business and industry
- urban growth
- changing technology and advances

Note that the topics listed above can also be used by the librarian to date, title, or describe unidentified photographs.

Typically, your users are the general public. They make photograph requests in a number of ways, from very specific to broad. One researcher may be looking for a specific individual, on a specific day, in a specific place. Another may want to see a range of photographs from a general location and may be open to your suggestions. In the latter case, one photograph can lead the individual in a direction not originally intended. This person may have wanted to see cityscapes and then settle on photographs of trees.

Unlike books, which have individual call numbers and designated shelf assignments, photographs require a more in-depth approach. When providing photograph reference, you will probably be required to look in different locations, pull multiple items, think quickly on your feet, provide advice, and communicate personal knowledge. Flexibility is the key.

Smart Collecting + Smart Processing = Access + Sustainability

Let's start with a few quick definitions:

- A *collection* is a group of materials with a common theme or unifying characteristics typically from a single donor or entity.
- An *artificial collection* is a group of materials assembled by the librarian after materials have been donated. You can create artificial collections from groupings of loose prints.
- *Aggregation* is the assembling of material both in the physical sense (sorting and storing like items together) and the intellectual sense (creating finding aids and catalog records).
- *Processing* entails housing in appropriate enclosures, arranging, and describing the material contained within a collection.
- A *finding aid* is a standardized template used to describe the context (includes donor notes, historical notes, and dates) and contents of a collection. Contents are typically described at a folder and box level, not item level.

> There are more than one hundred million new photographic images produced every day, and they begin to deteriorate almost immediately.

There are more than one hundred million new photographic images produced every day, and they begin to deteriorate almost immediately.[2] The good news is that you're not responsible for collecting all of them. Collecting photographs requires judgment and selectivity. Many photographs come to public libraries as piecemeal donations and rarely as complete collections.

While every librarian understands the need for collection development and management policies, guidelines for books and other routine library acquisitions are insufficient for special collections and photographs.

Do:

- Be aware of what other repositories are collecting. Avoid competition and duplication. It's costly in terms of time, expense, and goodwill.
- Be selective. You are under no obligation to accept every photograph offered.

- Make sure the photos complement your local history collections and are within your collecting scope. Be ready to refer a donor elsewhere if the photographs are not a fit.
- Actively solicit photographs that fill in gaps in the local historical record.
- Establish a clear written policy about what you do and don't collect. Make it transparent by posting it on your website. Stick to it.
- Develop a photograph reproduction policy that observes the U.S. copyright law in addition to creating revenue. Make sure that the deed of gift gives copyright to the library.
- Be aware that photographic reproductions are sources of revenue that help ensure long-term sustainability.

Don't:

- Collect anything you cannot support. If the collection is too large, requires extensive preservation, or there is no staff to process it or provide access to it, give it a pass unless the donor is willing and able to donate funds for its support.
- Stray from your collecting scope. Donors can be referred to other local historical societies, museums, or archives.
- Collect or accept photos in poor condition. Most public libraries don't have the budget for extensive conservation and restoration techniques.
- Collect or accept photographs that are mostly unidentified. This greatly decreases their research value. (See "Making the Most of What You Have," page 205.)
- Collect or accept duplicates of photos available elsewhere. Duplication of photographs decreases value and uniqueness and wastes time, money, and resources for the library and the patrons.
- Collect or accept photos that come with restrictions. This not only delays access but reduces library storage areas to warehouse status.
- Separate photographs from the original manuscript collections in order to start a photograph collection. Separating photos was a common practice until fairly recently. Separation destroys context.
- Alter the original image using Photoshop for reproduction requests. Keep it simple. Altering historic photos changes the integrity of the original.

Processing with Confidence

Prevention is the first step in preservation. Prevention means collecting, housing, and processing wisely. Modern public libraries have adequate climate controls that protect most materials from extreme temperature and humidity fluctuations. Photographic prints with gentle use can last indefinitely under these conditions.

The cost of processing a photograph collection will depend on the types and amounts of housing purchased. All materials purchased for photographs should be intended for that use. Supplies used for books are not always safe for use with photographs. A vendor's claim that supplies are archival does not always make them appropriate for photographs. Housing materials for photographs should meet the accepted archival standards as stated by the American National Standards Institute and pass the Photographic Activity Test (PAT). You should only order through reliable suppliers of archival materials.

Preservation:

- Most photographs in local history collections are prints on paper and require little special handling or training.
- Gloves should be worn by patrons and staff handling photographs. This prevents fingerprints and the transfer of dirt.
- Protect photographs from UV light. Do not leave original photos on permanent display. Brief exposure to UV light is generally acceptable.
- Storing photographs in acid-free paper envelopes or polyester sleeves is recommended.
- To limit the cost, use inert polyester sleeves only for images that are in poor condition, are rare, or are heavily used. Polyester or Mylar is the more expensive type of housing.
- Photographs should be "right reading" when placed in protective housing. This means image side to the front, facing right side up.
- Individual photographs found within manuscript collections should be sleeved for protection.
- Photographs should be examined by patrons under staff supervision. This will reduce damage caused by mishandling and the likelihood of theft.

Arrangement:

- Photographs of a similar process, size, or material can be stored together.
- Place as many sleeves within a folder as possible. Photographs stored vertically should be snug to prevent bowing or bending.
- Keep only the best image. Don't be afraid to weed multiple images.
- Use controlled vocabulary, such as Library of Congress headings, wherever possible. These subjects can be used to help identify and name series or groups of photographs, to catalog, and as folder titles on your finding aid. Note that these heading don't always work. Depending on the photos, other methods

used might be geographical or chronological. The librarian needs to decide which method provides the best research value.

- With direction and oversight volunteers or donors can be trained to process photograph collections.

Description:

- Cataloging or describing photographs is not like cataloging monographs. It requires a different mind-set.
- For local history collections, the goal is to get the patron close enough to browse the relevant subject material.
- Minimal description at the envelope, folder, or even collection level will work.
- Provide subjects, geographical locations, people's names, events, and date ranges when they are known.
- Assemble or aggregate similar groups of photographs together. If the images have the same subject, date, or location or are of the same person, they can be described as a group.
- Minimal description on a group vs. item level decreases duplicative descriptions in the catalog. It can also eliminate the need for special, expensive descriptive software that also comes with a steep learning curve.
- Use the technology you already have. Create finding aids (a standard guide to archival material) for photograph collections on Word using a standardized finding aid template. Convert it to PDF and upload to your website or catalog.
- Collection-level entries can be provided in library catalogs and linked to a simple PDF.

Making the Most of What You Have

Orphaned, unidentified, or uncataloged photographs typically languish in libraries. These photographs can be made into stronger, more useful collections by gathering them into an artificial general subject collection, also referred to as "ready reference." This allows you to turn something unusable or rarely used into a highly researched, heavily used collection.

- When creating an artificial collection, provide what information possible and group together by common themes.
- Reunite loose or removed photos with their original manuscript collections. If original context is lost, then you can create a new artificial collection. Use common themes or Library of Congress subject headings to organize, name,

and catalog. (For example, the Arizona Historical Foundation's Subject Photograph Collection is organized by broad subject categories including: animals, buildings, military, mining, people, places, plants, schools and universities, sports, and transportation, just to name a few.)

- Orphaned albums can also be grouped together into a general album collection. Provide album titles or general topics, dates, and condition.
- Postcards can be aggregated together into a ready reference collection.
- Photographs can be treated as a separate series within a larger manuscript collection. This allows for special housing and/or storage needs, but maintains context.

When is a collection not a collection? Your library must define what constitutes a collection. Bulk matters. Are individual photographs donated over time called a collection? Not usually. These would be considered fragmentary pieces, not stand-alone photograph collections. Just as a single book does not make a collection, a single photograph does not either. If possible, all collections should have a finding aid. A finding aid should describe a collection to the folder and box level, not item level. This is the way researchers will find their way to and through your collections. In the absence of a finding aid, your library can create a collection-level description.

Different levels of description will be used according to the importance or rarity of a collection. Collections will range in size and topic. Use your best judgment when processing.

The Strange, Unusual, and Misunderstood

While the majority of the photographs encountered in your collections are ordinary, there are those photographic processes, formats, or materials that will be unfamiliar. The following types of photographs are more common, but still may require special housing materials and/or consideration.

- Color photographs already exist in most history collections and their prevalence will only increase over time. Color photography is inherently unstable, and color images begin deteriorating immediately. The dyes used to create color images—yellow, magenta, and cyan—all fade at different rates, making preservation and conservation a real challenge. Even when stored in complete darkness, within proper housings, their deterioration is unavoidable. If available, cold storage can slow these effects, but not completely stop or reverse them.
- Albums with deteriorating pages, fading images, and highly acidic material such as newspaper clippings can be interleaved with tissue or acid-free paper. Large Mylar sheets can also be used but are expensive. Do not disassemble

albums or arbitrarily remove photographs. Albums are a single artifact. The removal or dissection of pages will result in the loss of context.

- Slides should be stored in slide pages and then kept in notebooks, hanging files, or filing cabinets. Always handle slides by their mounts.
- Negatives come in many different sizes. They should be handled with gloves and stored using specific negative sleeves. Due to different chemical compositions, deterioration rates, housing and temperature requirements, and handling concerns, negatives should be stored separately from prints.
- Cyanotypes (blueprints) can be ripped or torn easily. Careful handling should be observed.

These types of photographs are rare, fragile, and typically not for the generalist. Don't attempt to handle the following formats without consultation from an expert.

- Glass plate negatives are heavy and fragile and may be cracked or broken. They require specific cleaning techniques, housing materials, and storage space.
- Nitrate negatives can be identified by the word "Nitrate" stamped on the film edge, by identifying the notch code (a system of cutout patterns along the edge of the film), or by having a conservator conduct a burn test. They are flammable and potentially explosive. If you don't have cold storage such as a freezer, you need to segregate these negatives from other collections. Note: cold storage requires special boxes, bags, and humidity controls. Nitrate negatives should be stored in paper envelopes only.
- Daguerreotypes, ambrotypes, and tintypes are among the oldest and rarest photographic media. They are often found in a case and commonly referred to as cased images. If in a case, keep the image and case together as they are considered a single object. You should never attempt to clean these images.
- For anything else that doesn't look like film or print on paper, set aside and get an expert opinion.

Observations on Digitization

A balance must be struck between providing access for users while safeguarding the physical objects. When some librarians encounter photographs, they believe that they must digitize everything. This may include purchasing expensive proprietary software. In reality there are more factors to consider when deciding what to digitize, and it doesn't have to cost a lot. Creating digital scans of the photographs in your collections has many advantages, but beware of pitfalls.

- Not all photographs deserve to be digitized. Just because your library has the ability to scan and digitize every photograph doesn't mean you should. Digitization projects should be selective and planned. Consideration must be given to the long-term housing, upkeep, and migration of digital files.
- Take care of the physical objects before you go virtual.
- Digitization is an access tool.
- Digitization is not preservation. While digital images may relieve the stress of handling original photographs, originals still need proper housing, care, and management to ensure their longevity. Digital media is unstable and outdates quickly. It will probably deteriorate faster than your original photographs.
- Digitization can be useful as surrogates for fragile photos.
- Do not destroy the originals! The original photograph, not the digital file, is the historic object.
- Use digitization as a way to showcase samples of your best collections.
- Take advantage of state or regional digital consortia. Let them maintain, upgrade, and staff the technical infrastructure. You can point patrons or potential donors to the site, then sit back and admire your work.
- Digital reproductions can be used as revenue recovery for your library. Fees for photograph duplication and the use of your photos in publications can provide funds to buy supplies and pay for preservation projects or even staff positions.
- Check all copyright restrictions when posting photographs to the web. Make sure that they are in the public domain or that the copyright has been deeded to the library.
- If you digitize photographs, be prepared to respond to reference requests.

Conclusion

Photographs are primary documents, not afterthoughts. As such, they deserve the same consideration as print collections. Photographs are tools for both the patron and the library. They exist to provide information. By observing the above guidelines, the librarian will do little harm, greatly increase access, generate revenue, and increase the library's capacity to grow photograph collections that document the community's history. Libraries serve the community, and photograph collections maintained in libraries are a way of connecting to that community. Libraries contain many of the same books and databases. However, photographs and special collections are one-of-a-kind. They tell a unique story about local history. With a little attention, you can make your photograph collections a rich resource for your community.

Bibliography

McClung, Patricia. "RLG Symposium on Preservation of Photograph Collections in Research Libraries." In *Photograph Preservation and the Research Library,* edited by Bernard Reilly and Jennifer Porro, 53. Mountain View, Calif.: Research Libraries Group, 1991.

Sturgeon, Melanie I., and Linda A. Whitaker. "The Arizona Summit: Tough Times in a Tough Land." *Journal of Western Archives* 1, no. 1 (2010): 17.

Notes

1. Melanie I. Sturgeon and Linda A. Whitaker, "The Arizona Summit: Tough Times in a Tough Land," *Journal of Western Archives* 1, no. 1 (2010): 17.

2. Patricia McClung, "RLG Symposium on Preservation of Photograph Collections in Research Libraries," in *Photograph Preservation and the Research Library,* ed. Bernard Reilly and Jennifer Porro (Mountain View, Calif.: Research Libraries Group, 1991), 53.

PART VII
DIGITAL

CHAPTER 21

Digital Preservation of the Emilie Davis Diaries

Alexia Hudson

That a race forcibly transported to a state of slavery here . . . should not have been able to attain to an equality in morals with their intellectual superiors is not surprising. In fact, when we consider the obstacles which have interposed to impede their advancement, it must be admitted that their progress as a class has been great as circumstances would allow.

—Joseph Kennedy, United States Superintendent of the Census, comments about free Blacks in his introduction to the 1860 Census

Joseph Kennedy's comments regarding the long-term viability of America's free Black population echoed a common sentiment among some whites of the era. Although there was an acknowledgment of "a great number of excellent people included in that population,"[1] the philosophy of Black self-sufficiency was incomprehensible at that time.

Historical accounts from abolitionists and journalists of the period counter Kennedy's assessment. A vibrant, educated free Black community survived and thrived in many areas throughout the United States in the 1800s, in spite of limited social, economic, and educational opportunities. One of the major social centers for this group was Philadelphia, which had the largest population of Northern-based free Blacks during the Civil War era.[2]

However, the lack of primary resources from members of the free Black community during the antebellum and Civil War periods has impeded scholarly exploration on this group. This is why preserving the Emilie Davis Diaries is so important. The diaries not only expand current scholarly knowledge about two historically elusive groups in early America (women and free Blacks), but also gives a human voice to life in an urban center during the Civil War. From 1863 to 1865, Philadelphian Emilie Davis wrote in her diaries nearly every day about activities such as attending weddings and shopping with friends. Emilie also chronicled attending a lecture in Philadelphia by Frederick Douglass and her first-time use of a sewing machine. She traveled frequently to Harrisburg to visit her father and was a skilled seamstress.[3]

Of greatest historical significance is Emilie's description of key Civil War–related events, such as the human impact of the Battle of Gettysburg, the fall of Vicksburg, and the funeral procession of President Abraham Lincoln in addition to other incidents of the war. Through her eyes, readers also learn about some of the complexities of the time period, such as Black family fragmentation and the emotional difficulties of being a single wage-earning Black woman during the era of legalized slavery.

In mid-2009, I initiated a digital preservation project for the Emilie Davis Diaries that resulted in a ten-year partnership between the Pennsylvania State University Libraries and the Historical Society of Pennsylvania. This agreement allows for the digitalization, preservation, and promotion of the Davis diaries. The partnership is linked to several key strategic goals of Pennsylvania State University Libraries in terms of preserving valuable Pennsylvania historical documents in a digital format.

This chapter provides a brief history of Emilie Davis and Philadelphia's free Black community, the process of discovering the diaries, and the unique partnership developed between the Historical Society of Pennsylvania and the Pennsylvania State University Libraries to preserve the Emilie Davis diaries for future generations.

Emilie Davis's Story

During the late 1800s, Philadelphia was home to the largest population of free Blacks in the northern area of the United States.[4] Emilie Davis was one of six children in a working-class family. According to the diary, she worked as a wedding dress seamstress. Her father is listed as a waiter, her mother was a seamstress, and her sister Elizabeth was a domestic; Emilie wrote in her diaries that her brother Alfred was drafted into the military.[5]

The Census Data of 1860 places Emilie between the ages nineteen and twenty-one from 1863 to 1865. Emilie's race is classified as "mulatto" and her father is listed as "black." This strongly suggests that phenotypically, Emilie looked like a White or mixed-race woman to the Census taker, who probably used physical appearance to racially identify individuals.[6] However, Emilie refers to herself as "colored" in her diary entries and only makes mention of race when she is describing someone White.[7]

Emilie's family was middle class but was not a part of the elite free Black minority of Philadelphia. Members of this group included the Fortens (whose patriarch was millionaire shipping magnate and library patron James Forten), the Willsons (whose daughter Josephine married the first Black United States senator), and the Bustills (owners of a large-scale catering business). These individuals traveled abroad and were educated at prestigious universities such as the University of Pennsylvania.[8]

Emilie wrote that she attended night classes at the Institute of Colored Youth (now Cheyney University) and socialized with the Bustills. She may also have benefitted from the largest philanthropic activity of the elite free Black community of Philadelphia: the Philadelphia Library Company of Colored Persons, founded in 1833. This library circulated more than six hundred items, hosted lectures, and administered educational courses on reading and writing.[9]

These details shed light on how Emilie was able to write in such a narrative format. She was frequently surrounded by the educated elite of the free Black community and benefitted from formalized education at several points during her young life.

In 1863, Emilie decided to journal daily in a small pocket diary. She spent a great deal of time journaling and eloquently wrote from her emotional core. That year, she recounted the Battle of Aldie, the Skirmish of Sporting Hill, the New York City Draft Riots, and National Fast Day.

In 1864, Emilie's diary entries focused on the presidential election, along with a heightened emphasis on attending church and feeling "thankful." These changes may have developed in response to increasingly difficult circumstances that made Emilie's life even more challenging in the following year.

The year 1865 was emotionally taxing for Emilie. The majority of her entries focused on lamenting her loneliness. She appears to have lost continuous contact with her siblings Elizabeth, Nellie, and Alfred. Her mother appears to be an absentee figure. Her other brothers, Edmond and Thomas, are not mentioned. Her father, who was gravely ill, moved to Harrisburg.

Later that year, Emilie deeply mourned the death of her brother and the assassination of President Abraham Lincoln. She attended the funeral procession of President Lincoln in Philadelphia and waited two hours to view his body while it lay in state. She wrote, "In my sorrow and in my grief but here I am and all things have passed away."

The last full journal entry was written on April 15, 1865, which was the City of Philadelphia's official "Day of Mourning" following Lincoln's assassination. Then, the 1865 diary abruptly ends with Emilie's last written statement:

"All's well that ends well."[10] Shortly thereafter, she seems to disappear from all historical records, including the Census.

One can speculate that Emilie elected to "pass White" in order to pursue a better lifestyle. According to Black oral history accounts, it was a common practice for so-called mulatto Black women to conceal their identity and marry into a White family for financial security. When a family member elected to pass for White, the remaining Black family members kept a close guard on their secret, as exposure usually reaped dire consequences. Therefore, written records from individuals who elected to "pass" were not preserved.[11] Given the emotional distress Emilie was under, her last entry may have foreshadowed her heartrending decision to abandon her Black identity in search of a better future.

"Discovering" the Emilie Davis Diaries

The Emilie Davis Diaries were acquired from a private collector in 1999 and are currently housed at the Historical Society of Philadelphia. Because of the painstaking challenge of handling fragile, handwritten materials, the Davis diaries were not fully processed and incorporated into the Historical Society of Pennsylvania's collection until 2004. Transcription work was conducted on the diaries by public historian Dr. Kaye Wise Whitehead as a part of her doctoral fellowship with the Historical Society of Pennsylvania and the Library Company of Philadelphia.

I "discovered" these diaries on a private group tour of the Historical Society of Pennsylvania conducted by Lee Arnold, the Historical Society of Pennsylvania's library director, in February 2009. Arnold shared with the tour attendees that the diaries were in desperate need of preservation, as they were quickly fading and deteriorating. The Historical Society of Pennsylvania had been unsuccessful in securing sponsorship to pay for preservation and stabilization of the diaries and decided to appeal openly for assistance. The timing of this visit to the Historical Society of Pennsylvania and the discovery of the Davis Diaries coincided with an internal call for digital project proposals from the Pennsylvania State University Libraries.

I was captivated not only by the "find," but also by Emilie's writings, which flow from journalistic to poetic. The entries are written in nearly perfect standard American English at a time when the majority of Blacks and women were functionally illiterate.[12] Her daily life is captured in a manner that could illuminate new pathways on scholarship about women, free Blacks, education, and "social" librarianship in early America.

Understanding the rarity of such a discovery, I decided to broach the Historical Society of Pennsylvania's interest in a possible partnership with Penn

State Libraries to digitalize the diaries. They agreed favorably, and luckily so, as the proposal for Pennsylvania State University Libraries digital preservation projects was due in sixty days.

The Digital Preservation Projects of the Pennsylvania State University Libraries

The Pennsylvania State University Libraries has a commitment to preserve Pennsylvania's history for both scholarly purposes and "a public good that benefits society as well as higher education."[13] This objective is achieved through partnerships with various research libraries, historical repositories, and archival organizations as facilitated by members of the library faculty.

In 2005, the Pennsylvania State University Libraries launched its "Pennsylvania History Online Project"—a digital library project that provides Internet-based access to important research materials that chronicle Pennsylvania history. The launching of this site served as the catalyst for wider-reaching digital preservation projects that encompassed a variety of items such as maps, newspapers, images, and manuscripts.

A Digital Collections Review Team composed of librarians, archivists, digital curators, a metadata librarian, and members of the Digitalization and Preservation Team works with librarians of all subject expertise throughout the Penn State University system to identify projects for possible digital preservation collaborations. Preference is given to projects that illuminate new elements of Pennsylvania history and create partnerships with other historical organizations, libraries, and educational institutions.

The proposal for digitalization of the Emilie Davis Diaries was authored by myself along with Lee Arnold, the Historical Society of Pennsylvania's library director. The proposal requested digitalization and metadata development of all three of Emilie's diaries. Upon further examination, it was determined that the documents also required a stabilization process to undergo the preservation process. After review by the digital collections review team, the project proposal was unanimously approved pending legal agreements.

Executing the "Memorandum of Understanding"

The Historical Society of Pennsylvania and Pennsylvania State University Libraries conceptually agreed that entering into the partnership to digitalize the diaries was mutually beneficial. There was also an understanding of the unique historical value of the diaries and need to protect them throughout the digitalization process. After a series of conference calls and e-mail exchanges, both parties agreed to execute a nonexclusive memorandum of understanding (MOU).

The MOU was organized into seven sections: an outline of the project, goals, general terms, the digitalization process, ownership rights of the digital content, security of the physical diaries, and expectations of online access. The terms of the MOU describe this venture as a collaborative effort in order to "support educational and research needs worldwide," and cover a ten-year period starting in January 2010.

Ownership of the digital content is shared by both organizations. However, the arrangement specifies that the digital content will be posted for users to view only, not to download. The documents are cited on the Pennsylvania State University Libraries' web page as the property of the Historical Society of Pennsylvania.

The MOU also includes a clause indicating that amendments may be added periodically to cover situations and activities (e.g., technology changes) that may arise during the agreement period. It was approved by both organizations in February 2010, ten months after the initial proposal submission.[14]

Digitalizing and Preserving the Diaries

The next level of work focused on stabilizing and digitalizing the diaries. This leg of the process was managed by the Pennsylvania State University Libraries' Digitalization and Preservation Team. Pennsylvania State University Libraries uses OCLC's CONTENTdm for this digitalization project, which offers several benefits such as allowing for multiple workflows, interoperability, and synchronization of internally developed metadata with WorldCat.

After the diaries were sufficiently stabilized to withstand digitalization, pages were individually scanned and uploaded in uncompressed Tagged Image File Format (TIFF). TIFF files preserve high-quality images without pixelation and blurry images. The pages were also scanned at a high 600 dpi resolution, which allows readers to zoom into a document on their computer screens to see all of the fine document detail.

A persistent URL (PURL) is assigned to each digital collection so that it is both short and clearly distinguishable from the other collections. This simplifies cross-searching through the collections in both internal and external search engines. All three diaries are currently available to view online at www.libraries. psu.edu/psul/digital/davisdiaries.html.[15]

The next step in the process was creating the metadata for the diaries to enable better searching capabilities. A long, cumbersome process was anticipated, since many Civil War–era documents contain a significant amount of sociolect. To our delight, the Davis diaries are written in nearly perfect standard American English, so the initial metadata work was simple. As more specific information about people, places, and events becomes evident in the transcriptions, additional elements of the metadata will be added.

Future Plans for the Emilie Davis Diaries

A historical summary page about free Blacks in Philadelphia during the Civil War era with cross-references to the battles Emilie mentioned in her diaries is being created. This page will include images of free Blacks in Philadelphia and links to holdings in the Pennsylvania State University Libraries and various Civil War–related resources.

There is also a working outline to develop a series of K–12 teacher's guides highlighting the significance of firsthand accounts of a free Black woman, a history of free Blacks in Philadelphia, and the city's unique role in the abolitionist movement. The intention is to supplement these teacher's guides with a series of digital learning objects (such as vodcasts and interactive geographical maps).

Recommendations

The African proverb "it takes a village" could be applied to most large-scale digital preservation projects like the Emilie Davis diaries. More than fifteen individuals working for the Pennsylvania State University Libraries and/or the Historical Society of Pennsylvania have previous or current involvement with the Davis diaries in various professional capacities. As the initiator of this project, I interacted with most of these individuals, which was a challenge, given that my primary job description centers on undergraduate course-related reference and instructional support.

When considering implementation of a digital preservation project, consider the following recommendations for making the process of discovery, preparation, implementation, and completion run smoothly:

- Place yourself on the mailing list of local archival repositories and historical societies to receive invitations to lectures and presentations on their holdings.
- Verify that internal and external funding exists for your project before proceeding. The National Endowment for the Humanities and the Library

of Congress offer resources (and periodic grant-funding opportunities) for American preservation projects.

- Have "talking points" about the historical significance of your project prepared for presentation at any time, especially since you may have to answer the same questions repeatedly to different key stakeholders. Consistency is crucial in all communication about your proposed project.

- Familiarize yourself with your organization's preservation standards and technology so that you and your team can "speak the same language" when your preservation project begins.

- Establish team and individual timelines for preservation workloads before the actual preservation work begins. Be honest about how much of your time you can allocate to the project if preservation is not among your core job responsibilities.

- Consider negotiating a long-term agreement with all proposed partners that describes a plan for dealing with unforeseen technological advancements. As newer technologies are introduced, it will be helpful to include a clause that allows for readjustments and changes in preservation standards.

I wish to thank the following individuals for their efforts in making this project successful: Penn State University Libraries' former dean Nancy Eaton, associate dean Michael Furlough, Sue Kellerman, Albert Ruzo, Karen Schwentner, Patricia Hwse, the Department of Digitalization and Preservation, the Digital Collections Review Team of 2009–2010, and Penn State University's Legal Department.

Works Cited

Davis, Emilie. Diaries, Unpublished handwritten materials, January 1, 1863–December 31, 1865. Archives, Historical Society of Pennsylvania, Philadelphia, Pa. Electronically accessible via the Pennsylvania State University Libraries, www.libraries.psu.edu/psul/digital/davisdiaries.html (accessed December 12, 2010).

Dubois, W. E. B. *The Philadelphia Negro*. New York: Cosimo, 2007.

Gatewood, Willard B. *Aristocrats of Color: The Black Elite 1880–1920*. Fayetteville: University of Arkansas Press, 2000.

Hershberg, Theodore. "Free Blacks in Antebellum Philadelphia: A Study of Ex-Slaves, Freeborn, and Socioeconomic Decline." *Journal of Social History* 5, no. 2 (Winter 1971–1972): 183–209. www.jstor.org/stable/3786411 (accessed December 8, 2010).

Horton, James Oliver. "Freedom's Yoke: Gender Conventions among Antebellum Free Blacks." *Feminist Studies* 12, no. 1 (Spring 1986): 51–76. www.jstor.org/stable/3177983 (accessed on December 8, 2010).

Kennedy, Joseph. Introduction to *Population of the United States 1860; Compiled From the Original Returns of the Eighth Census*. Washington, D.C.: Government Printing

Office, 1864. www.archive.org/details/populationofusin00kennrich (accessed on August 28, 2010).

Lehuu, Isabelle, "Female Literacy," in *Historical Dictionary of Women's Education in the United States*, edited by Linda Eisenmann, 147–48. Westport, Conn.: Greenwood, 1998.

Miller, Randall M., and William Pencak. *Pennsylvania: A History of the Commonwealth*. University Park: The Pennsylvania State University Press and the Pennsylvania Historical and Museum Commission, 2002.

Pennsylvania State University Libraries. Strategic Plans 2002–2005; 2005–2008; 2008–2013.

Porter, Dorothy B. "The Organized Educational Activities of Negro Literary Societies, 1828–1846." *The Journal of Negro Education* 5, no. 4 (October 1936): 555–76. www.jstor.org/stable/2292029 (accessed on December 8, 2010).

Raimon, Eve Allegra. *The Tragic Mulatta Revisited: Race and Nationalism in Nineteenth-Century Antislavery Fiction*. New Brunswick, N.J.: Rutgers University Press, 2004.

Winch, Julie. *The Elite of Our People: Joseph Willson's Sketches of Black Upper Class Life in Antebellum Philadelphia*. University Park: The Pennsylvania State University Press, 2000.

———. *A Gentleman of Color: The Life of James Forten*. Oxford: Oxford University Press, 2002.

Whitehead, Kaye Wise. "They Both Got History: Using Diary Entries to Analyze the Written Language and Historical Significance of Free Black Philadelphia." *Language, Literacy, & Culture Review* (2009). Internal publication of the University of Maryland, Baltimore County. www.umbc.edu/llc/llcreview2009.html (accessed August 30, 2010).

Notes

1. Joseph Kennedy, introduction to *Population of the United States 1860; Compiled from the Original Returns of the Eighth Census* (Washington, D.C.: Government Printing Office, 1864), vi.

2. Randall M. Miller and William Pencak, *Pennsylvania: A History of the Commonwealth* (University Park: The Pennsylvania State University Press and the Pennsylvania Historical and Museum Commission, 2002), 191; Willard B. Gatewood, *Aristocrats of Color: The Black Elite 1880–1920* (Fayetteville: University of Arkansas Press, 2000), 97–104; Theodore Hershberg, "Free Blacks in Antebellum Philadelphia: A Study of Ex-Slaves, Freeborn, and Socioeconomic Decline," *Journal of Social History* 5, no. 2 (Winter 1971–1972): 183–209.

3. HSP Finding Aid.

4. Miller and Pencak. *Pennsylvania: A History of the Commonwealth*, 191; Gatewood, *Aristocrats of Color*, 97–104; Hershberg, "Free Blacks in Antebellum Philadelphia," 183–209.

5. Kaye Wise Whitehead, "They Both Got History: Using Diary Entries to Analyze the Written Language and Historical Significance of Free Black Philadelphia," *Language,*

Literacy, & Culture Review (2009), internal publication of the University of Maryland, Baltimore County, www.umbc.edu/llc/llcreview2009.html (accessed on August 30, 2010).

6. Whitehead, "They Both Got History"; Hershberg, "Free Blacks in Antebellum Philadelphia," 183–209.

7. Whitehead, "They Both Got History."

8. Gatewood, *Aristocrats of Color*, 97–104.

9. James Oliver Horton, "Freedom's Yoke: Gender Conventions among Antebellum Free Blacks," *Feminist Studies* 12, no. 1 (Spring 1986): 65; Dorothy B. Porter, "The Organized Educational Activities of Negro Literary Societies, 1828–1846," *The Journal of Negro Education* 5, no. 4 (October 1936): 555–76; Julie Winch, *The Elite of Our People: Joseph Willson's Sketches of Black Upper Class Life in Antebellum Philadelphia* (University Park: The Pennsylvania State University Press, 2000), 111–19.

10. Whitehead, "They Both Got History."

11. Gatewood, *Aristocrats of Color*, 181; Eva Allegra Raimon, *The Tragic Mulatta Revisited: Race and Nationalism in Nineteenth-Century Antislavery Fiction* (New Brunswick, N.J.: Rutgers University Press, 2004).

12. Isabelle Lehuu, "Female literacy," in *Historical Dictionary of Women's Education in the United States*, ed. Linda Eisenmann (Westport, Conn.: Greenwood, 1998), 147–48.

13. Pennsylvania State University Libraries. Strategic Plans 2002–2005; 2005–2008; 2008–2013 (internal documents).

14. Emilie Davis Diaries: Memorandum of Understanding between the Historical Society of Pennsylvania and the Pennsylvania State University Libraries, 2010 (internal document).

15. Emilie Davis Diaries: Memorandum of Understanding between the Historical Society of Pennsylvania and the Pennsylvania State University Libraries, 2010 (internal document).

CHAPTER 22

Preserving and "Publishing" Local Biographies

Elizabeth B. Cooksey

William Hunter's death (in 1802), which resulted from his duel with David Mitchell, gained national attention. Hunter was a successful Savannah merchant and politician.[1]

The Doctors McKane practiced medicine in Savannah in the late nineteenth and early twentieth centuries. . . . They were successful at a time in the history of America when African-Americans were encouraging each other to excel.[2]

These glimpses from the lives of early Savannah residents come from a collection of 414 biographies written between 1975 and 1994 by students at Armstrong Atlantic State University, located in Savannah, Georgia. Current Savannahians reap the benefits of forebears who founded the Georgia Historical Society in 1939. Its library is an ever-increasing trove of primary source material. This history has also been preserved in physical objects, everything from streets paved with cobblestones brought over as ballast in eighteenth-century ships to park squares ornamented with cannons from the American Revolution and Civil War.

With these resources, history students at Armstrong often work with primary sources. Several hundred of them, with the guidance of Professor Roger Warlick, PhD (1930–1998), produced more than four hundred biographies of local residents living in the city's first 250 years. Each student was assigned one person to research and write about. Each time Professor Warlick had collected a year's worth of papers, he brought them to the campus library (Lane Library) to be bound and added to our special collections. Introducing them, he wrote, "These biographies are of ordinary people from all walks of life who in some small way contributed to the history of the city of Savannah. It is the hope of the compiler that this collection of biographies not only will provide some pleasure to the casual reader, but also will prove to be of some value to the to the future researcher."[3] In about 2005, a volunteer gathered the tables of contents from each volume into a machine-readable index, which was posted on the library's website.

Another campus history department project selected some of the best biographies to scan for an online collection called "Savannah Images." The library staff created a link from the library's online Savannah Biographies index to the scanned papers in the Savannah Images Project. These scans were converted to a word processing format, but the early optical character recognition (OCR) was rough, creating what looked like typographical errors. Further, no attempt was made to get permission from the student authors of the selected papers for web posting. We believe the steps we took to make this collection easily available online worked well, and offer this summary of our procedures in hopes of helping all librarians who have similar collections.

As those of us who work with local history know, a sizable proportion of the population is focused on genealogy. When people started doing online genealogical research, some of them discovered the Savannah Biographies. They began asking Lane Library about access to the papers. Our head of special collections, Caroline Hopkinson, arranged for two photocopies of each of these requested papers, one for the requester and one to have scanned into a PDF for future purposes.

At this time, one of the librarians suggested the authors be approached for permission to post their biographies on our website. The university's attorney gave permission to use a form we created (see below). Although every effort was made to reach alumni authors, some permissions fell through the cracks. One of these was by an alumna in the process of a job search. Her paper was among those with the poorly rendered characters, making it look as if she had produced a typo-filled biography. Fearing this would harm her search for employment, she complained about its having been posted. As a result, the library director took down all posted biographies until a systematic request for permissions could be made. The now obligatory systematic procedure took place in 2011 when a temporary reference librarian stepped in as project coordinator. In hopes that a discussion of our methods may prove useful to others who hold similar collections, we present them here.

Materials Available to the Project Coordinator

- Twenty-five bound volumes as described above. These presented a few problems:
  - They were heavy and thus unwieldy.
  - They were often so tightly bound that it was hard to get straight photocopies from many of the papers.
  - The organization of contents from volume to volume was not uniform. For instance, some were arranged by last name of the biographee while others

were in author surname order. Still others were bound in chronological order by term/year (e.g., all papers from one year's winter term, then all of the year's spring term).

- A file of the early correspondence between Ms. Hopkinson and authors from whom she had sought/received permission in the previous iteration of this project. There were very few of these exchanges.
- The aforementioned index on the library's website
- The loose-leaf photocopies of some of the biographies

First Steps

- Double-checked the old tables of contents for accuracy, leafing through each volume to be sure its decades-old table of contents included each biographee and each author and that author and subject names were correctly spelled.
- Converted the website list into RTF and created a table in MS Word with these headings:
  - subject of biography [surname, given name]
  - volume number
  - surname of student author
  - first name of author
  - date [paper was] created

A printed copy of this table was used to pencil in corrections found during the checking process. Then we developed the most important tool for the project, a Microsoft Access database.

Converting a Word Table into an Access Database

To turn a Word 2007 table into an Access 2007 database using Windows 7, the following steps can be used (Windows XP users may find some slight differences, but the basic procedure is the same; a few of the less intuitive differences are explained here in parentheses after the Windows 7 instructions):

1. Open your Word table.
2. Convert it to a text file: use the Layout tab, choosing "separate text with tabs." (WinXP use Table Tools > Layout tab > Data tab. Change the drop-down box when saving the file to make it "Plain Text" to prevent defaulting to saving in Word.)
3. Save that text file; close Word.

4. Open Microsoft Access; choose "create a new table." (WinXP users will see "Blank Database," so choose "Create.")
5. Choose External Data tab, and then "text file."
6. Pop-up screen asks you to browse for the source. Do so, and choose "Import the source data into a new table in the current database."
7. Choose "delimited" (the default); click on "Next."
8. Choose "tab" (default); click on "Next."
9. The resulting pop-up lets you name your columns (defaults are "Field1," "Field2," etc.). Then choose the data types you want (drag-down arrow allows for yes/no, integers vs. text, currency, etc.). (It will use your column headings as the first cell in each one if you don't stop it.)
10. Let Access add the primary key or choose "no primary key."
11. Choose "Import to Table" and then "Finish."

When you've gone through these steps, your database will be ready to use.

We named our Access database "Savannah Biographies Table" and inserted fields in addition to the original five so that our final database contained the following columns:

- subject of biography [surname, given name]
- BD-DD [subject's birth and death years]
- surname [of student author at time paper was written]
- surname [current name of author]
- personal title [e.g., Mrs., Dr.]
- first name [of author]
- date [paper was] created
- volume number
- permission requested date
- permission granted date
- street
- city
- state
- ZIP
- phone
- author notes
- digitized already? [yes/no]
- paper avail? [yes/no]
- Linked [on website]? [yes/no]

Gathering Alumni Addresses

The natural place to begin gathering information about alumni authors' current addresses (and names) was the alumni relations department, called the Office of Advancement on our campus. Georgia Massey, one of its database coordinators, helped us track down current directory information for them. She used three databases to do so:

1. Blackbaud's "The Raiser's Edge"—a program designed for nonprofits to use in their fund-raising efforts.
2. Banner—Armstrong's directory of students from the 1980s to the present. This digital directory holds transcripts, class registrations, Social Security numbers (accessible only by qualified personnel), and student identification numbers. The ability to obtain Social Security numbers gives the most certain identification.
3. "Alumni Finder"—a commercial product (one of many available). Of the three used by Georgia, this has the best current address information.

COMMON PROBLEMS IN THE HUNT FOR ALUMNI

Even with these databases, there were still some problems finding alumni. The most common is determining the student's current name. Women, of course, traditionally take new surnames upon marriage, and both men and women often use nicknames.

Among solutions to those problems employed at Armstrong are the following:

- Try to match Social Security numbers, even if only partial is available.
- Try to match birthdates.
- Use class registration lists to determine what the chances are that the person listed was a history major or in a related field.
- Use old commencement programs to find nondigital records.

The Office of Advancement was happy to try to help us, but as they were busy with their own projects, we sometimes waited for weeks between the receipt of one set of names/addresses and the next. However, we were able to make a quantum leap in our progress by obtaining from them a complete set of more than eight hundred history majors in the Banner database. We used this to do a database-assisted matching project.

HOW WE COMBINED DATABASES TO SORT
FOR PERTINENT MATCHES

1. Converted the Excel file into an Access table. The procedure is similar to that used to go from a Word table to Access, discussed above. Taking care to adjust the original Excel columns to match those of our "Savannah Biographies" database, we named the second database "History Majors."
2. Merged the two databases into one temporary one.

We were able to streamline the process of matching authors from our list of more than four hundred names with more than eight hundred records containing address data sent by the Office of Advancement by:

- sorting by surname, looking at each associated first name for possible matches (e.g., Gladwell, James and Gladwell, Jimmy)
- sorting by given name, looking at other fields for clues (e.g., Susan F. Isola, class of 1980 and Susan Frick, paper completed in 1980)

Use of the sorting capabilities in Access was helpful in finding a large number of good "eduguesses."

APPROACHING FACULTY MEMBERS FOR LEADS

Another way we found current information for our authors was by approaching current and retired campus humanities professors. We mounted an attractive display in the History Department's office to encourage our history faculty to participate, later reusing its elements in a library exhibit about the project. As the addresses were found, we filled in our Access table, allowing us to automate much of the work of the mass mailing of requests. Each mailed packet consisted of:

- a one-page permission form
- a letter (on the library's letterhead)
- a self-addressed, stamped envelope

For the permission form, we revised an earlier document, including a new cover letter introducing the project and making an appeal to Dr. Warlick's former students to help fulfill his dream of making their work more available. We used MS Word's mail merge function to use data from our Access table in both our letter and the permission form. Following are example inserts for the mailing:

Example Letter for Permission

[Month/Day], 2011

1. _____
2. _____   Lines here are replaced by the requisite
3. _____   data using MS Word's merge function
4. _____   and our MS Access table.
5.
6. Dear _____

    The Librarians at Lane Library would like to fulfill the late Professor Roger Warlick's dream of making the biographies written by students in his Historical Methods course available to as wide an audience as possible.

    With this in mind, we are appealing to you for permission to post (on the library's website) a digital copy of the paper(s) you did for Dr. Warlick's course. We have the following biography by you in our Special Collections division:

    <u>Subject of biography</u>:   _____ Also completed automatically
    <u>Completed in (term)</u>:   _____ by the merge function
    <u>Student author</u>:   _____

    To give us your consent, simply fill out the enclosed form and return it to us in the envelope we have provided.

    It would be very helpful if we could gain your cooperation in this. Although it has now been some time since you made your efforts for the assignment, the work you did continues to be of value to those interested in Savannah history, and the project as a whole is a fine tribute to the memory of Dr. Warlick.

    Thank you so much—
    Caroline Hopkinson
    Head of Special Collections and Library Archives

Example Letter for Permission, Second Page Included in Mailing

    I hereby grant Armstrong Atlantic State University permission to digitize and post on the University's website the biography of _____ I wrote in Armstrong's Historical Methods course.

_____ (Signature)
[typed name as we have it]
(If your name has changed, please print it here: _____.)
_____ (Date signed)

We have done our best to match the student author names with current name/address information held by the university. If you think you have received this in error, we'd appreciate your letting us know.

Postage-paid envelope was subsidized by a private donor who loves Georgia history.

FACTORS LEADING TO HIGH POSITIVE RESPONSE RATE

The positive response rate to our requests for permission was fairly high, which we attribute to two factors:

1. Professor Warlick's personality: many students recounted fond memories and seemed to feel a sense of duty to help achieve his goal
2. our provision of self-addressed, stamped envelopes

ORGANIZATION OF THE FORMS RECEIVED

When the signed permission forms started arriving, we:

- labeled each by subject's name (surname first), storing them alphabetically in a three-ring binder.
- noted in our database the date each permission form was signed.

Web-Posting the Biographies

Concurrently, we needed our webmaster to post the "permitted to post" papers. Having noted in the database which papers were available in usable digital format and those for which we had copies in loose-leaf form, we could tell at a glance when a paper needed to be digitized as the permission arrived. For those not already in loose-leaf copy format, we retrieved the pertinent bound volumes and photocopied the entries we needed.

Using a multiple-sheet scanner, we digitized each paper, using the scanner's software to clean up the copies. The flowchart in figure 22.1 describes the steps of this process.

Ways to Communicate among the Team of Project Workers

Members of the library staff and faculty who worked with the project coordinator shared information in person, by telephone, but most frequently by e-mail. We also used the cloud, to give the project coordinator access to the databases, scans, and other material during slower times at the reference desk as well as in her office.

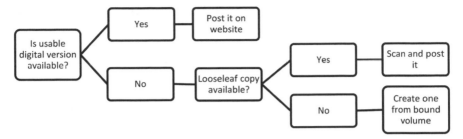

Figure 22.1.   Decision Flowchart for Posting.

Project Benefits

A number of benefits resulted beyond the value of making knowledge more widely accessible. One of the most satisfying was our receipt of many notes jotted by alumni on the permission forms remembering Roger Warlick, their classes, and our university with fondness and gratitude. The following are just a few of many such comments:

> As you may have heard, Dr. Warlick's class was one of the hardest on campus. . . . However, he had such a special demeanor about him, always on hand with a suggestion, an observation, correction or encouraging words on a research dead end day.[4]

> I have such fond memories of Dr. Warlick and my time at the Armstrong History Department. It was good training for my career and I'm sorry that Dr. Warlick passed at such a young age. Of course, I am happy to honor his wishes.[5]

> I am pleasantly surprised to receive this request. I remember the paper/ assignment. I can't imagine how anyone would find it valuable—but I hope this collection will honor Dr. Warlick well. . . . He was a good, kind, thoughtful, and able teacher. . . . He taught me skills in historical research I still use today.[6]

> He was a really great man. He believed in me. I'm thankful to God every day. I'll meet him one day in Heaven.[7]

Some of the authors whom we contacted told us a little about their current circumstances, enriching us with a fuller picture of their lives. We shared these updates on the success of the writers (including judges, historians, librarians/ archivists, and clergy) with the current and retired humanities professors and the staff who deal with alumni. We were a bit surprised to find that a very small subset of our author population (now in the teaching profession) didn't want their undergraduate papers on the web. Although we reached them without difficulty, we were unable to persuade them to allow their biographies to be published.

After our on-campus sources of information were thoroughly mined for alumni information, we still had a few writers to find. In hopes of doing so we sought further publicity for the project. One Alumni Affairs employee enthusiastically suggested introducing alumni authors to each other during Armstrong's alumni homecoming festivities. She also put us in contact with a local television writer/personality who agreed to help get the word out about the Savannah Biographies. Many of the Savannah Biography alumni writers entered professions in the field of history or information science. We hope some of them will come upon this chapter and let us know how to reach writers whose Savannah Biography papers are not yet posted on our website. This chapter itself, thus, becomes part of the publicity garnered for Lane Library by our local history project.

You can see the posted biographies at library.armstrong.edu/savannahbiographies.html.

Things We Might Have Done Differently

As the project went along, we discovered a few things we might have done differently.

- Get permissions while students are enrolled—Ask the student writers to sign permission slips while they are still on campus.
- Request electronic copies—Our earliest "Savannah Biographies" were written before personal computers were common, but those finished in the final years could have been submitted digitally.
- Make scans keyword-searchable.
- Work harder on publicity—To reach people who don't know the project exists, concentrate more heavily on local publicity, including placing advertisements in the alumni magazine and giving the work a more prominent place on the university's website.
- Obtain e-mail addresses to save time/funds—Ask the recipients if they want e-mail notification when their papers are posted.
- Sift through papers for best quality—Our choice of what is posted is based chiefly on who has given permission. In retrospect, it might have been better to have chosen the papers showing the best quality research and writing, asking permission to post from that subset.

- Explore the issue of copyright—We have not yet explored this facet, but are wondering whether it might not be a good idea.

A project of this kind really needs a coordinator who can be immersed in it—staying on top of the details and coordinating all the elements. A talented long-term volunteer could be given such a project and find it very rewarding. The beauty of such a project is that with very little financial outlay it can do a great service to a large population—reaching out to honor people in the past by keeping them in the minds of those in the future.

Notes

1. Samuel Martin, "William Hunter" Abstract, The Savannah Biographies, vol. 24 (Savannah, Ga.: Special Collections, Lane Library, Armstrong Atlantic State University, 1993).
2. Evelyn W. Parker, "The Doctors McKane," The Savannah Biographies, vol. 24 (1993), 1–2.
3. Roger Warlick, introduction to each volume of the Savannah Biographies collection.
4. Dee Mullis, author of Ellen McAlpin biography, March 12, 2011.
5. Deborah M. Nelson, author of Mordecai Myers biography, March 22, 2011.
6. Jeffrey E. Sanders, author of Morgan Rawls biography, February 25, 2011.
7. Rev. Dr. John T. Maddox, author of Anthony F. Mira biography, April 28, 2011.

CHAPTER 23

Promoting Local History through the Catablog

Cyndi Harbeson

Local history, genealogy, and photograph collections are rife with challenges. In many cases, librarians with little to no archival training are put in charge of their library's local history collection and must quickly learn how to handle and describe these unique and often fragile materials. Libraries face challenges dealing with archival materials due to staffing and technology limitations as well as those challenges inherent in the collections themselves, which do not lend themselves to basic cataloging. The learning curve for providing adequate description of these collections to promote access can be steep. A good way to level the playing field is through the use of blog technology, or software specifically developed to support regular entries of information, to create a catalog (aptly termed "catablog"[1]) of the local history collection.

A catablog is an easy, straightforward means of providing access to special collections. Unlike other discovery tools, such as library catalogs, finding aids, subject guides, or pathfinders, catablogs are dynamic and multipurpose. It is one of the most user-friendly ways to provide access to your collections. We've all heard the phrase "if it's not online, it doesn't exist," and this is especially true of special collections like local history, genealogy, or photographs. These types of materials are not easily accessed through a typical library catalog because they are not cataloged the same way as monographs or serials, which generally conform easily to the Anglo-American Cataloging Rules. For this reason, local history collections in public libraries often receive less attention from catalogers than other materials and remain inaccessible and invisible to researchers.

Benefits of the Catablog

The advantages of a catablog are myriad. Listed here are ten benefits of using a catablog as opposed to other more traditional discovery tools.

1. LOW-COST SOLUTION

Most important for a small library or historical society, blogs are a low-cost alternative to traditional software programs. Depending on the level of control you want to exert over the site, you can set up a blog at no cost or for as little as twenty to sixty dollars a year.[2] The blog is then hosted by a separate site, such as WordPress or Blogger, so the library is not responsible for the cost of server space.

2. LITTLE TO NO TECHNICAL EXPERTISE REQUIRED

Blogs also require very little technical expertise to set up. In a few easy steps, you can customize your blog's template to coincide with the look of your library's website. Knowledge of web languages such as HyperText Markup Language (HTML) or Cascading Style Sheets (CSS) is not necessary, although a cursory understanding is helpful. Maintenance of the site requires little time and attention. Blogging platforms host the site, and as a result, you are generally only responsible for maintaining the content. Support and troubleshooting guides are also available on all blogging platform sites.

3. CONSISTENT ACCESS TO COLLECTIONS

As an access tool, catablogs provide simple, consistent access to materials while maintaining distinct collections. Students, scholars, and the general public all have a certain familiarity with blogs and recognize the layout. Finding information on the catablog comes easily and without unsuccessful searching. This ease decreases the chance that users will leave your website before finding the information they wanted. The catablog is one of the most user-friendly methods to access collections.

4. PROMOTES USER INTERACTION

Catablogs also encourage direct interaction with our users through the use of comments and tags. In the case of archival materials, our users are often our best resource for providing the most in-depth and complete access. While librarians and archivists cannot be experts in every subject area, we can benefit from the expertise of our users. The catablog allows this knowledge to be seamlessly shared not only with us, but with the whole community. Although most comments are beneficial and add to the knowledge of the collection, they can be moderated for inappropriate messages, if that is a concern at your institution. Tags also allow for increased knowledge of collections by providing additional subject access. Users may also be more likely to use tags than to leave full comments on your site.

5. SUPERIOR SUBJECT ACCESS

Providing additional subject access is important, especially in cases where collections are primarily related to one topic, but also include some material or even one item on another subject. For example, in the Hans Schwieger Papers,[3] a collection documenting the work of a German conductor and containing primarily music-related materials, there is a letter describing the writer's reaction to President Kennedy's assassination. Without providing some subject access to this one item, no one would look in the Schwieger Papers for such information even though it could be beneficial to someone's research. Because archival collections are generally not processed to the item level, materials like this letter might not be identified in a catalog record or collection description. Tags and comments allow users who stumbled upon important finds in your collection to share their discoveries with other patrons.

6. EASILY APPRISES USERS OF COLLECTION UPDATES

The RSS (Really Simple Syndication) capability of catablogs also allows users to gain access to your collections without visiting the site directly. With the use of a web feed, collection updates can be instantly available to anyone interested. Using RSS feeds reduces the need to publicize changes or additions to the local history collection in other ways, such as news releases or e-mail notifications. The RSS feed can also be posted on your library's website to apprise visitors of updates to your local history collection. In the long term, this method can significantly save on staff time.

7. ACCESSIBLE VIA MOBILE DEVICES

With the rise in use of mobile devices, using a catablog rather than a library catalog, traditional web page, or a more static database decreases the need to maintain two separate sites, one for computers and another for handheld devices. Sites that host your catablog will automatically recognize that your site is being accessed by a mobile device and will adjust the display accordingly to create a separate, mobile-friendly version of the website. Use of mobile devices for web searching is definitely on the rise. Having mobile-friendly web pages is now almost a necessity for any library.

8. EASE OF SEARCHING

Catablogs also provide a high level of keyword searchability. When arriving at a web page, it is common to look first for a search box in which to enter keywords on a topic rather than browsing through the site. Because blogs are already inherently designed with a search capability, catablogs can be easily adapted for multiple types of searches. The information in the catablog is also searchable through a basic search engine, increasing the access points for every collection. People who may never have visited, or heard of, your library will be able to locate relevant materials in your collections and be in contact with you about using your resources.

9. SUPPORTS MULTIMEDIA

An advantage found in catablogs that is currently unavailable in many traditional catalogs is the ability to support multimedia. Digital images, audio files, and video can all be included directly in a catablog. In library catalogs, it is cumbersome to attach images directly to the catalog record. Including video or audio files is often impossible. With a catablog, digital images can be uploaded directly into the record. These images can then be displayed alongside collection descriptions. The same is true of audio and video files. With the additions of these types of files, the catablog becomes much more dynamic.

10. MULTIPLE BROWSING ABILITIES

While not the only tool with browsing capabilities, catablogs offer increased opportunities for perusing collections. Instead of searching by categories such as author, title, or subject, with a catablog you are able to browse through these categories as well as others like tag or material type. Browsing allows users without a specific research topic in mind to stumble upon hidden gems in your local history collection.

There are many advantages of catablogs versus depending solely on more traditional library catalogs and archival finding aids. But even with the many benefits, it is still important to carefully consider whether the catablog is the right discovery tool for your institution. And, if it is, just how do you go about launching one at your library?

First Steps to Creating a Catablog

Creating a catablog for your library is an easy and straightforward process. Whether you are just beginning work on your library's local history collection or have already developed some discovery tools, the process is the same. First steps should always include a survey of the collections. This survey should include a basic inventory with the collection title, extent, condition, and accession or collection number. As you work, develop a means of ranking the collections in terms of processing priority.

During this initial process, think about establishing standards for how information is going to be entered into your catablog, if these have not already been developed. Standards that determine how collections are accessed are important for every organization. The earlier these standards are developed, the better. Having set standards will allow for easier decision making in the long term. Examples of access standards include the types of keywords used, what information about a collection is included in the record, and how records are displayed to the public. Be consistent with how you enter information and what words you use when determining subject access. If you use the word "cat" as a subject term in one record, don't later use the word "feline." It may be helpful to keep a list of subject terms with references to the correct word to use in cases with many possible synonyms.

Each accession or collection in the inventory will get its own catablog entry. Even if the collection is unprocessed or not fully processed, it should receive a record in the catablog. These entries could range from preliminary descriptions to complete finding aids. While publicizing unprocessed collections in this manner may seem unorthodox, it is the only way to provide access to materials that may not be fully processed for months or even years. A brief description is infinitely better than no description.

After an inventory is completed, you can begin transferring any information that exists on your current website pertaining to the local history collection. Transferring this information can occur either through linking current web pages to the catablog or through migrating the content into the catablog itself. Examples of content you can transfer include:

- subject guides
- finding aids
- catalog records
- online exhibits
- collection descriptions

Once a collection inventory is complete, standards are established, and existing information is transferred, you can begin updating legacy finding aids and processing collections according to the rankings you established during inventorying. In the midst of this processing work, devote some time to making your catablog more dynamic. Add digital images to collection descriptions. Include links to other relevant sites. Create podcasts about interesting materials and embed them in the site. Use your imagination and creativity to produce a more robust instrument to access your collections.

Ten Steps to Catablog Creation

In just ten steps, you can create and implement a catablog for your local history collection.

1. DETERMINE THE TECHNICAL SKILLS OF YOUR STAFF

Is this your first web project? Are there members of your staff with web design knowledge or experience with blogs? Do you have a technology services department to provide support with your project? Don't be intimidated if this is your first, or one of your first, online projects. Blogs are now designed to be set up and maintained by people with little to no technical knowledge. Once you begin work, you will quickly pick up any needed skills.

2. CHOOSE YOUR BLOGGING PLATFORM

Think about what you want your catablog to look like. What functionality would you like to be included? What aspects of your discovery tool are nonnegotiables? Once you have had a chance to think about the end product of your catablog, take some time to explore different blogging platforms. Choose the one that will best support your vision. Now is also the time to decide whether the free version of the blogging platform will suit your needs. If you feel that you need more, explore the options of different platforms that offer upgrades for a fee. Many companies will allow you to start out with the free version and upgrade at a later time. However, it is more efficient in the long run to decide between the free version and the upgrades before you spend time customizing themes and adding data.

3. DECIDE ON A NAME

You will need to choose a web address for your catablog. Try to choose a name that is closely related to your institution's name. All web addresses must be unique. For this reason, you may have to use your second or third choice of name. Select your catablog's web address with care. Once you establish the address, it cannot be changed. Bear in mind that if you are choosing a free version, the name of the blogging platform's website will also appear in the web address.

4. CHOOSE YOUR THEME

There are dozens, if not hundreds, of themes available from which to choose. In my experience, a three-column theme with a customizable header works best, but a different layout may be a better fit for your library. Select a theme that complements your library's existing website, when possible. Don't be afraid to test out several different themes before officially launching your catablog. You can always change the theme if you find that a theme doesn't display as you'd hoped. Including an image from your collections or of your library in the header is always a good idea.

5. CUSTOMIZE YOUR CATABLOG

Now is the time to restructure your blog so that it looks and functions more like a catalog. Change the settings so posts display by title rather than date. Create a home page with search boxes, contact information, and tag selection bars. On the home page, you can include links to your policies and procedures as well as pages describing research services or guides. Clearly describe how to navigate through the catablog on the home page. Customize search functions by creating multiple search categories, including keyword, author, title, and material type. Add drop-down menus to allow users to select specific subjects or tags. Include prominent links to your library's main website, preferably in or near the header so the link appears on every page. Customization is the most time-consuming step in establishing your catablog, aside from data entry. It can also be somewhat frustrating since some trial and error may be necessary before you are satisfied with the end result.

6. TRANSFER EXISTING INFORMATION

Add any subject guides, catalog records, or collection descriptions to your new cat-ablog. Link to existing pages or paste the information directly into a catablog post. Incorporate any relevant collection information, including online exhibits that draw from your local history resources. Attach finding aids to the catablog, even if they are PDF or Microsoft Word files rather than EAD finding aids. Anything that will assist researchers in locating appropriate resources should be included in your catablog. You can always return to the linked pages and update them to fit more closely with the other content once the catablog has been launched.

7. ADD NEW RECORDS

Use the data compiled in your inventory to create records for each item or col-lection. Develop a standard form for entering this information in your catablog. Minimally, each record should include a title and brief description. Where pos-sible, also incorporate creator, dates, subjects, and extent into the record. Utilize volunteers or interns for the basic data entry. Establishing a basic record for every collection is the goal, rather than focusing on complete, detailed records for a few items. Once a collection is processed, additional information can be integrated into the record, such as a finding aid, related collections, material types, or access information.

8. INCREASE THE SITE'S MULTIMEDIA

After basic records exist in the catablog for every item or collection, turn your attention to adding images or audio and video files. Attaching images to your catablog records is an excellent way to increase your site's overall appeal. Even if your library does not have a digitization program, you can still scan photographs or manuscripts at relatively little cost to include digital images in your catablog. Ideally, every record should include an image to give users a sense of the collection.

9. CREATE AN INFRASTRUCTURE FOR GROWTH

After you have designed your catablog and added collection descriptions, form an institutional support structure to encourage further development of the system. Appoint at least two staff members to be in charge of the catablog. Include the catablog as part of your planning and assessment strategies. Incorporate mainte-nance of and additions to the catablog as part of your daily or weekly workflow.

10. PUBLICIZE YOUR CATABLOG AND COLLECTIONS

Advertise your catablog on your website and in news releases to library newsletters and local publications. Discuss the catablog with your patrons during reference interviews. Create bookmarks with the web address for the public to take home with them. Mention the catablog when discussing discovery tools with classes or during programs. Talk to other librarians in your area about the work you've done. Share feedback about the catablog with your colleagues. As you increase awareness of your catablog, you also spread knowledge about your local history collections. And enhanced awareness will translate into increased use of those materials, which is the ultimate goal.

Final Thoughts

The decision to use a relatively new technology to solve the problem of providing access to historical materials is not one to be made lightly. While the start-up and maintenance costs are relatively low, a serious commitment of staff time is necessary, at least at first. Catablogs can be an incredibly useful tool for those willing to harness the power of blog technology. Your collections will become more visible to your current audience and others will also learn of your resources because the records will appear in search engine results.

When resources are limited, catablogs offer the opportunity to maximize your results for minimal costs and equipment. After a few hours of research, you can begin the process of developing your own in-house, nonproprietary discovery tool. Discuss the benefits and the disadvantages of creating a catablog with your colleagues or staff before launching yourself into the process. Any project of this nature requires forethought and planning as well as a commitment to developing the standards, policies, and procedures that will ensure its success.

Notes

1. The term "catablog" was first coined by Robert S. Cox at the University of Massachusetts, Amherst.

2. Figure based on the cost of upgrades at the site WordPress.com (accessed July 2011).

3. The Hans Schwieger Papers are located in the Special Collections of Belk Library at Appalachian State University.

CHAPTER 24

Reinventing the Obituary File for the Digital Age

Kerry A. FitzGerald

A File Is Born

As a county seat, Grand Haven attracts and welcomes genealogists to West Michigan year-round. Its sandy beaches, art fairs, and festivals do nothing to detract from the popularity of the sleepy town, although they may distract the genealogist from venturing into serious research. But for those who soldier on, armed with notebook, laptop, and flash drive, Loutit District Library will not disappoint.

In the 1980s, the library set aside a small unstaffed room to house a budding local history and genealogy collection. Books, pamphlets, journals, clippings, historical photographs and documents, indexes, maps, atlases, microfilm of Census data, and the local newspaper were gathered together for the first time. Shortly thereafter, the Grand Haven Genealogical Society was formed, and members took it upon themselves to index all obituaries published in the *Grand Haven Tribune*, dating back to 1891. All issues of the paper were read, either via microfilm or bound hardcopy, and the pertinent information extracted. The society tackled the project with gusto, but when many cooks gather in the kitchen, there are many interpretations of the recipe. While the society succeeded in creating a traditional card-catalog system, inconsistencies in the depth of information collected cropped up here and there.

Under new library administration and a significantly increased budget, the humble little room was expanded to three times the size, its open hours were increased, and a staff member was assigned to man a service desk. The room was no longer a self-service storage room. Local History and Genealogy became an official department of the library and staff rolled up their sleeves.

Fifteen to twenty years into the obituary file project, typewriters were replaced by the softer clacking of keyboards and the cards superseded by a spreadsheet. The Genealogical Society formally disbanded, although a handful of hard-core members continued as library volunteers.

With the launch of the library's website, staff began to explore ways to make the local history and genealogy collection available online. One of the first projects genealogists encouraged us to tackle was the transformation of the old obituary file into a searchable online database. This chapter will describe the steps taken to see the project to completion, including the extraction and formatting of information, management of volunteer activities, and the preparation for web access.

Designing the Worksheet

As any genealogist will tell you, when it come to obituaries, less is definitely not more. Genealogists turn to published obituaries as a premier source for personal information about an ancestor and his or her surviving family members. An obituary not only confirms the deceased's place of residence but may also provide date and place of birth or the deceased's age, place of interment, name of spouse and date of marriage, along with names of parents, siblings (and their spouses), and offspring. The obituary may also provide the place of residence for each of the named survivors. And those are just the dry facts. Great-Grandfather's obituary might mention that he was a champion chess player or Aunt Maude's that she once raised $15,000 for the local Kiwanis Club.

With the plethora of information compiled in the typical obituary, where does one begin? If you're starting with an existing obituary file, most of the grunt work—accessing the published obituaries and extracting the information—has already been done. If you're not starting with an existing file, the steps and tips outlined in this chapter will allow you to create a digital file and provide remote access to it, if desired.

But let's take a step back for a moment to consider the source material—the newspaper. Even if you're starting with a card-catalog system, you'll want to have access to the newspaper—either in hardcopy or microfilm format—from which the obituary information was extracted. Why? Dates can be transposed, names mistyped or misspelled, and entire obituaries overlooked. For quality control, we highly recommend verifying the data. If you're starting this project from scratch, we also recommend that you begin working with the oldest issues of the newspaper, since these will be the most valued by the genealogist, and work your way to the present. You'll eventually reach a point where you can keep up with current obituaries published in hardcopy or online.

Now, let's assume you're working with a card file. The majority of the cards in our file system resemble the sample in figure 24.1.

This sample contains the name of the deceased, the date of birth, date of death, the date the obituary was published, the page and column(s) on which the obituary appeared, and the name of the newspaper. Other cards contain the entire text of the obituary—cut out of the paper (not the library's copy, of course) and glued to the card. Many of these complete cards sprouted legs over the years and walked out the door. Still other cards contain significantly less information—perhaps only the deceased's name and the date, page, and column of the obituary.

Realizing we had the perfect opportunity to reinvent this index, we designed a worksheet to gather as much personal information as possible about the deceased (see figure 24.2).

Grand Haven is a community primarily of Dutch descent, and the local residents adhered to standard naming practices, which present the genealogists with some unique problems. For example, it was common to name the first son after the paternal grandfather and the second son after the maternal grandfather. If Jan Vandermeiden's father was Willem, and Jan had four sons, the firstborn son of each of Jan's sons would be called Willem, so you can see how the generations might be confused. To aid our genealogists, the worksheet we created

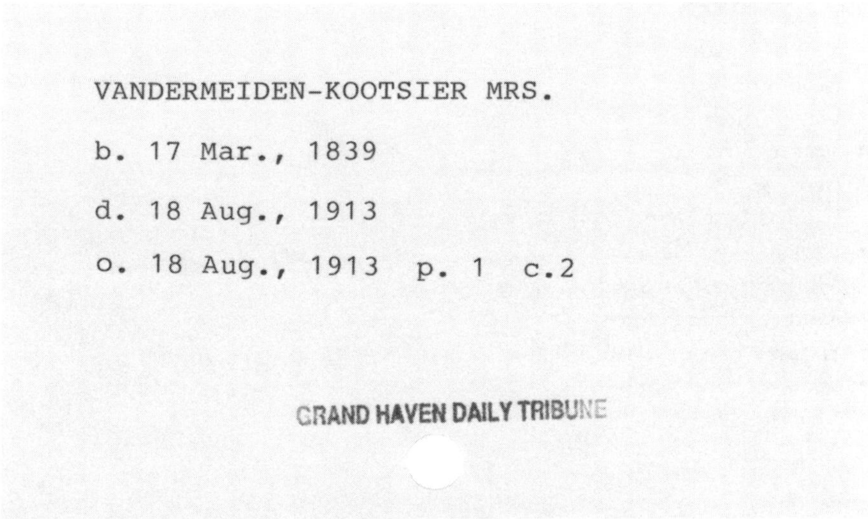

VANDERMEIDEN-KOOTSIER MRS.

b. 17 Mar., 1839

d. 18 Aug., 1913

o. 18 Aug., 1913   p. 1   c.2

GRAND HAVEN DAILY TRIBUNE

Figure 24.1.

DEATH INFORMATION LISTED IN THE GRAND HAVEN TRIBUNE																			
Last Name	First Name	Date of Paper	Pg/Col	Month of Death	Day of Death	Year of Death	Month of Birth	Day of Birth	Year of Birth	Age	Father Last Name	Father First Name	Mother Last or Maiden Name	Mother First Name	Spouse Last or Maiden Name	Spouse First Name	Marriage Date	Cemetery	

Figure 24.2.

consists of twenty columns, the headings for which are listed left to right across the top of the page:

• Last Name
• First Name
• Date of Paper
• Page/Column
• Month of Death
• Day of Death
• Year of Death
• Month of Birth
• Day of Birth
• Year of Birth
• Age
• Father's Last Name
• Father's First Name
• Mother's Last or Maiden Name
• Mother's First Name
• Spouse's Last or Maiden Name
• Spouse's First Name
• Marriage Date
• Cemetery

Each row in the data collection worksheet represents one obituary. A total of eleven obituaries can be extracted onto the legal-sized worksheet.

Thinking Digitally

The next tool you'll need is spreadsheet software. We used Microsoft Excel to create the worksheet and for final data entry. When we first started working with a spreadsheet, we made two significant blunders that became apparent when we engaged our web designers in discussion about reconfiguring the spreadsheet data into a searchable database. In our original worksheet, both last names and first names were entered together in one column. This arrangement prevented wild-card searching. In other words, the searcher had to enter the last name and first name exactly as typed to score a hit. If last name and first name are entered in separate columns, the user can search for all instances of a surname alone or truncate either name if an exact spelling isn't known. For example, if *berg* is entered into the search box, not only are entries for *Berg* and *Berger* retrieved but also all entries containing *berg*—like *Lindberg* and *Weinberger*. Likewise, *van* will retrieve not only *VanWieren* but also *Cavanaugh* and *Evans*.

We also gave consideration to spacing in surnames. In our obituary file, many local names begin with *Van*, *Van de*, *Van den*, or *Van der*, and all their variant spellings. We made the decision early on to record such names in our spreadsheet without any spacing between the elements. For example, *Vanden Berg* was entered as *VandenBerg*, *Van De Wege* as *VanDeWege*. Such name-entry standardization allows the searcher to retrieve all instances of a name regardless of variations in spacing occurring in the published obituary. Capitalization is ignored by the search engine. The genealogist visiting our website is advised to enter surnames into the obituary database without spaces.

The second mistake we made concerned date entry. In the original version of our worksheet, dates were entered as month-day-year in a single column in "date format." Formatting the birth, marriage, and death date columns as "dates" in Excel seemed logical. However, we soon discovered that Excel cannot recognize dates prior to 1900. A date entered as 04-16-1899 or 04/16/1899 is automatically converted into a formula. When a dash is used to separate date elements, Excel treats it as a subtraction process, and when backslashes are used, Excel treats it as a division process. In order to work around this problem, it was necessary to set the formatting of the date fields to "text." But taking this step created another set of problems, which will be discussed below.

We wanted to give our searchers the ability to limit a search to a specified year of birth and/or death, but with the date columns formatted as "text," we found we couldn't do so. Dates no longer functioned as "dates" in Excel. Therefore, we pushed up our sleeves to create another work-around solution. We achieved our goal by separating the month, day, and year into different columns of text. The end result allows the user to search for the John Robinson who died in 1954.

Extracting the Data

We were fortunate to have a number of dedicated volunteers to help record and process the enormous amount of data contained in 119 years of the *Grand Haven Tribune*. To ensure the accuracy of the data, we divided the project into the four phases, listed below.

- Phase 1: Volunteer 1 examines one month of the newspaper—April 1901, for example—and records on the extraction form every article published regarding a person's death. These articles may include a death notice, an obituary, a funeral notice, and any accompanying article about the deceased.
- Phase 2: Volunteer 2, with the newspaper and the extraction forms in hand, checks the information recorded by Volunteer 1 against the published copy and makes necessary corrections. If an article has been overlooked, Volunteer 2 records the data on a clean form.
- Phase 3: Volunteer 3 enters the data into Excel.
- Phase 4: Library staff proofreads the Excel spreadsheet and corrects data-entry errors. Library staff makes the final decisions regarding data inclusion (see discussion below).

As the volunteers extracted the data from the newspaper, the desire to fix typos and inaccurate information (as published in the newspaper) was strong. Likewise, patrons occasionally expressed the same urge, especially when the data in question pertained to the spelling of a loved one's name. While the staff is sensitive to the feelings of our clientele and the perfectionist tendencies of our helpful volunteers, the decision was made early on to record the data as it originally appeared in the newspaper. The rationale behind this procedure was that if the newspaper published a death notice for John Anderson under "Jon Andersen," the subsequent obituary and accompanying articles are likely to retain the incorrect spelling. Additionally, we feel the place for such corrections is in the research notes and publications of the genealogist.

Considering the Workload

As you think about assigning the extraction workload to staff and/or volunteers, here are some benchmarks from our project that may prove useful:

- The four workers mentioned in the extraction phases above typically recorded ten years of data from the newspaper in a year's time, averaging between fifteen to twenty hours per week.

- The *Grand Haven Tribune* is published six days a week, although prior to 1900, the frequency of publication varied.
- The *Tribune* currently serves a population of roughly 47,000.

Compare these factors against your own indexing project to get an idea of the time involved and the manpower needed.

Creating the Database

Although the library staff was not involved in the actual creation of the obituary database, the tech-minded reader might be interested in knowing the steps taken by our web designers in converting the Excel files into a searchable database. This is the don't-try-this-at-home part of the project, unless you or your staff possess some working knowledge of computer programming. If not, now's the time to call in the experts.

When we began entering data into Excel, we broke the data up into manageable files—usually a year's worth of information from the newspaper. Next, we e-mailed these files to our professional web designers who first converted the Excel files into CSV (comma-separated values) files. This process stripped away the columnar display and returned the data to its raw state. The next step was to re-create the files in MySQL to form the database. Finally, the data was interpreted from the database in the PHP scripting language to create the user interface. We would have liked to have visited the web designers' workplace to see their software and programming in action, but since the library was in the process of moving back into its expanded and remodeled facility, we didn't have the opportunity to do so.

While the creation of the database is the most technical and the most complicated step in the project, it's also the fastest if it's given into the right hands. Where do you find those hands? We had no trouble hiring programmers who understood our needs, even in our small town. If a professional web designer can't create the database for you, a good place to look for a programmer is a larger library system, a local college, or a university. If you're lucky, a student programmer might be willing to take on the project for free as a regular or extra-credit assignment.

Going Live

Now that you have your obituary database, you'll want to put it through its paces before you go live on your website or offer it to your users in house. Test the search engine against known obituaries from the old card catalog or newspaper. Does the database return the expected results? Is the response time adequate? Is the user interface self-explanatory, or do you need to provide instructions or search tips? In our example, the following text greets the visitor to the obituary database: "For best results, enter name elements without spaces. For example, enter *vandenberg* instead of *van den berg*. Capitalization is not necessary. This database is a work in

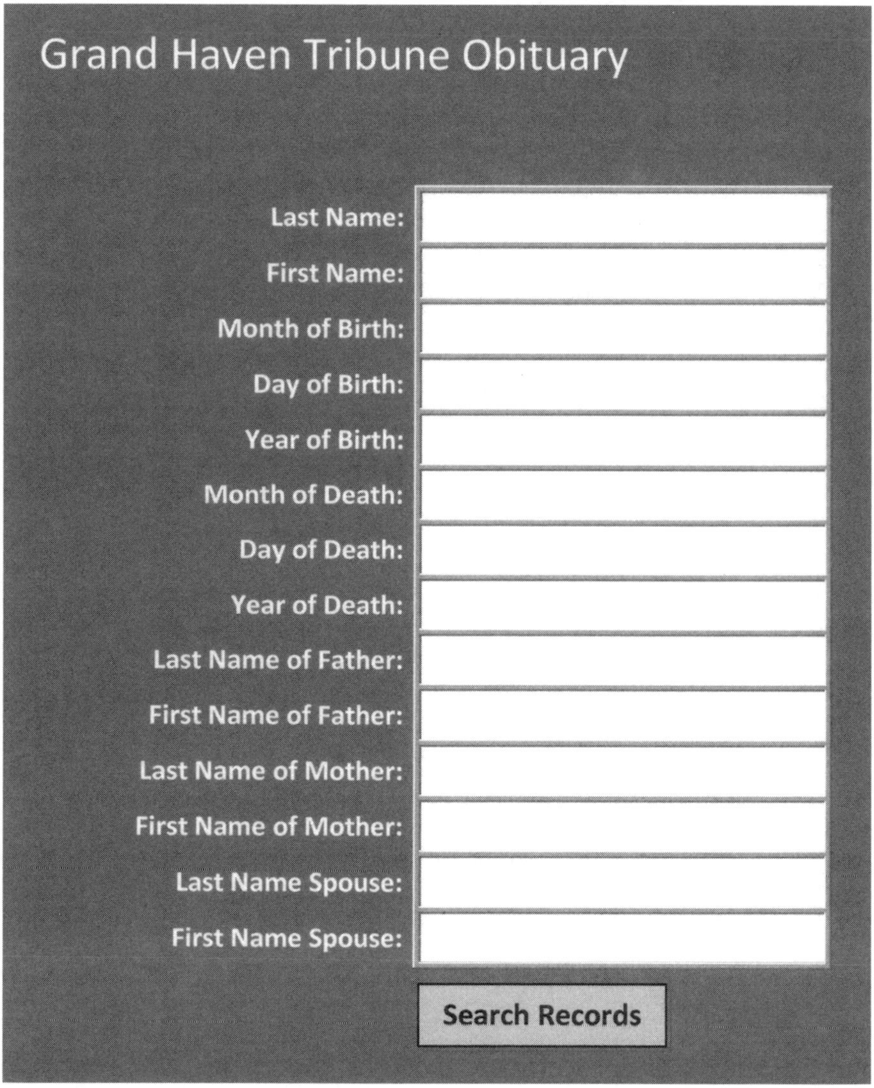

Grand Haven Tribune Obituary

Last Name:	
First Name:	
Month of Birth:	
Day of Birth:	
Year of Birth:	
Month of Death:	
Day of Death:	
Year of Death:	
Last Name of Father:	
First Name of Father:	
Last Name of Mother:	
First Name of Mother:	
Last Name Spouse:	
First Name Spouse:	

Search Records

Figure 24.3.

progress as we expand the years of newspaper coverage." Figure 24.3 is a snapshot of the user interface to the obituary file as it appears on our website.

A typical search result is shown in figure 24.4.

Now that you've brought your project to fruition, there's no time to waste resting on your laurels. You need to get the word out about your exciting new genealogy tool. Announce it on your website, write a blurb for your newsletter, send off a press release to the local paper, get the word out to local and regional genealogy societies and schools. You created it. They will come. They will search!

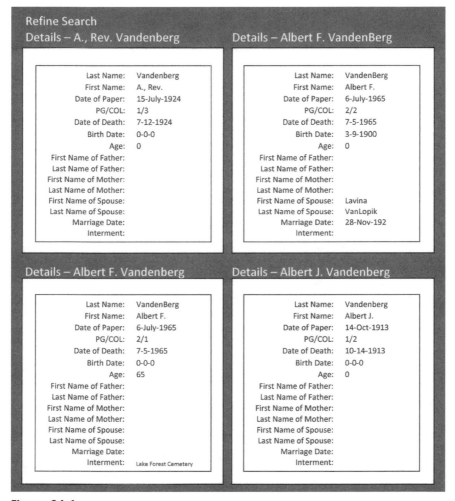

Figure 24.4.

Spin-Offs

You've successfully created one database to cater to the genealogist—why stop there? You're on a roll!

At Loutit District Library, we're in the midst of developing a database of local birth announcements—culled from the same old card file—and marching through the same steps we followed with the obituary file. After that, there's our marriage index file to reinvent.

Another source of vital records in our area is the Ottawa County Death Records. We receive an Excel file each month from the county clerk's office. The file provides the names of residents who passed away or nonresidents who died within the county limits, usually within the past month or two. For each deceased individual, the file lists place of residence and date of birth and date of death. Check with your county clerk to see what joint projects you can arrange. Talk to local cemeteries as well. We were able to obtain an Excel file of interments in several area cemeteries and created a database for them as well. You never know what's out there or what might be possible unless you ask.

You might take your own obituary database one step further than we did. Think how appreciative the genealogist would be to come across a database of complete obituaries, scanned from the local paper or captured from the newspaper's website. Before undertaking such a project, you'll need to secure permission from the publisher, of course.

Put your digital thinking cap on. The possibilities are endless for reinventing old files and outmoded formats for the digital age. Think outside the box and the usual sources genealogists turn to for information. For example, local church records and directories are an excellent source for establishing an ancestor's place of residence (not to mention denomination), but if an ancestor's church membership is not known, a visit to several area churches might be necessary for the genealogist. How wonderful would it be for him or her to discover all that information gathered together in one convenient location?

Project Checklist

To recap, here are the steps we followed to turn our old card-file system into an online database:

1. Obtain copies of the original source material—the newspaper—for the obituaries.
2. Design a worksheet for data extraction (see figure 24.2).
3. Assign the extraction workflow.

4. Proofread and correct the work.
5. Enter the data from the worksheets into a spreadsheet.
6. Proofread and correct the data-entry work.
7. Hire a computer programmer, if necessary, to convert the spreadsheet files into a relational database and to construct the user interface.
8. Test the final product.
9. Go live and spread the word!

As you undertake your own project, we would enjoy hearing from you. We welcome your questions and your unique ideas for other projects to help the genealogy researcher. Please visit the online version of our Local History and Genealogy Department, located at www.loutitlibrary.org. From the main page, click on the link to *Explore Your Past*, and then select *Genealogy Resources*. Click on the link to *Grand Haven Tribune Obituaries 1891–1979*. Stay awhile and play with the database. Who knows? You might find a long-lost relative in Ottawa County. Take a moment and let us know what you think about our final results.

Please e-mail thoughts and questions to Jeanette Weiden at jweiden@ loutitlibrary.org. Jeanette coordinates collection development, user instruction, and volunteer activities for Loutit District Library's Local History and Genealogy Department. She served as assistant curator of collections at the Tri-Cities Historical Museum for seven years and received her BS from Grand Valley State University. Through Jeanette's careful guidance, this project furthered the library's mission of providing quality materials and services to address the educational and informational needs of our community and the greater community beyond.

The author would also like to thank Jason and Rob at Iron Mountain Design for making this project an Internet reality.

PART VIII

ORAL HISTORIES

CHAPTER 25

Preserving Born-Digital Oral Histories

Juliana Nykolaiszyn

There is something special about listening to past events or ways of life from those that experienced it firsthand. Oral history provides a great outlet to not only fill gaps in primary source documents but also shed light on history that could possibly be forgotten. From family memories to community histories, oral history is something special. It's something powerful. And it is something that needs consideration when it comes to preservation.

Oral histories continue to gain in popularity, especially with recording equipment becoming more accessible and available due to technology costs decreasing. Many repositories have a collection of oral history interviews in some form. It is the "some form" that complicates matters when it comes to preservation. From paper transcripts to recorded media, oral histories pose unique preservation challenges based on the materials at hand. There are many options, ranging from high-dollar preservation efforts to low-cost budget solutions that can not only help save your stories, but also make your oral histories available for years to come.

Like most technology-based efforts, oral history has seen a rapid shift from recordings produced via physical objects, for example cassette tapes, to born-digital files and formats. And while these recordings may be generated on a physical object such as a flash-based memory card, the file may not reside on the physical card for long as interviews move through various phases of processing. While oral history preservation is not a new topic, taking care of born-digital materials in a technological age is, and with that, this chapter hopes to highlight strategies to think about when it comes to preserving such material in your repositories and archives.

Evaluating your Collections

In order to understand what you are working with, your oral history collections need to be evaluated. The best way to do this is by performing a thorough inventory of your materials. In inventorying, you should treat born-digital recordings just like traditional oral history recordings. In this phase you want to develop a list of recordings and denote location, file size, format, resolution, playability, and how each is stored. If guides such as finding aids, catalog records, and other inventory lists have been developed in the past, let those serve as road maps on your search, but it is best to physically evaluate each object. While it may be difficult to touch and feel the oral histories depending on the type of media they are stored upon, it helps to "lay hands" on these recordings as best you can to understand the extent of what you are dealing with. This also gives you a chance to double-check existing inventories.

LOCATION

The location of files could mean many things. You want to know basically where to find the recording in your collection. Is the born-digital file housed on a computer server? If so, note the path. If it is housed on flash memory, denote the type of memory card (Compact Flash, Secure Digital Card, MiniSD Card, MicroSD Card, etc.). If the born-digital files reside in multiple locations, note all locations, including CDs, DVDs, or other backups.

FILE SIZE

Recordings can range in size depending on the type of recorder used, recorder settings, and compression formats. For each recording, note the size of each file. This will help in determining future needs for possible migration efforts and server space allocation projections.

FORMAT

Recording audio in .wav format is the current archival standard, especially when it comes to oral histories. While it is preferred that audio is recorded in such a format for depositing to libraries and archives, it may be possible to have audio in many different formats, including compressed versions such as .mp3. Video can also range in format depending on encoding and compression. Since video tends to bring up interesting challenges, it will be discussed later in the chapter.

Overall, remember to document the format for every oral history in your collection, both audio and video. This information will also come in handy not only for future migration efforts, but also in evaluating future use.

RESOLUTION

When you think of resolution, photographs may come to mind, but in the world of audio recording (and audio tracks on video recordings), it refers to something different. Both sample rate and bit depth provide additional insight into your audio and are important to note on your inventory list. Sample rate refers to the number of times per second your audio is captured. This is measured in kilohertz (kHz). Bit depth refers to the number of bits recorded in a sample. Depending on the types of recorders used in the oral history process, sample rate and bit depth will vary from collection to collection based on the unit's settings. The higher your sample rate and bit depth, the more space will be required to store your audio files. If you are not aware of the settings on your recording units, you can always check sample rate and bit depth using audio editing software, including freeware products such as Audacity.

PLAYABILITY

A goal is to make sure the digital recordings in your collection can be played. This may sound like a no-brainer, but it can also pose unique challenges. If your audio or video is recorded in an obscure format, or your computer is not equipped with a program to play the files, it will be hard to listen to interviews and subsequently difficult to provide access to patrons looking to utilize your oral history content. If you cannot play a file, do a little research on the recording format. While you never want to alter, save over, or delete the original recording, if you are having difficulties, try converting the file to another format by creating a use copy or duplicate copy. While this use copy may not be created in a desired "archival" format, it could possibly result in a playable file, which is important in providing access. In analyzing playability, you can record the duration or how long the interview runs. This information could come in handy when preparing metadata for your collection later in the process.

STORAGE

Born-digital recordings can be stored in a variety of ways, which is one of the more challenging aspects of preservation. The recordings can very well be stored on the original recording media, such as a flash memory card. Or the recordings could be transferred from the recording media to a variety of places, including storage on portable hard drives, computer servers, CD/DVDs, and the list goes on and on. For the recordings in your oral history collection, note where the item is stored, even if multiple copies reside in different locations within your repository. For example, you may have the original recording stored on a computer server, which is backed up every two days. In addition, you may have additional copies of the master recording burned to CD or DVD, and yet another copy stored on a portable hard drive in your office.

Storage is a big part of long-term preservation, especially when it comes to born-digital files. The next section will go into greater detail in examining storage, including a variety of solutions based on budgetary considerations.

Storage Options

Born-digital files will more than likely transfer locations several times before finding their archival home. This is because the files will need to be moved off the recording device or memory card to other long-term storage options. This is not a bad thing, since it makes sense to reuse and free up memory when recording. The big thing to think about is where to put the files once recording has been completed. This can be handled several ways, such as burning to recordable media; transferring to computer servers, portable media, or off-site storage; or using a combination of backup options.

RECORDABLE MEDIA

Storing on recordable media includes transferring the audio recordings to either compact discs (CDs) or digital video discs (DVDs). A standard CD can hold approximately 700 megabytes of data storage while a single-layer DVD can hold up to 4.7 gigabytes of data. There is quite a difference in space and cost between the two, but you also have to consider not just purchasing standard CDs and DVDs but also exploring archival CDs and DVDs. While archival gold CDs, such as those manufactured by Mitsui, have a long shelf life, some archivists are still undecided about this type of technology. In this case, it would be advantageous to explore creating multiple copies, for example, burning use copies on standard CDs or DVDs and master files on gold CDs or DVDs.

COMPUTER SERVERS

If you have the space available, keep a master copy housed on your repository's computer servers. In most cases, it helps if it is RAID-based. RAID stands for "redundant array of independent disks." And while RAID systems vary in operation, in the simplest of terms they have protections built into the system that reduce your chance of losing data in case of disk failure. Since operations and costs vary, it is always a good idea to consult your repository's systems department to make sure adequate protections are in place if you start storing your master files on organizational servers.

PORTABLE MEDIA

Portable media refers to external hard drives. These types of drives continue to come down in cost and increase in disk space. External drives provide a great low-cost option, especially if your repository does not have the funds to invest in a computer server. But, just like a regular hard drive on your computer, these drives can also fail, so it is important to have a backup on another media, in addition.

OFF-SITE STORAGE

This is one of the more expensive options in preserving not only your oral history material, but on a grander scale, your repository's electronic content. Off-site storage provides a way for you to send your files to a secure server location, usually in another part of the state or country. Your files are backed up on a network of drives, and if the system notices any differences, the files are then replaced with another copy of the content, similar to the redundancy you find with RAID servers but on a much larger scale. You may wonder why this is beneficial, but if a fire or disaster impacts your facility, your data will remain safe and intact at another location.

BEST OPTIONS

In looking at your options, the best choice could very well be a combination of what has been discussed so far. For low-cost options, it may be best to back up your files not only on an external drive, but also on CDs or DVDs. For mid-level protection, back up files on your repository's RAID server in addition to burning backup copies in the form of CDs or DVDs. The most costly option is off-site storage, which is great for larger well-funded organizations or those who live in areas of increasing natural disaster threats.

Video Oral Histories: Preservation in Flux

It is very common today to have a collection of video-based oral history interviews, with no additional audio component. This material could very well be recorded straight to the hard drive of the camera, on removable media such as flash-based memory, or via digital video tape. Regardless, there are many questions about video, especially when it comes to archival standards. In fact, the jury is still out on the best way to archive video. The archival community is currently reviewing archival standards and best practices for video preservation. The best advice to follow is to be consistent and, in the future, be prepared to migrate your video collection once a standard is finalized.

Archiving video collections is challenging, but not impossible. Your institution can take active steps toward preservation, even if a standardized format is still being decided by the archival community. Let's review some of the key terms you may have heard about when researching digital preservation revolving around video production.

COMPRESSION

When you make a DVD from your video files, you are creating media in a compressed format. When you make a video for viewing on the Internet, you are creating media in a compressed format, too. Even when you upload a video to YouTube or Vimeo, Internet platforms for viewing videos on a wide range of subjects and topics, yes, you are dealing with video files that have been compressed. Now compression is not necessarily a bad thing when it comes to working with video. Video in its raw form is very large and takes up a serious amount of computer resources, and depending on the type of video camera used in production, your video file could be pretty big if shot in standard definition or really, really big if shot in high definition. We're not talking megabytes, but many, many gigabytes. Regardless, compression allows us to make the video more versatile for use in different ways, including online or in exhibits.

Understanding Codecs and Containers and Wrappers

Compression can be hard to explain. So here is a simple overview of the process. A codec stands for "compressor-decompressor" or "coder-decoder." It basically provides the instructions that tell the computer how the file has been compressed upon creation and, in addition, how to decompress when played back. There are lossy and lossless codecs, depending on your overall outcome or needs. Compression schemes include H.264, H.263, MXF, Sorenson, MPEG-4, MPEG-2, and JPEG 2000 (among others).

Containers and wrappers are essentially the same thing. You want to think of containers and wrappers like a .zip file. A .zip file may contain many different files in various formats. In the case of video, a container or wrapper holds the information needed to transmit the video on your computer screen. This information includes audio, video, captions, subtitles, menus, metadata, and so on. Common containers/wrappers include .mp4, .mov, .wmv, .avi, .ogg, .flv, .mpeg, and .mxf (among others).

One quick note: only certain wrappers may work with specific codecs. Most video editing programs will provide codec-wrapper options or combinations to aid in selecting compatible matches. It is getting easier, but it is still possible to compress a file using codecs and wrappers that do not talk to each other!

Here's an example. When producing video for web-based viewing, you are taking all of the files generated by your video camera (such as audio, metadata, video, etc.) and compressing each asset into one file, for example, using H.264 codec. The compressed file is then wrapped in a container, such as an .mp4, allowing for playback.

It is easy to get confused quickly when exploring codecs and containers/ wrappers, especially since some of the codecs use the same names as some of the containers/wrappers. While the discussion of compression, codecs, and containers and wrappers can be quite daunting, remember if you remain consistent in your decisions, it will be easier to not only manage your data but also to migrate collections in the future.

More Considerations

The following tips provide items to think about when considering digital preservation of oral histories:

BEST PRACTICES

While best practices for dealing with archival audio exist, working with video still remains a topic of great discussion. The best suggestion is to remain consistent in your efforts and be prepared for future migration. Making a DVD of your video oral histories is one option, and while DVDs contain a compressed picture, it is just another way to provide not only access to your collection but also a backup copy of your material in case electronic files or digital video tapes become damaged.

ORIGINAL EQUIPMENT

Since most libraries, historical societies, and other repositories serve as holders of oral history materials, your organization may also be the creator of the recordings. In this case, it is advantageous to always keep the recording equipment when possible. As the years go by, this may sound wasteful in times of limited space, but by keeping the recording equipment, you increase your ability to play (and therefore transfer) recordings on media that may eventually become obsolete. Again, especially if you are the creator of the material, retain not only audio recorders but video recorders that were used in the oral history process. This is especially true when thinking about analog materials generated by cassette players or reel-to-reels. These machines are becoming more and more obsolete in libraries and increasingly handy if you want to provide access to older recordings or for future conversion to digital formats.

ASKING FOR HELP

A statewide oral history survey conducted by members of the Oklahoma Oral History Research Program at the OSU Library in 2008 found many Oklahoma respondents unsure of how to preserve oral history collections. Some small to mid-sized libraries and repositories expressed questions about preservation, noting materials stored in shoeboxes, in homes, or buried on shelves, in addition to organizations taking active steps in archiving oral histories with respect to proper care and condition. While the repositories surveyed included a mix of analog and digital collections in their oral history holdings, researchers noticed a need for increased preservation education, especially with respect to audio-visual materials. Many statewide organizations exist to help repositories locate answers to preservation questions or find contacts to assist. Turn to your state-based historical records advisory board, state library, college or university archival departments, or oral history programs in your area for additional guidance or consultation.

The Future of Digital Preservation

From dealing with paper to computer bits and bytes, digital preservation may seem daunting but it is possible. Let's face it, technology can be scary. But it allows us to do new and exciting things, for example, preserve everything from fragile paper collections to the recorded voice or video of oral history interviews. Knowing this rich material will be around for future use is reason enough to tackle challenges in preservation. There will always be new technologies to conquer, but careful planning, migrating, and adapting to changes as they come along will all help ensure your born-digital recordings and oral history collections will be around for generations to come.

For More Information

The following resources are a great place to start when exploring oral history and information about digital preservation:

Oral History Association
www.oralhistory.org

H-Oralhist Listserv
www.h-net.org/~oralhist

Oral History in the Digital Age Wiki
wiki.ohda.matrix.msu.edu

CHAPTER 26

Preserving Indiana Women's Voices: A University Oral History Project

Theresa McDevitt

Those who visit the oldest building on the Indiana University of Pennsylvania (IUP) campus will see adorning the walls the photographs of the men who served as principals and presidents during its 135-year history. Histories of IUP, which trace its development from a normal school to a teachers' college and then finally to a university, note the significant role that these men played in the history of the institution. While the story of these men is important, its elite focus documents only one aspect of the history of the school. In fact, there is another less well-known and appreciated story that should also be documented, and without which, the true history of the institution will not be known. That is the story of the female students, professors, and administrators who led and attended the school during the same period.

In the early 1880s female students and faculty began to outnumber male students and faculty on the Indiana campus. For nearly one hundred years, through the First and Second World Wars, until the GI Bill and concomitant crowding in the college classrooms of the nation led to a demographic shift in the schools' population, female students continued to dominate the student body by large percentages and female faculty continued to outnumber males. In spite of this, awareness of the female-centric history of the institution has been all but lost. Unfortunately, students, faculty, and administrators at the institution are generally ignorant of this significant history, and this is a loss particularly for young women who might be inspired by the stories of their predecessors. The focus of the project that will be described in this chapter was to investigate and document the rich history of women students, faculty, and administrators at IUP before the primary sources are lost forever.

Though the project is ongoing, thus far it has resulted in the collection of a diverse group of analog tapes and digital audio and video recorded interviews and other documents that record the experiences and impact of women at IUP from the 1920s to the present day. Though this collection is small and incomplete, it is a beginning. Current faculty in women's studies and public history are also working on oral and public history projects, including additional interviews and an exhibit on the history of women at IUP. These projects will be added to the existing collection and bring the stories included in them to the attention of a broader audience.

Inspiration for the Project

This project began in the spring of 2005 when I began working as acting special collections and archives librarian. My appointment coincided with the arrival of a new university president who had a keen interest in preserving and promoting the history of the university, but it was his wife that inspired me. Sometime that semester when I met the new president's wife, she asked me for information on the roles and stories of women who been married to IUP presidents to provide background for a presentation she was planning. Not surprisingly, though there are two histories of IUP, neither had much information on women's experience and neither could even provide the first names of the first ladies, let alone any details of their time here. Though I was easily able to locate hundreds of archival boxes of documentation on the lives of the principals and presidents, there was practically nothing that documented the lives of the women who in many cases had played important roles in their husbands' administrations.

Looking through the school's newspaper yielded a bit of information on these shadowy figures as hostesses or leaders and creators of campus and community organizations, but my search was yielding little of any use. When I took my dilemma to one of the other librarians, she suggested that retired faculty and administrators who were still living in the area could probably provide information on the first ladies, if only I asked. I did ask and they were eager to talk about these women, and even provided me photographs, news clippings, and actual letters that documented their lives. Armed with the information they provided I had much to assist me in finding more in university publications and other printed records. Putting the two together, I was able to provide the president's wife with at least a bit of the history she had asked for. The difficulty in locating this information opened my eyes to the larger problem of the lack of documentation in primary or secondary sources of the experience of women at our institution and led me to resolve to do something about it.

Collaboration

My experience was not unique. It is often difficult to find information on women's experience at colleges and universities, and experiences such as mine have led women archivists and historians across the country to begin gathering documentation on the hidden experience of women at colleges and universities and writing books to document them. For example, Carol Sonenklar, a historian at Penn State University, wrote *We Are a Strong, Articulate Voice: A History of Women at Penn State* (Penn State University Press, 2006). This book was written to commemorate the twenty-fifth anniversary of the creation of women's studies at Penn State and was funded by a grant from the school's women's commission.

I was inspired by works like that of Sonenklar, and began to consider working on such a project. I recognized that our collection had many primary sources upon which to build such a history but also that there was much missing. I turned to a colleague who had been the first director of the IUP Women's Studies Department and who was also enthusiastic about a similar history being written about IUP. At her suggestion, I was asked to join IUP's President's Commission on the Status of Women, where the project received enthusiastic endorsement. With her support and the support of the commission, I was able to apply for funding to pay a graduate assistant to help me do oral history interviews and for a sabbatical to begin writing the history.

Getting Started

For many years historians deemed women's lives and experience as historically insignificant, so records documenting their lives were not preserved. With female students and administrators in the majority at our institution, this was a unique opportunity to find and preserve stories useful not only to those interested in their history, but also those interested in the history of women at similar institutions.

Recognizing how important the oral histories were as a starting point for research, I decided to begin collecting oral histories of women students, faculty, and administrators. Though I had a PhD in history, I had no training in doing oral history, so before I began interviews in earnest, I learned what I could about best practices of oral history collection. First, I consulted with a sociology professor who had done considerable oral history collection and who had taught classes where students collected oral histories. He suggested I watch a film called *An Oral Historian's Work with Dr. Edward Ives* (Northeast Archives of Folklore and Oral History, 1987), which provided me with a good introduction. The university's public history professor also provided me with a useful list of readings. An up-to-date list of readings on oral history can be found at the Center for Oral History Research at the UCLA Library's web page (oralhistory.library.ucla.edu/bibliography.html#basic) and the Oral History Association's Resources website (www.oralhistory.org/resources). Such sites are gold mines of information on how to get started, common barriers to be overcome, consent forms, and tips on preserving, indexing, and transcribing. I was also able to attend a workshop on doing oral history. Such workshops are commonly offered by historical societies and are invaluable to getting started.

Two important things to consider when doing such interviews are issues of privacy and the rights of the interviewee to protect their utterances, which are their intellectual property. At a college or university it is important to determine if you will be required to get Institutional Review Board (IRB) approval for the interviews. Some institutions will require these but others will not. If you are associated with a college or university, you should check with the appropriate authorities before you begin.

Interview Tips

Whatever equipment you have chosen, make sure you know how to use it and have everything you will need for an interview longer than what you have planned, including extra tapes, batteries, a microphone, and so on. Nothing will undermine the interview more than you appearing not to know how to operate your equipment, and nothing is worse than doing a great interview and losing it because you did not know how to use your equipment. For example, once I did an interview with an elderly professor with Parkinson's disease. The professor struggled through and provided a brilliant interview, and then I realized that my equipment had malfunctioned and I didn't have it recorded. Most people who have done interviews have similar stories.

This is equally true of consent forms. If you don't have signed consent forms from those you interview, you may limit the ability of researchers to use the information contained in the interviews in their writings.

Learn all you can about the topic you will be asking about *before* you begin interviewing subjects. It will provide context for you and make the interview more meaningful. It may help you to craft questions. You may even have questions that you can ask the interviewee about background sources that you find confusing.

Begin the interview asking the subject for his or her name, date, and place of birth. This will help to identify the subject and prevent confusion with someone else with a similar name.

Have questions ready beforehand (if you are required to get IRB approval, this will probably be required). It you send the questions to your subject ahead of time, it may even make the interview more productive.

Don't interrupt your subject when he or she is telling a story and resist the temptation to tell your own stories. The interview is about their experiences, not yours!

Take notes and write down any questions that occur to you so you can ask them at the end of the interview.

Ask if the subject has any photographs or other documentation that illustrate his or her story. Offer to scan and return them or even better take a digital camera and photograph the subject and the documentation. Ultimately, the subject may give you the originals but don't pass up the chance to get copies while you have it.

Show the subject the consent form ahead of time but don't ask him or her to sign until after the interview is finished.

Offer to give the subject a copy of the interview when you are done and to show him or her any articles or other publications that may result from the interviews before they are published. This will avoid your including things in a publication that were not correct interpretations of what the subject told you, shows respect for your subject, and might even lead to the subject remembering more useful information when reading the article.

Explain to the subject where and if the recordings will be available to researchers, and give him or her the option of sealing them for a certain amount of time if they so desire.

Equipment

We are living at a wonderful time to do oral history. New digital equipment is replacing analog devices with increasing frequency. When I began doing interviews, I used a tape recorder. Tapes were for many years the recommended format for doing and preserving oral history interviews, and are still considered by many to be the best means of preserving recordings. The ease of use of digital recording devices, the excellent fidelity of recordings, and the increasing scarcity of tape recorders to play analog interviews led me to switch to digital recording equipment very soon after I began my project. (For a comparison of the positive and negative aspects of analog and digital recording equipment, readers can consult the Nebraska State Historical So-

ciety's *Capturing the Living Past* website available at: www.nebraskahistory
.org/lib-arch/research/audiovis/oral_history/equipment.htm, which provides
a concise and understandable overview of equipment choices.) The important
thing to remember is to use the best equipment available, use standard equipment, make duplicate copies, and preserve them in the best way possible at
the present time.

In addition to equipment to do the interviews, transcribing equipment can
also benefit the researcher. While a good index of interviews immensely increases
their value for researchers, a transcription of the interview is even better. Unfortunately, transcriptions are terribly time consuming, requiring much more time
than the interviews themselves.

I was able to write a grant to purchase Start-Stop UNIVERSAL Transcription System, a PC-based, foot-pedal-controlled transcriber that allows you to
control the speed and playback of digital recordings. While still time consuming, such transcription equipment allowed me to pause, play, go back, and fast
forward without taking my hands from the keys and greatly facilitated the transcription of the interviews.

Finding the Money

As already mentioned, I was able to work with female faculty, administrators,
and organizations from women's studies to the President's Commission on the
Status of Women to get support for the project. I was able to write grants that
financed transcribing equipment, digital recording equipment, disks on which
to do backup recordings, and a graduate student to film, transcribe, and index
the interviews. The grants were made much stronger by letters of support from
these women and organizations.

Never written a grant? Consider why you want to do the research. Be able
to articulate an interesting question that you want to answer that you find fascinating. If you do not find the subject interesting, it is unlikely that others will
want to fund it.

Look to others for support in your grant writing. Colleges and universities often have a grants office to support such efforts and will help you locate
a funding source, compose and correctly complete the application, and track
expenditures and do required reports.

Looking for funding sources? Consider: Your own college or university very
likely has money available to support faculty research projects or some office may
be interested in doing oral histories to document its history. This is becoming
increasingly popular. Alumni groups and the Alumni Office might also have
money to support your effort.

Federal, state, and local history government agencies may offer local history project grants money. Private individuals or associations may offer funding, particularly if you will be collecting information relating to the organization's history.

Do a Google search and look for similar projects and see where they were able to find funding and do not hesitate to call the project director and ask for advice. Most people are happy to provide assistance, and some funding agencies actually require those who receive awards to help others.

Baylor's "Funding for Digital Oral History Projects" page includes the names of funders that provide money for oral histories, a description of each, and their URLs. It is available at: www.baylor.edu/content/services/document.php/79844.pdf.

Finding the People to Interview

The same people who wrote letters of recommendation for the grants I wrote to do the project were also able to provide the names of wonderful willing subjects to interview and were able to introduce me to them. The University's Alumni Office also encouraged the project and provided invaluable introductions to alumni who were interested in being interviewed for the project. Alumni events are natural venues for meeting with people who love to talk about university history.

Outcomes

The outcomes of the project have been multifold. Doing oral history with women is extremely gratifying. They loved being interviewed, and they had such interesting stories to tell. In addition to the historical information I was able to gather, I met wonderful, inspiring women. There are three material outcomes of the project that I will discuss here: The Indiana Women's Voices Oral History Collection, *A Women's History of IUP* e-book, and an exhibit that will commemorate the twenty-fifth anniversary of the start of women's studies at IUP.

INDIANA WOMEN'S VOICES

Indiana Women's Voices Oral History Project was carried out in the summer of 2008 and was made possible by an IUP senate faculty research grant. It began as a project to document the history of the Women's Studies Program and the President's Commission on the Status of Women and involved conducting oral history interviews with retired and current IUP faculty and administrators that were involved in their development. I was joined by a graduate student, and together we conducted eight interviews with digital recording equipment. The interviews were transferred to appropriate archival storage media, transcribed, and indexed for inclusion in university archives. This formed the nucleus of the collection. The graduate student also found earlier local history interviews with female students and faculty that dated back to the early part of the twentieth century. These were transferred to digital format and copies were included in the collection. We also included interviews with other students and faculty from the 1940s and 1950s that I had done earlier. The result was a collection that spanned much of the twentieth century and will provide useful information on the history of women at IUP for future researchers. The inventory for the collection can be viewed at: http://www.lib.iup.edu/depts/speccol/All%20Finding%20Aids/Finding%20aids/MG%20or%20Col/MG149.doc.

A WOMEN'S HISTORY OF IUP

In the fall of 2009, I was able to take a sabbatical to do the research for a history of women at IUP. The result of the sabbatical was an article and an e-book that are available from a Libguide to commemorate the twenty-fifth anniversary of the start of the Women's Studies Department at IUP. (The Libguide is available at: libraryguides.lib.iup.edu/content.php?pid=214839.) As I did the research I was able to do more interviews with IUP alumni and retired faculty.

MUSEUM EXHIBIT

The latest project relating to women at IUP is a museum exhibit that will be designed by students in a graduate public history class as their semester-long research project. The students will do an exhibit based upon the material available from our archives, including the oral histories already available. They will also interview other students and faculty who have not been interviewed yet. The recordings will be added to the Women's Voices Collection. The exhibit will document the history of women's studies at IUP and will be available on the Internet and physically if grant funding permits.

Tips for Doing an Oral History Project

Preserve material first that you know people are interested in and that therefore fulfills a preexisting need. In this case it was information that documented the lives of presidents' wives, but it could be anything. This gives legitimacy to your project and can provide you with allies in pursuing your project.

Work with women leaders and women's groups and organizations to assist you in raising interest and obtaining funding and personnel to carry out a project.

Learn what you can about oral history practice before you begin; whether through books, articles, or websites, much information is available.

In choosing equipment for oral history interviews, use the best recording equipment available at the time, make duplicate copies, and preserve them in the best way possible. Transcription equipment can also ease the time-consuming but very useful process of transcription.

Apply for grants to get funding to pay for the equipment, materials, and personnel (including your own time) that make the project possible.

Work with people familiar with university history, particularly the Alumni Office, to find individuals to be interviewed.

Additional Resources

Baum, Willa K. *Transcribing and Editing Oral History.* Walnut Creek, Calif.: AltaMira Press, 1991.

Gluck, Sherna, and Daphne Patai, ed. *Women's Words: The Feminist Practice of Oral History.* New York: Routledge, 1991.

Ritchie, Donald A. *Doing Oral History* New York: Twayne Publishers, 1995.

Sommer, Barbara W., and Mary Kay Quinlan. *The Oral History Manual.* Walnut Creek, Calif.: AltaMira Press, 2002.

Thompson, Paul. *The Voice of the Past: Oral History.* 3d ed. Oxford: Oxford University Press, 2000.

Yow, Valerie Raleigh. *Recording Oral History: A Practical Guide for Social Scientists.* Thousand Oaks, Calif.: Sage Publications, 1994.

CHAPTER 27

Steps in Preserving Oral Histories

Suellyn Lathrop

Cultural institutions have unique collections that are invaluable to those interested in studying local history. The key is providing access to those collections for researchers while preserving them for the next generation. This chapter reviews the how-to's of conducting an oral history through transcribing and preserving oral histories, creating an oral history collection inventory, and assessing as well as digitizing existing oral histories. Following these steps allows for better access to and more use of your oral history collection by researchers.

The Interview

The first step is deciding who to interview. Everyone has memories of the past, but not everyone can tell a story in a way that is worth recording. Talking with potential interviewees a few times will give you a sense of their style and storytelling abilities. Building a relationship prior to an interview helps the subject open up and trust the interviewer.

Research the topics you will discuss prior to the interview. Use this research in writing your questions. Ask action questions that require more than a yes or no answer and lead to more conversation. Employ who, what, when, where, why, how, and tell me about questions and statements to elicit the most information.

Sample questions and follow-up:

- Who has been most influential in your life? In what ways did they influence you?
- Tell me about your first job. What did you like about it? What did you dislike about it?
- What did you do for fun as a child?
- How did you decide to become x?
- Why did you do x?

Make an appointment for the interview and set a clear time limit of a half hour or hour. The rule of thumb is the older the interviewee, the shorter the interview should be. The maximum recommended interview length is an hour and a half. You can make follow-up appointments as needed. Preparing the interviewee for the general topics that you would like to discuss with him or her will maximize a short interview period.

Choose a quiet space away from traffic, noise, and other people. Get comfortable and keep your equipment within easy reach. Setting up your equipment is a good time to reassure the interviewee that he or she will soon forget the tape recorder is in the room. Always test your equipment with a short test recording. Play it back, checking the volume setting and listening for background noise. Fill out an oral history release form with the subject.

The form should indicate the name of the interviewer and interviewee, the location, date, and a copyright and use statement.

Prior to the first question, create an introduction on the recording medium by stating your name, the date, the location, the subject's name, and the reason for the interview. Asking biographical questions up front will lay the foundation for the rest of the interview. Don't fear the silences. Allowing your interviewee time to think through answers will result in a better interview. Watch and allow him or her to complete each answer before asking a follow-up or the next question. Being flexible when the conversation goes in a different direction may also result in a more interesting interview than anticipated. Answers to early questions may actually come later as you progress through your conversation, and some questions planned for later may be answered before asked. Come prepared with more questions than you think you need to allow for these scenarios. Bring a pad of paper and pen, jotting down new questions sparked by the answers you are getting. Don't interrupt the storyteller unless they are very far off track.

Providing old photographs and documents can jog memories. Narrate as needed when looking through photos. Statements like "Tell me about this photograph of you at school. What year was this taken?" allow a later listener to understand the context of the conversation without the images. Whenever pos-

Sample Oral History Release Form

Organization Name and Contact Information

Project Name: _____

Date: _____

Interviewer: _____

Tape Number: _____

Name of Person(s) Interviewed: _____

Address/Telephone: _____

Interview Location: _____

By signing the form below, you give permission for any tapes and/or photographs made during this project to be used by researchers and the public for educational purposes including publications, exhibitions, World Wide Web, and presentations. By giving your permission, you do not give up any copyright or performance rights that you may hold.

I agree to the uses of these materials described above, except for any restrictions, noted below.

Name (please print):_____

Signature: _____

Date: _____

Interviewer's Signature: _____

Date: _____

sible, make copies of the photographs and documents used during the interview. These will enhance the researchers' understanding. Numbering the images or documents in the order that they appear on the tape will assist future researchers.

After the interview, label the recordings clearly using whatever system your local historical society employs for oral histories and the word *MASTER*. Write on the label prior to affixing it to an audio or video tape. Use pencil or permanent marker.

Make a duplicate of the recording as quickly as possible and label it in the same way, this time use the word *COPY* 1. A high-speed duplicator may be a good investment. Break off the record tabs on all copies to prevent accidentally recording over them when playing. All collections should be stored in a secure location. Master tapes should be stored separate from the copies and possibly off-site. Both sets should be in a stable, dry, cool environment averaging 65 to 70 degrees and 30 percent humidity whenever possible. A slightly higher humidity may be tolerated in a cool climate. Under the best conditions an audiotape will last approximately thirty years. Making copies periodically throughout the life span of a tape will transfer the information forward.

Use Copy 1 to create additional copies, indicating the generation of each tape from the master. These copies will be used to transcribe the interview. As a courtesy, send one copy of the interview to the subject along with the abstract, index, or transcription, whichever is created.

While Blockbuster may believe that it is a kindness to rewind, the audio or videotape does not. Repeated high-speed rewinding shortens the life span of tape. The tape is wound too tightly and unevenly on the spool and the sudden stop puts additional stress on the tape that will eventually stretch and may even break it. The best practice is to allow the tape to play to the end and rewind just prior to listening, stopping a couple times to slow down the rewinding. Always keep tapes in cases when not in use to keep dust and dirt out. Avoid touching the tape as fingerprints can distort the recording and damage the tape.

Abstracting, Indexing, or Transcribing

The briefest description to be created is the abstract. This can be one or two paragraphs indicating the time period(s), names of significant people, events, and locations discussed. This brief description can be used in creating bibliographic records. It will enable researchers to quickly see which tapes intersect with their research interests. An abstract is best created by the interviewer while the interview is still fresh in their mind.

Example:

> Oral History Interview # 341, Mark Smith interviewed by Frank White on May 15 and June 1, 2011, at the Mark Smith residence, 111 Rainbow Road, Bowling Green, Kentucky. This interview consists of two 60-minute tapes, approximately 1 hour and 20 minutes. Personal history and reminisces of Mr. Smith from 1928 to 1970 includes early childhood in Smiths Grove, World War II home front, marriage to Sally Jones, banking career in Bowling Green, KY through retirement in 1970.

Another quick way to give researchers access to an oral history tape is creating an index. This will take about one and a half times longer than the interview. An index captures the essence of the interview by logging names, dates, places, and topics discussed and matching them to the counter number on the tape recorder. Researchers can fast-forward to sections that most interest them. The indexing can be done using a word processing program or a database. Create a heading using the tape number, interviewer and interviewee, date, and location. Using a tape recorder with a tape counter, set the counter to 0000 and begin playing, taking note of topics and when they change. Reset the counter for each side and each tape in the set.

> Oral History Interview # 341, Mark Smith interviewed by Frank White on May 15 and June 1, 2011, at the Mark Smith residence, 111 Rainbow Road, Bowling Green, Kentucky. This interview consists of two 60-minute tapes, approximately 1 hour and 20 minutes.
> Tape 1, Side 1
> 0000–0010 Introduction
> 0011–0030 biographical background, born Nov. 3, 1928, Smiths Grove, Kentucky, father Joe Smith, mother Josephine Taylor Smith, siblings Jack Smith, Sue Smith, and Mary Smith
> 0031–0050 experiences in school at Smiths Grove, favorite teacher John Brown
> 0051–0078 memories of World War II home front in Smiths Grove, Kentucky
> Tape 1, Side 2
> 0000–0100 marriage to Sally Jones, August 5, 1950, moving to Bowling Green, Kentucky
> 0101–0223 working as banker in Bowling Green, Kentucky

Transcribing an oral history is more labor intensive than either an index or abstract. The rule of thumb is six hours of transcribing time for every one hour of tape. The tape is listened to over and over, stopping and starting while the transcriber types verbatim what is being said. A transcription machine with a foot pedal is a great tool. The machine has a variable speed and the foot pedal can be used to slow down or speed up the tape as needed. After the first draft is transcribed, it is a good idea to have another person knowledgeable about the topics discussed listen to the tape while reading and marking the transcript. The end result is a research surrogate for the actual tape. Tapes are rarely pulled for researchers when a transcript exists. Due to the cost of both time and money in transcribing, implementing an appraisal system can help identify the tapes to transcribe first, especially in the case of a backlog.

A copy of the transcript should be sent to the interviewee. They can indicate proper spellings of names and places, as well as correct errors in the transcription. In some cases the interviewee will request that sections be deleted. An oral history tape should not be altered. An edited transcript can be supplied to researchers to protect confidential information for a reasonable period of time. The best course may be to have another interview session and allow the interviewee to make additional comments.

Digital Recording Options

Oral history recordings can be made using magnetic audio or video tape and relatively inexpensive recorders. An alternative is to create a digital recording. According to the Oral History Association there are currently four types of digital recording devices on the market. Each has its pros and cons.

Solid state recorders, also known as flash memory recorders, are reusable and portable and create a high-quality recording. They are relatively cheap and are becoming cheaper to obtain. Files created are uploaded to computer for storage, playback, and manipulation.

Hard disc drive recorders can record for longer periods and create high-quality recording; however, they can also record more background noise. Again files created are uploaded to computer for storage, playback, and manipulation.

Compact disc records are relatively inexpensive, but CDs are beginning to go out of vogue. CDs can also be a fickle recording medium as the disc may not take anything.

Direct-to-computer can create longer high-quality recordings. This requires an audio interface with good mic preamps. An external mic is recommended to avoid recording the internal noise such as the fan from the computer.

Digital recordings can be created in several formats. For archival purposes it is best to create uncompressed master recordings. Compression can degrade the audio recording, which will be compounded on each subsequent copy. Compressed copies of a master file have their uses in making oral history recordings available online.

The Oral History Association recommends the use of headphones when setting up a digitally recorded interview. This allows the interviewer to adjust the recording levels and mic placement more accurately. They also recommend using AC power whenever possible, but also keeping fresh batteries in the recorder as a backup. Any interruption of power can destroy the recording in process. Record uncompressed .wav files at a minimum quality setting of 16-bit/44.1 KHz. Last, turn off all cell phones while interviewing. Cell phones set on vibrate will communicate with local towers occasionally. That signal will be picked up in a digital recording.

Digital files of all kinds can be stored on compact discs, DVDs, or external hard drives. As storage space becomes cheaper, it is worthwhile to look into off-site storage or contract with a commercial data storage company. A data storage company can maintain the files on a server, provide encrypted secure storage, and create regular data backups, enabling file recovery in the event of disaster.

Digitization of Existing Oral History Tapes

Creating an inventory of the existing oral history tapes will help a great deal in the prioritization of existing tapes for digitization and/or full transcription as well as in making the collection available to researchers. A simple list capturing the following information is all that is needed to create the inventory.

Collection name: name of the collection the tape is part of

Tape number/Identification code: identifying information of a particular tape

Label information: copy the label information or note absence of label

Location: physical location where the tape is stored; this can be a room and box number

Interviewer: name of the person conducting the interview

Interviewee: name of person being interviewed

Date: date this tape was made, will vary from copy to copy

Master/Copy: is this copy the master or a copy?

Contents: check abstracts, indexes, or transcriptions for the most important or fully discussed topics

Abstract/Index/Transcription: which of these exist for this tape?

Format: reel-to-reel tape, cassette tape, microcassette, videotape, VHS, Beta, other

Length of tape: 30-, 60-, 90-, 120-minute tape, other length; use diameter and reel size for reel-to-reel tapes

Length of interview: length of actual recorded material

Condition: excellent, good, fair, poor, broken tape, broken cassette; note dirt or dust, mold, pests, etc.

Oral history release form: yes, we have this; no, we don't have this

The information collected in the inventory can be used to rank the tapes on content, interviewee, format, age, and condition. Assigning a number to each category and totaling those for each tape creates a fairly straightforward prioritization list. The tapes with the highest numbers need more immediate attention than those ranked at the bottom.

Content: rank 1 = low value, 2 = intermediate value, 3 = high value

- How does the content fit into your organization's overall collection policy?
- How accurate is the account? How important is that?
- How well and completely does an oral history tell the story of a particular aspect of local history?

- How unique or common is the interviewee's experiences in relation to others in the community? Which is more important to you?
- Is this information available in other sources such as books, diaries, manuscripts, or photographs?
- Are these topics currently being researched at your facility?
- If topics are not currently being researched, ask why. Is it because of lack of accessibility to the collection? Would accessibility of this content increase interest in the topic?

Interviewee: rank 1 = unimportant, 2 = average 3 = very important

- How does this person fit into your organization's overall collection policy?
- Is the interviewee a person with deep roots in the community?
- Is the interviewee a known expert on the topic(s) discussed on the tape?
- What was the person's age at the time of the interview? Did that put them in contact with a generation beyond anyone else in the community at that time?
- Is the interviewee a relative newcomer in the community? Does this add to the understanding of the community?
- Does the interviewee represent a minority group in the community?

Format: rank 1 = cassette tape, rank 2 = reel-to-reel tape, rank 3 = older/obsolete format
Age of the tape: rank 1 = 1–10 years old, 2 = 11–20 years old, 3 = 21 years or older
Condition of the tape: rank 1 = excellent, 2 = good, 3 = fair, 4 = poor

Digitization can be done in-house or contracted out. In order to do it yourself, you will need to acquire some equipment and software. You may be able to rent or borrow a dual cassette deck and USB audio interface from a state or regional oral history association, state archives, or local organization for a short-term project. You will still need to have a computer and purchase recording, editing, and mastering software and compact discs. The process is easy to learn; however, a person does need to be present to monitor each tape while being digitized.

Monetary assistance for digitization projects is available through state and federal agencies such as state archives, the Institute of Museum and Library Services, and the National Endowment for the Humanities. The data collected in the inventory and prioritization process can be used as the basis of a grant proposal. Technical assistance for digitization is available through the Oral History Association, state and regional oral history associations, and your state archives.

Oral histories are a unique and valuable resource giving insight into local history, culture, and customs. They are recorded on a nonpermanent medium that requires special care and handling in order to prolong its life span and can be a bit intimidating to work with. With the correct preparation, description, transcription, and preservation, oral histories can be made accessible for local historians well into the future.

Additional Resources

Allen, Barbara, and William Lynwood Montell. *From Memory to History: Using Oral Sources in Local Historical Research*. Nashville: American Association for State and Local History, ca. 1981.

American Association for State and Local History. aaslh.org.

Baum, Willa K. *Transcribing and Editing Oral History*. Nashville: American Association for State and Local History, 1981.

Caunce, Stephen. *Oral History and the Local Historian*. New York: Longman, 1994.

"Columbia University Libraries Preservation and Digital Conversion Division, Audio/Video Survey." library.columbia.edu/services/preservation/audiosurvey.html.

"Digitization." www.baylor.edu/content/services/document.php/79806.pdf.

Ives, Edward. *The Tape-Recorded Interview: A Manual for Field Workers in Folklore and Oral History*. Knoxville: University of Tennessee Press, ca. 1980.

Mackay, Nancy. *Curating Oral Histories: From Interview to Archive*. Walnut Creek, Calif.: Left Coast Press, 2006.

Moyer, Judith. "Step-by-Step Oral History." Last modified 1999. dohistory.org/on_your_own/toolkit/oralHistory.html.

"Oral History Association," http://www.oralhistory.org/, last modified 2011.

Oral History Association. *OHA Newsletter*. Last modified 2011. www.oralhistory.org/publications/oha-newsletter.

Oral History Association. *Oral History Evaluation Guidelines*, Pamphlet Number 3. Adopted 1989, revised September 2000. www.oralhistory.org/wiki/index.php/Evaluation_Guide.

Ritchie, Donald, ed. *Oxford Handbook of Oral History*. New York: Oxford University Press, 2011.

Society of American Archivists, Oral History Section. www2.archivists.org/groups/oral-history-section.

Thompson, Paul Richard. *The Voice of the Past: Oral History*. New York: Oxford University Press, 1978.

PART IX

APPROACHES TO PRESERVATION

CHAPTER 28

Affiliation Agreements

Tomaro I. Taylor

The year is 2010, and the economic climate—though rebounding—is dismal. Faced with the continuing shortage of both financial and human resources, organizations are testing and implementing practices, policies, and procedures to ensure their consumers receive continuity of service. In smaller organizations, such as libraries, archives, historical societies, and museums, the "tightening of the belt" can have a significant (and sometimes detrimental) effect on service provision. Institutions engaged in the dispensation of cultural heritage knowledge may not be seeing as rapid a return as other businesses experiencing the ever-so-slight monetary benefits of cutting corners. With consumers finding myriad ways to secure the items they need, smaller organizations must be creative in how they provide access to the resources that traditionally they have made readily available. Many institutions may elect to stretch their budgets without sacrificing the things for which their customers rely on them most—accessible products, available services, and timely turnaround.

But what happens when the things they need most are the most likely to disappear? When a budget that can no longer support buying resources can barely support maintaining them? Libraries, archives, museums, and their sister organizations may turn to other, similar institutions for cooperative assistance. Assistance often can be found in the form of an affiliation agreement. In a time of need, affiliation agreements can help institutions, especially those designed to help preserve cultural heritage materials, ensure the longevity of their collections while guaranteeing their availability and usability for years to come. They can build new or extend existing partnerships and can turn significant disadvantages into demonstrable advantages.

What Is an Affiliation Agreement?

The term "affiliation agreement" also may be referred to as "institutional affiliation," "contract agreement," "reciprocal relationship," or "program agreement," depending on the institutions involved and the type of agreement established.

An affiliation agreement is a mutually beneficial partnership in which two or more organizations accept the responsibility of providing the support needed by each partner to accomplish specific goals. The goals outlined may be large or small, integral to the basic operations of an organization or designed as a special project with specific outcomes in mind. In all instances, the agreement is structured to alleviate institutional constraints, be they monetary or human in nature. At the basis, an affiliation agreement should increase an organization's productivity by not only providing fiscal and physical (i.e., hands-on) support but also by encouraging each of the involved parties to focus more readily on the successful accomplishment of their respective goals.

In a smaller environment, such as a historical society or local museum, an affiliation agreement can make a difference in whether larger-scale projects or projects requiring select levels of expertise are even considered. As smaller institutions typically may not employ experts in all areas of operation at all times—sometimes deferring, instead, to the Jack (or Jill)-of-all-trades model—professionals in those settings may not have the skills needed to engage in and work through to completion certain projects. This is especially important when considering such activities as preservation and preservation management, whereby materials and those attending to their care are extremely vulnerable to even the simplest of mistakes. Consequently, it is imperative that institutions—and particularly those working with special or rare objects—secure the assistance of those whose abilities are in line with the objectives needing to be met. More than a piece of paper, an affiliation agreement becomes an interinstitutional support network in which the interests of participating organizations are realized, culminating in targeted and specific goals. Long- or short-term, continuous or time-limited, an affiliation agreement can provide its partners with clearly defined objectives, real accomplishments, a shared sense of ownership and responsibility, and dedicated results for all, combined. An affiliation agreement is an effective and reasonable way to meet institutional objectives without sacrificing the resources that may or may not exist.

Components of an Affiliation Agreement

An affiliation agreement should consist of at least three main components:

- an overview of each partner organization and their role(s);
- a brief description of the potential benefits provided or attained by each institution; and
- a chronology of termination, review, and amendment deadlines.

More detailed agreements may include mission and goal statements, detailed project descriptions and timelines, and proposed outcomes for each institution. Institutions may wish to include statements regarding organizational infrastructure, staff support or engagement, fiscal responsibilities, and potential liabilities. However the agreement is drafted, representatives from each partner organization should review, sign, and date the agreement once it is finalized.

Finding, Developing, and Sustaining Partnerships

According to an article by Randall Longenecker, one of the first steps in the affiliation process is "getting acquainted, forming alliances, [and] building credibility and value."[1] In the real world, this constitutes building a social and professional network that can be tapped for ideas and actions. However, institutions considering partnership agreements should have their own goals in focus before soliciting cooperative ventures. Clear and open discussions in-house should occur prior to the identification of potential partners and should include a frank discussion about the goals to be accomplished. These discussions should include staff at all levels of the organization's hierarchical structure as well as any volunteer or paid stakeholders, such as advisory groups.

Many smaller organizations benefit from close proximity to larger institutions and the interest of community leaders. A museum society, for example, may employ the volunteer services of an executive board or council with ties to local corporations, governments, or academe. Outside of the boardroom, each of these individuals should actively promote and solicit for the betterment of the organization. However, it is not the sole responsibility of boards or of designated committees to develop and sustain connections between the organization they represent and potential partners. Staff and administrators must be just as vigilant at identifying affiliates that will support their endeavors as readily as their organization can help them.

> When choosing a partner organization, institutions must ensure their goals and objectives are complementary with their potential affiliate's. They also should ensure that staff on both sides of the agreement have the knowledge and time needed to support the contract.

Successful partnerships are built on solid projections, common and complementary goals, and plans that just "make sense." Partners must be cognizant of each others' needs and be open to discussing them directly while working together toward their successful accomplishment.[2] Regarding the physical preservation of archival collections and related items, it is typical to find one institution in possession of materials needing remediation and one institution that has the materials and staff expertise needed to provide preservation services. Although this "quick and dirty" fit may seem an easy solution, both potential partners should ask a number of questions before jumping in and solidifying a relationship:

- Does this organization have our best interests in mind?
- How many projects (similar or otherwise) has this organization completed successfully in the past five years?
- Over the past five years, how many times has this organization's leadership changed? How has it affected the organization?
- Who will lead this project? Which organization has the primary responsibility of ensuring deadlines and goals are met?
- How will this project be funded? How will funds be split? How will monetary support be secured if additional funding is needed?
- Who will maintain budgetary oversight?
- What levels of expertise are available at each institution? Who will be responsible for maintaining each part of the project? How many people from each institution will be participating in this project? What will be their roles? How much time will each institution allot to this project?
- What outcomes can be anticipated? How will the end product be used by the partners?
- How will these items be maintained post-project?
- Who will ensure the continued safety of the preserved materials?
- What happens if additional remediation is required post-project?

- What if the project is not completed successfully or to the satisfaction of one or both partners?
- How will progress be assessed? Who will complete the assessment?
- What happens if/when other, related projects are identified during the course of this project? How will those be managed? Concurrently or separately?
- Under what circumstances will the project be reevaluated?

It is impossible to address every question that might arise. What is possible, though, is being prepared for the types of situations that might develop out of a proposed agreement. A little foresight will prepare partners for both minor and major impediments to success and help them see where issues might occur. As such, it is imperative that partnering institutions work together to draft and finalize an agreement that is flexible enough to work around potential problems but solid enough to minimize risks.

Institutional Objectives and the Preservation of Cultural Heritage

The United Nations Educational, Scientific and Cultural Organization (UNESCO) defines cultural heritage as "encompass[ing] several main categories of heritage," including both tangible (e.g., manuscripts, works of art, archaeological sites) and intangible (e.g., oral histories, performance pieces) traditions.[3] Cultural heritage *institutions*, therefore, are organizations that identify, document, collect, and preserve those items, often for research, exhibition, and other educational purposes. How an institution chooses to maintain and provide access to collections is just as important as the type of collections constituting its holdings. When planning preservation projects, the following may be considered:

1. identification of the collection(s) or item(s) requiring preservation;
2. assessment of the collection environment in order to determine viability of remediation;
3. tiered delineation of projects and level of preservation concern (e.g., stable or critical);
4. detailed schedule, including completion date, outlining all activities to be accomplished;
5. high and low projected budgets, including cost estimates for supplies and equipment, professional assistance, etc.; and
6. identification of in-house personnel to support the named projects.

Other considerations may include the implementation of policies or procedures designed to protect collection items from improper handling or use or re-housing of materials to slow or prevent environmental damages. If an organization cannot or will not trust every Tom, Dick, or Mary with handling or using their collections, then they should not entrust the care and physical preservation of those items to every organization with which they might work.

An affiliation agreement will help partnering institutions identify and work toward common goals. The level and type of involvement provided will depend on the needs and expectations of each affiliate. In preservation, this may be as simple as providing the tangible resources necessary for the completion of particular projects or as complex as aiding in the reduction of one partner's staffing deficiencies through the allocation of staff time. At the University of South Florida (USF) Libraries, collaborative preservation projects have included the following types of activities, with USF and its partners accepting specific responsibilities to accomplish the goals outlined:

- de-acidification and encapsulation
- document repair
- digitization
- identification and assessment of damaged or damaging materials
- the provision of a stable environment and appropriate controls (e.g., acid- and pH-neutral archival containers).

Many of these projects were accomplished with fewer than two or three people assigned; they also were completed without individuals' primary responsibilities being overshadowed.

Successful Agreements: An Example

The University of South Florida is an academic research institution serving nearly fifty thousand students across multiple campuses within the Tampa Bay area. The Tampa Library, the university's main library, serves the university community, scholarly researchers, and the general public through the provision of both print and electronic resources accessible on-site and remotely. The Special and Digital Collections Unit of the Tampa Library is home to a variety of printed, archival, ephemeral, and artifactual materials, many of which focus on Florida history ("Floridiana"). A significant portion of the Floridiana archives detail the lives and activities of individuals living, working, and visiting historic Ybor City, a small community established by immigrants during the 1880s as a cigar-manufacturing town. The collections, just like the history of Ybor, are varied and range from family papers to the records of defunct businesses to cigar art and memorabilia. Many of the items constituting these collections are used regularly for research and exhibition.

The Ybor City Museum Society, also located in Tampa, Florida, serves as the support organization for the Ybor City Museum State Park. Established nearly one hundred years after the founding of Ybor City, the museum society is recognized for providing documentation and education that serve to preserve the community's diverse history. The society and the museum work together to sponsor programs—including exhibitions—that foster a greater understanding and appreciation for both historic and modern Ybor City.

Not surprisingly, an interesting and fruitful partnership between the USF Special and Digital Collections and the Ybor City Museum Society (YCMS) began during the mid-2000s. The museum society's outreach director, who frequented Special Collections regularly to conduct research and select materials for exhibition, developed a working relationship with the library's preservationist and one of the Special Collections librarians. While working with the outreach director, the librarian learned that an affiliation agreement had been drafted by the directors of both institutions but never finalized. After a short period of time, the society's outreach director and executive director asked the librarian to serve on the museum society's board of directors. This role provided numerous opportunities to enhance the university's presence within the community, affording greater exposure of Special Collections' holdings and allowing the university library to have a stake in the society's programming and organizational direction. In turn, adding a librarian to the museum society's board increased their academic presence and reach, allowing them to connect with a more expansive audience. In many ways, this position—with or without an official collaborative venture—would end up being a win-win situation for both parties.

However, while serving on the board, the librarian decided to follow up with the museum society and Special Collections directors in order to make this increasingly developing—though still somewhat informal—collaboration more permanent. Serving as the liaison between the two institutions, she reviewed the existing document, worked with the directors to revise and update their goals and expectations, and helped to finalize the agreement that would inform a number of projects over the next few years. The resulting formalization of a more permanent affiliation now provides each institution the advantages of partnering with an organization outwardly different from theirs but decidedly similar in terms of mission and goals.

The affiliation agreement between the Ybor City Museum Society and the University of South Florida Tampa Library Special and Digital Collections highlighted the practical expertise of individuals at both organizations, with particular emphasis being placed on access to both resources and personnel capable of supporting a range of short- and long-term goals. Of utmost utility for the museum society was the availability of library staff who could provide the technology and expertise needed to properly maintain collections. "Access to the Preservation facilities at the USF Tampa Library, including assessments, consultations, encapsulation and deacidification technology for fragile manuscript materials"[4] as well as "housing and preservation of manuscript collections in the USF Tampa Library,"[5] were included as benefits of the society's affiliation with the university. Accordingly, Special and Digital Collections benefitted from "increased recognition and promotion"[6] and the "placement of interns at a local historical institution."[7] Among the mutual benefits outlined, both the museum society and Special Collections could expect "collaborative work between the staff to identify joint projects that further the mission and goals of each institution."[8]

One of the first major projects conducted under the affiliation umbrella utilized the librarian's skills as an archivist and the outreach director's skills as a historian to identify and preserve collections of importance. An intern was selected from the university's library and information science graduate program.[9] The librarian regularly met with the intern at the museum society to provide archival instruction and guidance. Together, they identified important records, interesting documents, and a number of preservation concerns. The items in need of preservation/conservation were taken to the USF Tampa Library, where the intern was trained to de-acidify, encapsulate, and provide basic remediation for loose-leaf, paper-based documents. By engaging in this project, the museum society gained greater physical and intellectual control over one of their more valuable collections, and both institutions were able to experience direct benefits from their affiliation, resulting in another win-win situation for all involved.

Conclusion

As institutions increasingly are expected to reconsider and reprioritize budgets, projects, and staff time, it is important that they identify ways to facilitate basic operations while continuing to find means of progress. By thinking "outside of the building" and working with organizational partners to support and enhance institutional goals, libraries, archives, museums, and related cultural heritage societies will be better able to withstand decreasing financial and physical resources. Affiliation agreements are just one of the ways that institutions can provide or receive the support needed to sustain operations, particularly as related to projects necessitating specialized resources and knowledge. As cultural heritage professionals know, preservation activities are not to be undertaken lightly under any circumstance. As such, preservation provides a great opportunity for institutions to share their materials *and* expertise while working toward the common goal of ensuring the continued viability of special and specialized collections. These types of activities not only create the perfect environment for institutions to develop collaborative partnerships and support each others' endeavors in the cultural heritage realm but also the ideal conditions to develop sustainable agreements that will serve in good times and bad.

Notes

1. Randall Longenecker, "Crafting an Affiliation Agreement: Academic-Community Collaboration in a Rural Track Family Practice Residency Program," *The Journal of Rural Health* 16, no. 3 (2000): 237–42.

2. Florence Turcotte, "Partnering with a Local Park or Historical Agency," in *Librarians as Community Partners: An Outreach Handbook* (Chicago: American Library Association, 2010), 179–82.

3. "Culture: Definition of Cultural Heritage (2008)." United Nations Educational, Scientific and Cultural Organizations, portal.unesco.org/culture/en/ev.php-URL_ID=34050&URL_DO-DO_PRINTPAGE&URL_SECTION=2.01. (accessed December 7, 2010).

4. "Affiliation Agreement between the Ybor City Museum Society and the University of South Florida Tampa Library Special and Digital Collections and Florida Studies Center," revised September 28, 2009, by Dr. Mark Greenberg, Chantal Hevia, Tomaro Taylor, and Elizabeth McCoy (p. 2).

5. Ibid.

6. Ibid.

7. Ibid, 3.

8. Ibid.

9. The name of this program recently changed from the School of Library and Information Science to the School of Information.

CHAPTER 29

Educating the Community: Preserving Tomorrow's Treasures Today

Jessica Phillips

When people wish to learn about their community or family history, they probably head out to the local museum, library, archive, or genealogical society. This is a logical starting point, and when they get there, they likely expect the collections to be in good condition so they may easily access the information they need. Librarians, curators, archivists, and volunteers work hard to conserve and preserve materials as they are added to their collections, ensuring that the materials can be safely used. However, not all genealogical and historical information is held in cultural institutions; unknown numbers of valuable information sources reside with individuals and in residences. By educating the community today on how to protect the treasures in their care, we have the potential to minimize the repairs needed for these items in the future. In planning community instruction, it is important to consider why we are doing it, what audience to target, and what we need to teach them.

Why Should We Educate?

There are two basic reasons we should teach our community members about best practices in preservation. While libraries, archives, genealogical societies, and museums do hold a wealth of information, there is also an abundance of photographs, writings, wedding dresses, newspaper clippings, and quilts sitting in the closets, basements, and attics of amateur historians who may not know how to best protect the items in their care. People who have an interest in his-

296

tory, genealogy, or cultural memory already have a vested interest in protecting their records and artifacts, so by raising awareness of best practices, we can equip these people to properly preserve these items.

The second reason to educate the community follows from the first. Teaching others how to care for their items simply makes our jobs as professionals easier in the long run. When attic treasures eventually make their way into either the hands of descendants or into a cultural institution, they are more likely to be in good condition and require less repair work to keep the materials usable if we make efforts today toward education.

Who Should We Target?

In an ideal world, we would teach our entire communities how to best preserve the items in their care. Realistically, however, while we can certainly put on programs and invite the general community, we may be more effective in our educational outreach efforts if we instead target specific groups. Whenever I give presentations or workshops for targeted groups, I also make these sessions available to the general public. This allows those who are not members of an organization to be included in these targeted educational outreach efforts.

But who should we target in our instructional programs? As we have primary responsibility for public collections, our first students should be ourselves: the librarians, archivists, and museum curators of the world. Before we can teach others to protect their current and potential heirlooms, we need to make sure we really know that what we are teaching is accurate to the best of our knowledge. Beyond these professionals, however, there are many groups that we can target who should have an interest in protecting their collections for the future. We need to look at organizations that collectively hold and maintain materials as well as groups in which the organization's members own materials individually.

GENEALOGICAL SOCIETIES

These groups hold a wealth of information, and by their nature, they already exhibit an interest in the long-term preservation of information. These societies could have a wide variety of materials to protect, including but not limited to paper documents, photographs, wedding dresses, family quilts, home movies, and digital pictures. Some materials, like reference resources, may be held collectively; however, the majority of items will belong to individuals.

HISTORICAL SOCIETIES

Much like genealogical societies, local historical societies will likely have holdings of paper documents, photographs, scrapbooks, and historic textiles. They may also have collections of artwork, pottery, ephemera, and local artifacts. These items belong to the organization, and its members will often be responsible for the care of the collective materials.

QUILT GUILDS

When working with quilting groups, you should expect a wide variety of textiles, some photographs, and paper documents. There may be loose patterns, newsletters, magazines or books, needles, thimbles, threads, instructional DVDs, and plastic quilters' templates, as well as wooden or PVC quilting frames.

THEATER GROUPS

These organizations will likely have a large number of costumes, a variety of props and scenery made from many different materials, photographs, video recordings, posters, playbills, and scripts—possibly with annotations. Many of the items held by community theaters may be considered ephemeral in nature, as items like scenery or costumes are likely to be painted over or altered many times throughout their usable lifetimes. This ephemeral quality must be respected, yet there are still means of preserving the information, if not the object, through initiatives to document and photograph materials deemed significant—yet not so significant as to protect from reuse.

LOCAL WRITING CLUBS

These groups should be fairly straightforward, holding mostly paper documents and electronic files. There could also be photographs of club activities, newsletters, or newspaper clippings.

PHOTOGRAPHIC SOCIETIES

The holdings of these organizations are generally held by members rather than collectively, and they can vary widely. This group will undoubtedly have collections of modern photographs and digital images, but they will likely also have older photographic forms, such as daguerreotypes, glass plate negatives, tintypes, and albumin prints. Those interested in photography could also have items such as early cameras, magic lanterns, and modern slide projectors.

This is but a brief outlining of groups that would likely have an interest in preserving their collections for the future. Certainly there are other groups as well that we could target who would have an interest in protecting their treasures. Any organization that has an interest in history and heritage or in collecting or creating something with potentially historical value could be a target for an educational campaign to teach people about preservation.

What Should We Teach?

Now that we have identified some of the types of groups it would be beneficial to target with educational programs, we need to look at the kinds of information these groups will need to know in order to protect their treasures. Initiatives such as ALA's annual National Preservation Week[1] have provided opportunities and motivation for preservation professionals to go out of their normal sphere of influence to talk to community groups about preservation. When giving these presentations, I begin by leading a discussion about common sources of damage for many items and then follow that up with ways to counteract and prevent future damage. I do not advocate that people attempt to repair any damaged item, since oftentimes these efforts, when not performed by a professional, will lead to further damage.

Before starting a conversation about preservation for people not trained in this field, I find it helpful to clarify some of the terms at the heart of preservation.

- Preservation: Measures taken to maintain a collection or an item in its current condition and to prevent any further deterioration. Given that the expected audience for these presentations will be untrained in appropriate repair techniques, this definition should not be broadened to include invasive measures. The focus is on climate control, proper storage, and handling.
- Conservation: Measures taken to restore or repair materials. This should only be undertaken by a trained professional.
- Acid-free: Materials that have a neutral or alkaline pH, 7 or higher on the pH scale.
- Lignin: Lignin is a natural substance found in wood pulp that contributes to the breakdown of paper and board fibers. Storage materials should be both acid-free and lignin-free.
- Archival Quality: This term is unregulated. Some materials marketed as archival quality may not be safe for your collections. Be wary of supplies that do not contain the terms acid-free and lignin-free.

- Buffered: This indicates that an alkaline buffer has been added to the materials to help neutralize acids released by the objects they house. Buffered materials are generally a good choice for storage; however, be aware that some items can be damaged by the alkaline buffer.
- Unbuffered: This indicates that no alkaline buffer has been added to the materials. These items can absorb acidity over time. Unbuffered boxes and papers are preferred for some textiles as well as for certain older photographs, as these can be damaged by alkaline buffers.
- Photo Activity Test[2] (PAT): Items used to house photographs should state that they have passed the PAT, which indicates that these materials have been tested by the Image Permanence Institute[3] and were found safe for long-term use with photographic materials.

Common Sources of Damage

LIGHT

Items allowed exposure to light will often suffer from light damage observed as fading or discoloration. In addition to this, there can also be structural damage not easily seen that is caused by a combination of the light and its accompanying heat. The harmful effects of ultraviolet rays in natural and artificial lighting can be minimized through the use of special filters that cover windows and light-bulbs. Light damage is irreversible.

PARTICULATES AND DUST

These are not merely unsightly; they are also abrasive and conducive to mold growth and can form a mildly acidic solution when they combine with humidity in the air. This acidity may be absorbed by your materials, leading to discoloration and embrittlement. Be wary of using feather dusters to clean, as these can scratch valuables and are generally ineffective cleaning tools. A soft cloth will be a safer option for dusting valuables.

HUMIDITY

Humidity is especially problematic for collections. High relative humidity encourages pest infestations and aids in mold growth; low relative humidity can lead to embrittlement. Fluctuating humidity is associated with accelerated aging, as the varying levels of moisture held within the objects will cause materials to expand and contract, which increases the risk of damage. This risk is elevated when multimedia materials are involved, since different materials will expand and contract at different rates.

TEMPERATURE

Elevated temperatures accelerate the aging process of the items in our care. Lower temperatures are better for the long-term health of collections. Fluctuations in temperature are problematic because temperature is directly related to relative humidity. It is difficult to maintain a stable relative humidity level when temperatures are fluctuating.

PESTS

Most of our collections of importance to local history are organic in nature. Insects love the organic materials found in books and textiles, and some types will lay their eggs in these materials. When the larvae hatch, they will eat their way through these materials until they reach adulthood. Rodents, another common pest, can damage your collections, but they are also an indication that you may have an insect problem as well. Rodent and insect droppings can stain your materials.

WATER

With almost any major disaster or minor emergency, water will nearly always be involved at some point. Water will cause porous materials to expand and can lead to warping, curling, fading, softening, ink migration, and the separation of materials into multiple layers, as with photographs. Items that are not dried thoroughly or quickly can become a host for mold.

"INHERENT VICE"

These are naturally occurring qualities that cause items to change or break down over time. Properties such as acidity found in wood pulp papers or the instability of dyes used to create color photographs are examples of inherent vices. Some of these effects can be slowed through proper climate control.

Ways to Counteract and Prevent Damage

CLIMATE CONTROL

Maintaining a steady and acceptable temperature and relative humidity is essential to the long-term preservation of any collection. Fluctuating temperature and humidity are closely associated with accelerated aging of and increased damage to materials. The American Institute for Conservation website[4] provides information about ideal temperatures and relative humidity levels for a variety of materials.

PROPER STORAGE

Storage materials should be constructed from acid- and lignin-free materials. If you are housing photographs, these materials should also have passed the Photographic Activity Test. It is important to do a little research into your items before deciding between buffered and unbuffered storage materials. Storage boxes should be close in size to the pieces being stored, and items should be stored with like materials as well as with materials of similar size. Ideal storage spaces will be cool, dry, dark, and elevated at least a few inches above the floor to mitigate the risk of water damage and to discourage pests. You should not store valuable or important items in basements, garages, or attics, as these areas tend to have greater risks for water leaks, pests, and uncontrolled temperature and humidity.

HANDLING

Cotton gloves should be used whenever handling photographs, as oils that transfer from hands can cause damage to these materials. You should wash and dry your hands well before handling other materials; however, gloves are not usually necessary. Gloved hands pose a potential danger to fragile papers and textiles since the glove has the unfortunate effect of limiting tactile sensation. This can cause inadvertent roughness by leading you to grip items more tightly than necessary. Remove any jewelry and extraneous items and be aware of loose clothing when working with materials to reduce the risk of scratching or snagging fragile items.

- Pottery: Carry with both hands on the main body of the piece, and avoid lifting by handles or spouts, as these areas are often the weakest parts of the artwork.
- Textiles: These materials will be most fragile when wet. To reduce the possibility of creating new rips or tears, you should always support weak textiles when moving them.

- Photographs: Wear white cotton gloves, and hold photographs only by the edges or supported from behind.
- Paintings: Carry small paintings with one hand on each side of the frame with the painting facing your body. Get assistance when moving larger paintings.
- Documents: Support fragile paper when turning pages or moving documents, and avoid folding documents, even if previously folded, as the crease breaks paper fibers and creates vulnerabilities. The use of paper clips, staples, and sticky notes also poses dangers to paper and should be discouraged.
- Books: Grasp books from the center to remove from shelves. Pulling on the endcaps can cause damage to the book's spine. Do not fold page corners to mark your place, as these corners often break away when the paper becomes brittle. Resist the urge to store books spine up, as gravity will work against the book structure to pull the text block from its covers.

LOCKSS THEORY

LOCKSS,[5] or Lots of Copies Keep Stuff Safe, is typically associated with electronic journals; however, its principles hold true for physical items as well. By making duplicates of important materials through photocopying, digitizing, or photographing the items, we can store the originals and use the surrogates as access copies. This protects from unnecessary handling of the original while still providing access to the information. Duplication does not, however, constitute preservation. It is still important to store the originals properly and to check them regularly to ensure that pests are not present.

Conclusion

There are many opportunities throughout our communities to educate people about the importance of preservation. By alerting today's holders of tomorrow's treasures about common threats to their collections, we can raise awareness about common risks and train people concerning best practices in preservation. Through these efforts, we can help to mitigate damage caused by improper storage or from uninformed, though well-intentioned, attempts at repair. These educational efforts will be invaluable as they prolong the useful life of many important historical documents and artifacts. This chapter has looked at the "why, who, and what" of preservation education. It is up to you to determine the when and where.

Suggested Resources

Albright, Gary, and Monique Fischer. "Types of Photographs." Northeast Document Conservation Center, Preservation Leaflets. www.nedcc.org/resources/leaflets/5Photo graphs/02TypesOfPhotos.php (accessed February 23, 2011).

This article makes clear distinctions between different photographic forms, providing a quick and simple means to identify photographs.

American Institute for Conservation of Historic and Artistic Works. "Caring for Your Treasures: Guides for Taking Care of Your Personal Heritage." www.conservation-us .org/index.cfm?fuseaction=Page.viewPage&pageId=497&parentID=472 (accessed February 25, 2011).

The AIC provides a number of guides written for the general public that touch on ideal temperatures, humidity, storage, proper handling, and initial disaster recovery efforts for a wide variety of materials. These documents also provide guidelines about when to consult a conservator and how to choose the appropriate one for your materials.

National Park Service, Museum Management Program. Conserve O Grams. www.nps .gov/museum/publications/conserveogram/cons_toc.html (accessed February 22, 2011).

This site has concise, informative leaflets on collections care. The leaflets are published for museum curators in the National Park Service, but many topics covered are useful for individuals as well. You will find information on protecting furniture, baskets, leather, metal, stone, paintings, photographs, textiles, and electronic records.

Northeast Document Conservation Center. Preservation Leaflets. www.nedcc.org/ resources/leaflets.list.php (accessed February 22, 2011).

The Northeast Document Conservation Center provides excellent leaflets on several preservation-related topics. These leaflets cover optimal environmental conditions, storage, handling, and photographs in addition to leaflets geared more toward the management of a preservation program.

Ritzenthaler, Mary Lynn. *Preserving Archives and Manuscripts*. 2d ed. Chicago: Society of American Archivists, 2010.

While this volume has those working in archives as its intended audience, the chapters "Archival Materials as Physical Objects" and "Causes of Deterioration and Damage" will be especially useful to individuals and organizations wishing to better understand and protect their collections. These chapters provide in-depth yet clear examinations of the history and chemical makeup of paper, inks, photographs, textiles, adhesives, and animal skins as well as common sources of damage for these materials.

Notes

1. www.ala.org/preservationweek.
2. www.imagepermanenceinstitute.org/testing/pat.
3. www.imagepermanenceinstitute.org.
4. www.conservation-us.org.
5. lockss.stanford.edu.

CHAPTER 30

Historical Sheet Music Collections: Practical Wisdom, Racial Sensitivity

Karl Madden

This chapter documents a project to archive music materials from the estate of a music teacher active in the mid-twentieth century in the rural Midwestern United States. It provides a categorization schema—with examples—for the archiving of local collections of American popular sheet music and teaching materials. It presents perspectives about items that require racial sensitivity, a small number of which were found in the collection.

The materials—eight hundred items of popular sheet music, folios, and teaching materials—date from the early to mid-twentieth century, with some examples from the nineteenth century. The materials had been used in schools, by local music groups, and for private teaching.

The chapter will guide local archivists unfamiliar with music classification. For local collections, archivists should tailor personalized schemas based on materials, collections, missions, and patronage. The schema provided in this chapter is for collections of rural music teachers. It also provides perspectives on the management of music materials with racist content. It suggests ways to preface collections with impartial acknowledgment of offensiveness, yet with balance according to the purpose of the archive.

American popular music history includes the pre–American Civil War blackface minstrel genre, the postwar "new minstrelsy" (involving African American performers), the subsequent vaudeville genre, and the Broadway and Hollywood musicals of both world wars. This material is of multidimensional historic importance. It evidences a hundred-year period that includes the earliest mass dissemination of popular culture, provides primary source material for the study of momentous events in American political history, and documents the turbulent birth of the blues and jazz.

Minstrel songs—including the so-called coon songs—were published and disseminated in sheet music form by the millions and remain a troubling record of the cultural climate. Local archive patrons encounter song titles such as "All Coons Look Alike to Me," with cover images of stereotypical, racist caricatures and lyrics such as "All coons look alike to me / I've got another beau, you see / and he's just as good to me / as you, nig! Ever tried to be."[1]

Continuing scholarship is important for understanding the meaning of the songs—and how they were performed. Patricia Schroeder, in her article "Passing for Black: Coon Songs and the Performance of Race," has found new contexts for the songs that deepen our understanding of how American culture has evolved.[2]

Blackface minstrelsy may be considered the first truly American theatrical form.[3] From the 1830s through the late 1800s, it was the most popular form of entertainment in the United States. Eventually it gave way in popularity to vaudeville, but remained alive to the mid-twentieth century in high school and local theatrical productions. It provided, for much of the country, the only lens—fundamentally racist—through which African American culture was viewed.

Carefully worded prefaces with impartial, neutral descriptions provide appropriate educational framework for such material. Archivists should write prefaces according to ethical standards of the profession and according to current research. Patrons will therefore be exposed to various historical and sociological perspectives, and not be presented with simplistic views of racism. The rich significance of this form of popular culture may therefore be fairly appreciated, with public wisdom following.

Abbott and Seroff call attention to the fact that the most popular songs from the ragtime era were not the piano rags of Scott Joplin, but coon songs.[4] Precursors to the blues and jazz, coon songs are crucial to the history of black popular entertainment. The racism inherent to the genre—certainly offensive in its day—was nevertheless of a different quality than perceived by modern standards. It is not simply a matter of being racist or not; so much depends on the context in which the entertainment was performed and disseminated.

At the time, music was disseminated mostly (apart from live performances and word-of-mouth) by means of sheet music advertising and sales.[5] Pop music was as much a part of life then as in modern society.

Schema

When archiving materials of music teachers, consider how they were used. Music teachers organize their materials according to their personal needs. Personalized schemas may change according to use. Some categorize generally along grade/level, others along general performing force (piano, choral, etc). Most often there is a combination. This collection is divided by performing force—with some special categories—and may be subdivided according to level.

Typical Midwestern music teachers of the early twentieth century traveled many miles every day to a variety of schools and maintained private teaching studios in their homes. This collection included traditional school choral and piano music and popular songs. Mark McKnight's *Music Classification Systems* explains that in musicology the fundamental division in type of song is sacred/secular.[6] However, for archiving rural teaching collections, sacred/secular—or any subject/genre division (folk, children's, American Indian, etc.)—is impractical, with the one exception of Christmas music, which may need its own category. Item value as stand-alone cultural artifacts must be weighed within the context of the purpose of the archival project and the mission of the institution. A balanced practical organizational schema with conceptual perspectives for sensitive historical items is the goal.

Materials

The collection consisted of mostly out-of-print sheet music, anthologies, hymnals, music education materials, handwritten music, and miscellaneous ephemera such as program notes, student papers, and elements of music-related periodicals. The material had been heavily used and was in varying stages of decay (from excellent quality to hopelessly crumbling). Most was in satisfactory shape. Some items printed on linen paper of the nineteenth century were in excellent condition and of significant historical/aesthetic value. The collection was mostly piano notation (solo, accompaniment), with instrumental and choral music included. Most of the material dated from the early to middle twentieth century, some from the nineteenth century, and some from the 1970s.

It was decided to organize this collection according to performing force (solo piano, piano/vocal song, etc.), with a special categories for Christmas and Halloween. This allows the patron to peruse the collection as it was probably used by the teacher.

Generally, modern sheet music songs are designated PV (Piano/Vocal) or PVG (Piano/Vocal/Guitar) format. Usually, guitar chords are added features. If songs are specifically in guitar notation or tablature (fingering chart) without piano notation, they should have their own category. Popular sheet music prior to the 1970s is unlikely to involve guitar tablature. For this collection, PV and PVG do not require separate categories.

Categories

choral
Christmas/religious/seasonal
organ anthologies
piano anthologies
piano lessons
piano solo sheets
piano/vocal anthologies (PVA)
piano/vocal sheets (PVS)
special (operettas, band, etc.)
teaching materials

The following are sample records for each category (note the variable fields):

Table 30.1.

CHORAL	
Title	*Boll Weevil, The: Southern Folksong*
Format	Two-Part Treble Voices (S.A.)
Author, etc.	Arr. by Ellen Jane Loren
Date	1946
Notes	5 copies

CHRISTMAS/RELIGIOUS/SEASONAL	
Title	*Christ, the lord, is risen today*
Format	PV sheet torn from *ToDays' Magazine*
Author, etc.	Lange, C.
Date	1911
Notes	Fragile, ripped, folded

ORGAN ANTHOLOGIES	
Title	*Flexible Meditations for Organ*
Author, etc.	Various: Compiled and Edited by Denes Agay
Date	1986
Level	Intermediate
Pages	48
Notes	For general worship, weddings, or funerals

PIANO ANTHOLOGIES	
Title	*Easy Classics to Moderns*
Author, etc	Various: Compiled and Edited by Denes Agay
Date	1956
Level	Intermediate/Advanced

| Pages | 160 |
| Notes | Music for Millions Series Volume 17 |

PIANO LESSONS
Title	*John W. Schaum Piano Course*
Volume	Pre-A Book
Author	Schaum, J. W.
Date	1945
Pages	43
Notes	A preparatory book for the earliest beginner

PIANO SOLO SHEETS
Title	*Country Gardens*
Composer	Grainger, P. A.
Date	1919
Level	Advanced
Notes	From "British Folk-Music Settings" No. 22

PIANO/VOCAL ANTHOLOGIES (PVA)
Title	*Songs Everybody Sings*
Author, etc.	Jacobs-Bond, Carrie
Date	1925
Level	Advanced
Pages	96
Notes	w/ voice ranges. Includes photos, biographical sketch

PIANO/VOCAL SHEETS (PVS)
Title	*Ac-cent-tchu-ate the Positive*
Author, etc.	Mercer, J. & Arlen, H.
Date	1944
Level	Advanced
Notes	w/ guitar chords. From the movie *Here Come the Waves* with Bing Crosby and Betty Hutton

SPECIAL (OPERETTAS, BAND, ETC.)
Title	*Blackface and Music: A New Minstrel*
Format	Folio
Author, etc.	Paskman, D.
Date	1936
Pages	47
Notes	songs and a full show (ready for performance)

TEACHING MATERIALS
Title	*Music Book for the Radio Classroom*
Format	Melodies of well-known songs
Author, etc.	Strouse, C. E.
Date	1946
Notes	Kansas State Teachers College. 9 copies

Minstrel Songs and Archiving

Imagine the ubiquitous popular songs of the nineteenth century—songs familiar to all, such as "Camptown Races"—tinkling away on private parlor pianos and player pianos. As ingrained into American consciousness as these songs were, add to the scene the mind-set that Blacks were second-class citizens—this view born in part from the clowning, idiotic caricatures of comedic entertainment. Instead of being avoided, this offensiveness must be confronted, placed in context, and learned from. One walks a fine line in passing judgment; personal opinions are inevitable, but they should be constantly reconsidered, through education and experience. For example, Schroeder argues, regarding racial caricature, that these songs—and minstrelsy in general—in addition to being entertainment for Whites, were also sometimes used by Blacks—for Black audiences—as a form of ironic, satirical political activism—to challenge the racial status quo.[7] Perhaps progressive, conscientious people of various races appreciated such contexts at the time. Such is the nature of art, where provocative contexts may apply (e.g., controversial language in modern popular music such as rap and hip-hop).

Civil War

The American Civil War provided a great boost to the music business and sheet music propagation. Pathetic soldier ballads and songs dealing with home and family grew in popularity along with marching songs, rallying songs, and propagandistic patriotic music. The music of this time, played and sung by the public, provided a feeling of participation in the great struggle. Minstrel songs, for better or worse, should be understood within this context, as well.

Of interest to the context of prewar attitudes to minstrelsy is that every part of the blackface minstrel show involved racist caricature as an ongoing subject. As the political tensions of the 1850s grew, minstrelsy propagandized racial themes, such as the portrayal of unhappy escaped slaves who longed to be back on their plantations. It distorted the antislavery messages of *Uncle Tom's Cabin*, portraying docile characters such as the "Happy Uncle Tom." Minstrelsy misrepresented African Americans to northern audiences by portraying them as simple-minded people who did not belong in the North. After the Civil War, minstrelsy continued its misrepresentation, furthering the prejudice of the Jim Crow era. Ironically, after the Civil War, African Americans themselves became minstrels (among the only entertainment work available to them). Although the new minstrelsy (advertised as "bona fide" or "genuine") altered subject and portrayal (e.g., the incorporation of Negro Spirituals) and used ironic satire (satirizing White misperceptions born of minstrel caricatures), in reality, it exacerbated stereotyping.

By the end of the century, the minstrelsy faded, as Black dialect and performers integrated into vaudeville, but stereotypes and prejudice remained. By the end of vaudeville and into the world wars, coon songs and the minstrelsy were still alive and were considered lowbrow comedy. It caused problems during the Second World War. For example, the Hollywood cartoon *Coal Black and de Sebben Dwarfs*, with its racist caricaturing of African American troops, was banned, owing to the protests of the NAACP and concerns of the U.S. war effort that it would lower the morale of troops.[8]

Purpose

The archive is a site of ambiguity. It is best understood as a contested terrain for memory construction that in turn shapes contemporary understanding of society.

—Report, Nelson Mandela Foundation, 2005[9]

Collections that include offensive sheet music should be prefaced with carefully worded introductions, depending on the decisions of local archivists, in adherence to professional ethical codes of impartiality. They should provide context, but should not draw too much attention to individual items. When one comes upon a racist item (a sheet music cover page with a racist caricature, a title with a slur, racist lyrics, etc.), one's inclination is to separate it; one subconsciously places emphasis—special significance—to the item. However, the collection as a whole does not benefit from this, as such attention obscures the meaning of the collection. The subject becomes racism, where the subject should be, for example, music. Therefore, context of the archive mission and the historical context of the material need to be clearly presented. Unless the purpose of the collection is racism, organize such collections according to purpose, without drawing particular attention to racist elements of individual items. In the following example, note the neutral tone of the notes:

Vlach describes how in some surviving antebellum plantations that have been turned into museums, there is a tendency to avoid detailed descriptions of

Table 30.2.

PIANO/VOCAL SHEETS (PVS)	
Title	*All Coons Look Alike to Me (A Darkey Misunderstanding)*
Format	PV Sheet
Author, etc.	Hogan, Ernest
Date	1896
Notes	Stereotypical black caricatures on cover

the conditions suffered by slaves.[10] This kind of avoidance—trivialization—is a legacy of inadequate American historical education, where slavery and racism is abbreviated and marginalized as a brief anomalous period rapidly remedied with emancipation. Vlach suggests that such avoidance is a main reason the country remains divided.

There should be neutral accounting for racist artifacts in any institutional collection, whether or not the material forms the essential content or purpose, and regardless of personal opinions, archivists and museum curators should take ethical initiative in presenting this material to the public. However, Randall Jimerson, in his 2009 book *Archives Power*, in discussing the political power of archives, finds the notion of neutrality an illusion, stating that "archivists cannot avoid leaving their own imprint on these powerful sources of knowledge and identity."[11]

Archivists should not hide behind a façade of impartiality but rather, as stewards of the public record empowered by education, take responsibility for sound ethical decisions. Items should not be placed into context for the avoidance of judgment, but rather for the wisest possible judgment. How should offensive material be handled? Answers depend on the mission of the archive, the purpose of the collection, the nature of the items and their context in the collection, the archive, history, and ethics.

The Jim Crow Museum of Racist Memorabilia at Ferris State University, in Big Rapids, Michigan, is an archive specifically for racist material. Its objectives focus on education regarding racism.[12] When the Jim Crow Museum takes a piece of sheet music, its purpose is to show the inherent racism, but if that same piece of sheet music is included in a different kind of archive (e.g. a local archive), the purpose is different, because the objectives of the institution are different. There should be preparation for racist content, but not as the primary focus.

The Library of Congress and the Yale University Archives contain two well-worded descriptions.[13] Local archivists may tailor personalized versions for their collections. The Library of Congress has appropriated a collection from the Brown University Library consisting of 1,305 pieces of African American–related sheet music from 1850 through 1920. Note the neutral tone in the following excerpt:

> Particularly significant in this collection are the visual depictions of African Americans which provide much information about racial attitudes over the course of the nineteenth and early twentieth century.

Similarly, Yale appropriates from an essay by Sarah Haley that accompanies a collection titled *Let it Resound: Sheet Music in the James Weldon Johnson Memo-*

rial Collection. The preface to the minstrelsy section of the collection is titled "Minstrelsy: 1830s to 1900s." The following excerpt shows deft handling of the subject:

> The genre highlighted the abounding class, gender, and racial conflict that defined the era, and repressed conflict by invoking the romantic imagery of plantation tranquility. Minstrelsy gained a reputation ridden with contradiction, simultaneously scorned as a vulgar practice of the working class, and exalted as a national art.

Ethics

Locke Morrisey, head of Collections, Reference, and Research Services at Gleeson Library of the University of San Francisco, states, in an article on ethics and collection development, "Ultimately, ethics is a personal choice."[14] It is the responsibility of the archivist to make sense of these codes according to the unique circumstances of any archive and its items. The American Library Association and the Society of American Archivists have similar codes of ethics.[15]

From ALA:

> We distinguish between our personal convictions and professional duties and do not allow our personal beliefs to interfere with fair representation of the aims of our institutions or the provision of access to their information resources.

From SAA:

> Archivists should exercise professional judgment in acquiring, appraising, and processing historical materials. They should not allow personal beliefs or perspectives to affect their decisions.

Teaching Minstrel Music

Teaching minstrel music provides opportunities for thought-provoking learning about how it helped to shape social construction of race in an important period in American history. Richard Hughes provides teaching activities for songs of the minstrelsy. He suggests that teachers explain to their classes that the material is offensive by today's standards, and that the misuse of the material has the potential to deepen racial prejudice.[16]

Summary

Practical schemas for local archiving of the materials of rural music teachers are designed for experiencing the collection from a socio-historical standpoint, by imagining how the material may have been used, and organized by performance and teaching criteria, instead of by musicological criteria.

Perspective on the archiving of songs of the American nineteenth century with offensive racial stereotypes and caricatures suggests that such offensiveness should not be given too much attention as such, unless the purpose of the collection is the subject of racism. Instead, collections that contain such material should be prefaced with carefully worded introductions that educate the public about historical context within the purpose of the collection and the mission of the institution. Prefaces should strive for impartial, neutral terminology, with the understanding that absolute neutrality is probably theoretically impossible. This may guide the work of the archivist in organizing similar collections, for ethically sound enhancement of historical value to our cultural record.

Notes

1. William John Schafer and Johannes Riedel, *The Art of Ragtime: Form and Meaning of an Original Black American Art* (Baton Rouge: Louisiana State University Press, 1973), 26.

2. Patricia R. Schroeder, "Passing for Black: Coon Songs and the Performance of Race." *Journal of American Culture* 33, no. 2 (2010): 139–53.

3. Robert C. Toll, "Minstrels/Minstrelsy," in *Encyclopedia of African-American Culture and History*, ed. Colin A. Palmer, 2d ed., vol. 4 (Detroit: Macmillan Reference USA, 2006), 1456.

4. Lynn Abbott and Doug Seroff, *Ragged but Right: Black Traveling Shows, "Coon Songs," and the Dark Pathway to Blues and Jazz* (Jackson: University Press of Mississippi, 2007), 3.

5. Richard Jackson, *Popular Songs of Nineteenth-Century America: Complete Original Sheet Music for 64 Songs* (New York: Dover Publications, 1976), vi.

6. Mark McKnight, *Music Classification Systems* (Lanham, Md.: Scarecrow Press, 2002), 83.

7. Schroeder, "Passing for Black," 143–44.

8. Christopher P. Lehman, *The Colored Cartoon: Black Representation in American Animated Short Films, 1907–1954* (Amherst: University of Massachusetts Press, 2007), 78–79.

9. Nelson Mandela Foundation, "Memory for Justice: Report on a Colloquium," August 18, 2005, quoted in Elena S. Danielson, *The Ethical Archivist* (Chicago: Society of American Archivists, 2010), 1.

10. John Michael Vlach, "The Last Great Taboo Subject: Exhibiting Slavery at the Library of Congress," in *Slavery and Public History: The Tough Stuff of American Memory*, ed. James Oliver Horton and Lois E. Horton (New York: New Press. 2006), 57–58.

11. Randall C. Jimerson, *Archives Power: Memory, Accountability, and Social Justice* (Chicago: Society of American Archivists, 2009), 133–40.

12. David Pilgrim, *Objectives of the Jim Crow Museum* (Big Rapids, Mich.: Ferris State University, Jim Crow Museum of Racist Memorabilia, 2010), www.ferris.edu/jimcrow/menu.htm (accessed January 5, 2011).

13. Library of Congress, *African-American Sheet Music, 1850–1920*, from the Collections of Brown University, memory.loc.gov/ammem/collections/sheetmusic/brown (accessed December 31, 2010); Sarah Haley, *Let It Resound: James Weldon Johnson and Black Popular Music*, from Yale University Archives, beinecke.library.yale.edu/LetItResound/min_genre.html (accessed December 31, 2010).

14. Locke J. Morrisey, "Ethical Issues in Collection Development," *Journal of Library Administration* 47, no. 3/4 (2008): 163–71.

15. American Library Association, "ALA Code of Ethics," in *ALA Policy Manual* (2008), www.ala.org/ala/issuesadvocacy/proethics/codeofethics/codeethics.cfm (accessed December 31, 2010); Society of American Archivists, "SAA Code of Ethics for Archivists," in *SAA Council Handbook* (2008), www.archivists.org/governance/handbook/app_ethics.asp (accessed December 31, 2010).

16. Richard L. Hughes, "Minstrel Music: The Sounds and Images of Race in Antebellum America," *History Teacher* 40, no. 1 (2006): 29.

CHAPTER 31

Tracing History through Nontraditional Methods

Emily Griffin

When local citizens abandon their small town for fame and fortune elsewhere, you assume you can find a lot of information about them within their former community. You expect to receive stories from people who knew them, easily locate existing family members, and dig your way through photographs, letters, and scrapbooks. Unfortunately, that just isn't the case when the town has likewise abandoned noteworthy figures. Instead, leads grow cold and no new developments are made. As a librarian, you must broaden the scope of your search for local biographies to include nontraditional online resources.

The citizens of Crawfordsville, Indiana, take pride in the rich political and literary history of their community. With public attention placed on General Lew Wallace (author of *Ben-Hur*) and Senator Henry S. Lane through historical markers and museums, it is only natural that the reference department at the Crawfordsville District Public Library (CDPL) handles a majority of local history and genealogy-related questions. The reference department assists patrons in copying and/or scanning birth and death records, newspaper obituaries or announcements, and marriage records. We also find images, land records, and family charts. When we are not completing impromptu research for individuals, CDPL librarians enjoy researching lesser-known figures in order to discover new information about the community and supplement the collection of local history items. Often we are able to fully research a local figure by utilizing our own physical collection. This traditional method of in-house research typically includes the following tasks:

- searching our online databases for vital statistics (birth, marriage, death);
- accessing historical newspapers, birth records, and death records via microfilm;
- identifying local ties and life histories through family group charts, genealogy vertical files, and biography files;
- combing our image database for original photos of related people, houses, buildings, and events;
- publicizing our research and seeking assistance from the community via local newspapers.

Some research topics require additional searching, however. Biographical research on two local figures underrepresented in CDPL's physical collection caused me to look for concrete information in nontraditional online resources. Authoritative sources have always been a concern for librarians using traditional resources. What makes an authoritative online source? Online sources should be current (frequently and recently updated) and have a clear focus or purpose (check to see if there are any goals or intentions stated on the page). The source should be free of spelling and grammatical errors and have an overall uniform web design. The author or authors of the site should be easily identified and knowledgeable about the subject.

Through the online searching of websites and journals, message boards and forums, and social networking sites, I was able to establish connections with people who knew or had information about my subjects. The two subjects researched left Crawfordsville at an early age. Maurine Watkins, famed playwright of *Chicago*, attended Crawfordsville High School, but relocated to pursue a career in journalism after graduation in 1914. Stephen Crane was briefly featured in three B motion pictures before establishing himself as a high-profile restaurateur, but film enthusiasts know him best as one of Lana Turner's ex-husbands. Crane left Crawfordsville for Hollywood within a few years of graduating in 1937 from Wabash College. Watkins left no family in Crawfordsville, and Crane had no contact with the distant family members that still reside here. Although both locals were active in the city (Watkins was often cited in the newspaper for her contributions at the local school, and Crane ran the well-known, family-owned cigar store), each are basically unknown to today's population, despite their local roles and major achievements in their fields.

Nontraditional Resources

UTILIZING WEBSITES AND MESSAGE BOARDS

Among the online community, forgotten local subjects are likely to be well-known and their lives well-documented. I began by using Google and Bing search engines. By entering multiple combinations of search phrases, keywords, and Boolean logic, I was able to locate websites and forums that expanded my knowledge and spurred my projects forward. Biographical websites typically include photographs, published articles, and career histories, as well as contact information for the site's author and links to external information. Check the author information of each website to ensure credibility of your source. Make sure the author is identified on the site, has provided contact information, and has included any credentials or affiliations. You may find (as I did with a website on Maurine Watkins) that the website creator is a noted researcher on your topic and has a great deal of information to offer.

Do not be discouraged if you do not find any websites. The information you need may be hiding on forums and message boards. For example, I had no knowledge of Stephen Crane's lasting legacy until a Google search turned up several forums and message boards on his career in the restaurant business. Message boards can include news articles, candid and career-oriented photographs, and personal stories and experiences. Using the message boards can actually lead to the discovery of marriages (with names of spouses and dates), career locations and legacy, and life outside of your area. When using message boards for local history research:

- post specific questions about dates, events, and people for the group to answer;
- reveal your own knowledge to avoid getting the answers you already know;
- post images you have collected as well as scans to identify artifacts;
- look for source links that may provide further information.

ONLINE NEWSPAPER ARCHIVES

Google News has a large collection of articles available in their archive collection online. The articles span from the early 1800s to the present day, covering over forty languages. Unfortunately, Google announced in 2011 that it will no longer index and digitize additional historical newspapers. According to Google, you will still be able to access the existing archives, but no new items will be added in the future. Although the future of any free proprietary resource can be uncertain, Google News Archive's existing collection is still a useful resource for local history research. If your library does not have their archived newspapers indexed or available, this resource can be a great tool for quickly finding local articles. CDPL does not have events prior to 1973 indexed, but searches in Google News' index showed that relevant articles from 1911 were available in our microfilm collection. If local newspapers do not provide any assistance, search for local topics in nonlocal sources. You may unexpectedly find a lengthy article on your subject in the *New York Times* or the *Palm Beach Daily News*. In the Advanced News Archive Search, you can limit your search by keyword, date range, source, and price (many articles are freely available). In my work, a search for articles including the exact phrase "Maurine Watkins," published between 1920 and 1970, and limited to those free of charge, resulted in 36 articles. If you want to see pay-per-view articles, the same search results in 256 articles. Adding one of Watkins's play or screenplay titles to the search will decrease your total number, but will focus article browsing to columns, reviews, and news directly related to certain stages of the writer's life.

With a common name and famous literary connection, a search for the phrase "Stephen Crane" returns more than one thousand results, many of which do not pertain to my person of interest but rather to the more well-known writer. When dealing with a common name, it is best to do multiple searches with different keywords and limiters. You can complete advanced Boolean searches to narrow your results. Google News Archive supports the use of "+" (and), "-" (not), "OR," and exact phrase searches. You can also search with multiple keywords. For example, searching for Crane with the keywords "film," "Hollywood," or "Columbia" (Columbia Pictures) resulted in relevant articles on his movie career (as well as lots of amusing Hollywood gossip columns). Searches including "Lana Turner" returned articles published during Crane's two marriages to Turner and the subsequent divorces and press coverage of the murder hearing involving Crane and Turner's child. Using the knowledge of Crane's restaurants gained through online message boards, I searched for articles using the names and locations of his restaurants to find articles pertaining to the last thirty years of Crane's life. It may take time and multiple search strategies to produce relevant results, but searching Google News is well worth the historical articles you will retrieve.

An alternative to Google News Archive, the Library of Congress's Chronicling America is a free archive of historical newspapers made possible by the National Digital Newspaper Program (a partnership between the Library of Congress and the National Endowment for the Humanities). Unlike the unpredictability of Google's archives, the Library of Congress will permanently maintain this collection of newspapers that spans from 1860 until 1922 and is slated to expand its collection to include newspapers from 1836 to 1860 in the future. In 2011, the archive included 503 newspapers and more than three million pages. You are able to complete a basic search of the collection by entering keyword, state, or date range. The advanced search option allows you to narrow by specific newspaper titles, specific newspaper pages, and phrases. Because Maurine Watkins and Stephen Crane's careers happened after 1922, I did a keyword search for Ferris Hartman, another Crawfordsville citizen who was a respected comedian in the late nineteenth and early twentieth centuries. Searching all states and dates, a basic query for Ferris Hartman returned 1,864 newspaper pages! An advanced search of the phrase "Ferris Hartman" and the keyword "Tivoli" (an opera house in which he performed) limited solely to California newspapers resulted in 439 pages. Google News only allows you to share their newspaper pages via a hyperlink, while the Library of Congress permits viewing their newspapers as a text or PDF file, downloading the page to your hard drive, or printing an image of the page.

BLOGS

Many libraries use blogs as a way to connect with the community, increase publicity, and provide readers' advisory. Blogs can also be an effective networking tool for local history research. Results on search engines may turn up quite a few related professional and personal blog entries. Although an entry may be on your subject, that does not mean that the entire blog will be related. On the other hand, you may find that an entire blog is devoted to your subject or at least his or her industry. Search within the blog to see if there are any more relevant results before moving on to a new site.

Searching Blogs for Content

The most popular (and free!) blog publishers are WordPress and Blogger. If you want to search blogs for related content, go to WordPress and Blogger's home pages and use the "search blogs" features. Also, Google Blog Search allows you to complete basic and advanced searches for blog content. Narrow your search by blog title, post title, author's name, and date range for optimal results.

Always read the comments attached to relevant posts. You may find that commentators are family members, friends, or acquaintances who are sharing personal stories or correcting facts. Many online users log in with their e-mail addresses to leave comments or share their full name and e-mail address within their comment. Contact anyone whose post or comments seem valid and important to your research. If a post references an interview or meeting with a relative or colleague of your subject, contact the blogger and explain your project. During my investigation of Stephen Crane, I was able to conduct, via telephone, extensive interviews with two key figures in my subject's life following the assistance of an initial post and referral e-mails from a blogger.

If your library does not own a blog, consider setting up an account. Library blogs will be read by patrons in the community who frequent your website in addition to being listed in the results of major search engines. Use your blog as a platform to voice your questions about a local person, place, or business. Let the community know what you've found so far and encourage readers to share any knowledge they may have of the subject. Monitor your comments for possible leads and contact readers who express interest.

FACEBOOK AND TWITTER

Like blogs, social networking sites can connect people with similar interests. Facebook and Twitter are the most popular sites for social networking at this writing. More than likely, you or your library already have either a Facebook or Twitter account or both. Decide whether you want to connect with project participants via your personal page or your library's fan page. Some libraries may prefer to maintain pages for event announcements only, so librarians may want to use their own accounts to contact participants. Make sure you are professional but approachable in your own postings. Depending on the site you use, include a complete bio or info section that states your affiliation, establishes your credibility, and includes contact information.

On Facebook, announce your project on your wall and post links to your library's website (and local history pages, if you have them). Become a "fan" of pages related to your subject and a "friend" to people who knew your subject. By joining fan pages, you will have access to other fans who become contributors to your project. You are currently limited to 140 characters on Twitter posts, so choose your words wisely! Get straight to the point and make sure to "follow" (the equivalent to becoming a friend or fan on Facebook) relevant people or organizations. Tweeting and having your tweets read by important followers can lead to further e-mail, telephone, and in-person contact.

What if your local person was born in the late 1800s or early 1900s? Use your Census records and obituary notices to trace the family to the present day. Search for living relatives on Facebook and Twitter (name searches on Google typically result in corresponding social networking pages as well). Many relatives will be excited that the library is researching their great-great-grandfather (and impressed that you were able to locate them!) and will offer their assistance.

EBAY

eBay is a useful resource for libraries that actively collect local history artifacts. If your library has the budget for collecting relics of your town's history, eBay can be a treasure trove. A handful of the items CDPL has added to the collection thanks to eBay includes rare photographs, letters, business tokens, matchbooks, and scrapbooks . . . but it has taken time and many searches! Because of its non-intuitive search capabilities, eBay, like Google News Archive, requires multiple search strategies to gain the best result. A simple search for your subject's name may return pages of undesired and unrelated items. Although your returns may appear to be across-the-board, significant items may be missing. Surprisingly, a basic search of first and last name may not result in the photographs you will find if you add the keyword "photo" to the full name. Countless spelling errors in the listings can deter your search. Crawfordsville becomes "Crawfordville" and Indiana is sometimes "Indiaiana." Name searches often do not result in any items at all. For example, searches for Maurine Watkins almost always return zero items. In this case, keywords of related play or film titles will gain better results. eBay users are much more likely to title their item "*Chicago* playbill" rather than "1927 *Chicago* playbill Maurine Watkins." Remember that the sellers on eBay are not professional catalogers, so you have to be creative in how you search and anticipate unusual variations.

eBay searchers must definitely be patient and persistent in order to find the perfect item, but the time and effort are worth it. You might not find what you are looking for overnight. The listings on eBay are constantly changing and new items are continually added. To really make the most of eBay, searchers should check the listings regularly. Searching eBay has allowed CDPL to collect essential local items that were missing in the community from individuals and dealers across the United States and Canada.

Using eBay for Networking and Collection Development

eBay is an effective hub for local history activity. Search for your town, county, an old business, or person, and you'll be surprised at the items available. Don't have the library budget to purchase items? Contact the seller and explain your library's project. CDPL has found that many sellers are willing to donate listed items to and reserve future items for our library in exchange for a tax-deductible receipt.

Sharing Information through Online Encyclopedias and Databases

Give back to the online community by sharing the information you've discovered. You can find many user-centered encyclopedias and databases on the Internet. Create an account with online encyclopedias, such as Wikipedia, and compose an original entry on your noted citizen. If the person already has a created entry, add interesting facts that are not included and correct any factual errors. Add links to your created entry on the pages for your town and county. For example, Maurine Watkins and Stephen Crane are both listed under the Notable Natives and Residents section of the Crawfordsville page.

Online databases such as IMDb (The Internet Movie Database) and IBDB (Internet Broadway Database) allow you to add information and trivia or make corrections to their existing pages. Depending on the site, you may see your updates instantly or your additions may be visible after verification. Read the online information available on your subject and determine what needs to be included. Consider creating a research page on your library's website. Include basic facts, interesting discoveries, and scans of the items you've collected. Whether you choose to add a page to your library's site or to add information to existing online websites, make sure that your subject is well-documented and accurately represented online.

Publicizing the Project through Social Networking Sites and Blogs

You've acquired firsthand accounts from online contacts, obtained artifacts on eBay, and have put together a large collection of items on the subject. Now it's time to let the community know. CDPL often showcases research findings in a display and has found this an aesthetic way to publicize local history projects in-house. Contacting the local newspaper is still a viable option for spreading the news, but online publicity should be considered as well. Once you've completed your display and/or added your newly cataloged items to the collection, post updates on your Facebook wall or in your Twitter feed. Publicize your display with short, timely messages on Twitter: "Don't forget to check out the Maurine Watkins display at CDPL! Jan 8-Feb 28 on the 2nd floor." On Facebook, send event invitations that contain event, date, and time to friends or fans.

Publicizing Your Project Online

Seeking stories or information from local citizens? An announcement in your local paper is always helpful, but don't forget to reach out to your online community as well. Publicize your project via your library's website, blog, Twitter account, and/or Facebook account to increase your audience and receive a larger response. Keep online announcements simple and straight to the point! Remember to include information for multiple modes of contact: telephone, physical address, e-mail address, IM/chat username, and so forth.

If your library has its own blog, post announcements and photographs about your research there. CDPL has a Local History @ CDPL blog where staff members post new discoveries within our collection and recent acquisitions from donors or via eBay purchases. We have a separate blog, What's New @ CDPL?, where we announce upcoming displays and collection additions and query the public for participation. If you've already made connections with external blog owners, contact them when your project is finished. They may be interested in using your information in an upcoming post. Dealing with more famous subjects, you may find that your project garners a great deal of nonlocal attention online. In CDPL's case, a popular tiki culture blog spotlighted one of our projects and included a photo of our display in a post. Bottom line: Use all of the traditional and nontraditional methods at your disposal to spread the word about your research.

Why Nontraditional Works

You may not have local resources at hand to complete historical research, but the Internet can provide instant access to a bounty of relevant sources. If you have ever researched local citizens who ended up spending a majority of their life somewhere else, left little family, or gained recognition on a national scale, you have probably found it difficult to rely on local resources alone. Nontraditional resources, such as social networking sites, online news archives, websites, message boards, blogs, and online auction sites, can make local history research on forgotten local figures a more completely investigated process and rewarding experience for librarians. Through Internet searching, you can build connections with family, colleagues, classmates, and collectors whose contributions can add significance to your project and make your final presentation more compelling to your community. Nontraditional is not just for nonlocal information. Search online even when you do have local resources and participation. Combining traditional and newer methods will only strengthen your research and, in the end, enrich the library's local history collection.

Afterword

Preservation has long been a key responsibility for libraries. As information proliferates along with the forms in which it comes, and as the nature of information grows increasingly ephemeral, the role of librarians is more important than ever. Internally, librarians seek to preserve their existing unique holdings; externally, they work with the community to identify and preserve key collections. In both cases, they provide access through catalogs, finding aids, websites, or other access tools, as appropriate. This book on preservation, covering everything from the basics to the born-digital, is, therefore, very timely and offers readers practical advice rooted in the realities of individual libraries and the authors' experiences and expertise.

The chapters are organized to provide a logical trajectory for the subject of preservation. The book begins with everyday issues, such as basic repairs and managing in an environment of budget austerity. The reader is then taken through sections on community partnerships, approaches to preservation, and the unique aspects that apply to various formats. Following that, authors discuss the critical issues in digital transitions and maintenance and provide concrete examples through particular projects. Throughout, the authors provide innovative ways to take advantage of Web 2.0 tools and social networking for resources and for dissemination of completed and ongoing projects.

The authors are librarians with training and expertise in preservation, archiving, and conservation. Many studied history, but their backgrounds also include African American studies, anthropology, English literature, fine arts,

French, information technology, and music, all of which inform their perspectives on this complex topic. Their work in their subject areas informs their chapters, and they offer suggestions that emanate from their daily work and projects in a wide variety of libraries—public and academic, large and small. Examples of the libraries in which they currently work include the Friench Simpson Memorial Library in Hallettsville, Texas; the University of Illinois, Urbana-Champaign; the Loutit District Library in Grand Haven, Michigan; the Open Polytechnic of New Zealand (Auckland); and Covenant University, Ota, Nigeria.

Both novices and experienced preservationists will find information of value in this volume. In addition to the basic and more complex specifics of the preservation process, authors discuss the creation of policies and guidelines, the preparation of affiliation agreements for community partnerships, and various principles of preservation management that should be considered. After studying the book, readers will gain an understanding of the complete preservation picture from conception to finished product: management, budget, sources of financial and other help, contracts, working with donors and staff, training options, traditional and nontraditional processes, publicity and promotion, whatever they need to undertake a project on their own.

Whether their projects are large or small, readers will find a road map to guide them through the steps ahead. They will be aware of the issues they should anticipate, learn how to tackle them, and gain connections to a community of resources for help.

—Aline Soules, University Libraries, California State University, East Bay

Index

abstracting, oral interviews, 278
acid-free, term, 77, 299
acquisitions: environment for, 7; prompt response to, 8. *See also* collections policy
adhesives, *17*; in scrapbooks, 98
advisory boards, for historical newspaper selection, 49–51; surveying, 51–53
affiliation agreements, 287–95; components of, 289; definition of, 288–89; example of, 292–94
Africa, newspaper preservation in, 63–72
African American history, preservation of, 213–22
aggregation, definition of, 202
air conditioners, 6
albumen photographs, 121, 183; care instructions for, 186
albums, 206–7
ambrotype photographs, 121, 183; care instructions for, 186, 207
American Institute for Conservation of Historic and Artistic Works, 303–4

American Library Association, 181; code of ethics, 313; National Preservation Week, 299
American Memory Project, 40
American National Standards Institute, 204
archival quality, term, 299
archives: access to, 156; acquisition of, 148–52; appraisal of, 149–52; management, in local history collections, 146–56; natural versus artificial, 192; organization of, 152–53; of sheet music, racial issues in, 305–15; storage of, 155; term, 147–48; transfer to local history collections, 152
Archivist's Code, 124
Arizona Historical Foundation, Subject Photograph Collection, 206
Armstrong Atlantic State University, 223–33
Arnold, Lee, 216
artifacts: attachment of, 97–98; scrapbooks as, 76, 82–83; scrapbooks housing, 78–81, 98–100

artificial collections, 192; definition of, 202

binding: for newspaper preservation, 68; and scrapbook preservation, 94–95
biographies, 223–33; nontraditional methods for, 316–24
birth announcements, database of, 252
Black history, preservation of, 213–22
blogs: catablog, 234–42; and historical research, 320–21; platform for, 239–40
blueprints, 16; gifts policy and, 40; storage environment for, 37
book(s): gifts policy and, 40; handling instructions for, 303; by local authors, 119–20; storage environment for, 36
book repair, in-house, 11–21; procedures for, *19*
boxes/boxing, *18*; for newspaper preservation, 68; for scrapbooks, 100–101
Brigham Young University, 169
Brown, Karen E. K., 11–21, 337–38
Brown University, 312
browsing, catablog and, 237
budget issues: and book and paper repair, 11–20; and collection development, 110–11; and collections care, 3–10; and gifts policy, 38–39; and newspaper collections, 64; and records retention, 137–45. *See also* low-cost options
buffered, term, 300
bugs. *See* pests
Bybee, Howard C., 169–76, 338

California Preservation Program, 32
Canadian Conservation Institute, 23
card file, for obituaries, 245
cassette tapes: gifts policy and, 40; storage environment for, 36
catablog: advantages of, 235–38; creation of, 238–42; and local history, 234–42; term, 242n1

cataloging: archives, 153–55; photographs, 205; scrapbooks, 92
CDs. *See* compact discs
cellulose acetate film, 184; care instructions for, 186
cellulose nitrate film, 184, 207; care instructions for, 186
Chafe, William, 134
Civil War, and sheet music, 310–11
climate control, 302
clipping files, 119
cloud storage, 174–75
codec, term, 262–63
code linkages, for archives, 154–55
collaboration. *See* partnerships
collection, definition of, 202
collections care, 3–5; low-cost options for, 3–10
collections development: eBay and, 322; priorities for, 28–29
collections policy, 8; development of, 107–12; for photographs, 180–81, 190, 202–3. *See also* gifts policy
color photographs, 206
commercial binding, *15*
community outreach: genealogical societies and, 165; on preservation, 296–304
compact discs (CDs), 173–74, 260, 280; for newspaper preservation, 67
compression, 262–63, 280
computer servers, for oral history storage, 261
consent forms, for oral interviews, 269, 276–77
conservation, definition of, 185, 299
Conservation Center for Art & Historic Artifacts, 29
Conservation OnLine, 32
conservation services, *15*
contact information, 27
containers, 262–63
Cooksey, Elizabeth B., 223–33, 338
Coordinated Statewide Emergency Preparedness, 32

copyright issues: and archives, 152; and digitizing photographs, 208; holder of, 129–30; and local biographies, 224, 229, 233; and local history collections, 127–32, 135

corner reinforcement, *19*

correspondence: gifts policy on, 37–38; privacy issues and, 133

Council of State Archivists (COSA), 26, 32–33

Cox, Robert S., 242n1

Crane, Stephen, 317

Crawfordsville Distric Public Library, 316–24

cultural copyright, 152

cultural heritage: definition of, 291; preservation of, 291–92

cyanotype photographs, 121, 183; care instructions for, 186, 207

Daguerreotype photographs, 121, 182–83; care instructions for, 186, 207

damage: prevention and treatment, 302–3; sources of, 300–301

databases: for local biographies, 225–26; for newspaper indexing, 60–61; for obituaries, 247, 249–52; online, 323; for photograph index, 197; testing, 249–50

data storage, for family history material, 173–75

Davis, Emilie: preservation of, diaries of, 213–22; story of, 214–16

de-accessioning: and collection development, 112; and family history items, 41–42

death records, database of, 252

deed of gift, 111, 130

dehumidifiers, 6

developing countries: economic issues in, 64; newspaper preservation in, 63–72; term, 65

diaries, digital preservation of, 213–22

digital photographs, 184; care instructions for, 186

digital preservation, 211–53; of biographies, 223–33; definition of, 68; of diaries, 213–22; future of, 264–65; of newspapers, 68–69; of obituary files, 243–53; recommendations for, 175, 219–20; versus digitization, 208

digital recording equipment, 280

digitization: copyright issues and, 127–32; definition of, 170; ethical issues and, 134–35; of family history material, 169–73; and gifts policy, 41; items unsuitable for, 53–54; of newspapers, 47–54, 67; of oral history tapes, 281–83; of photographs, 122–23, 185, 208; of scrapbooks, 82–83; specifications for and title selection, 51

disaster, definition of, 22

Disaster Mitigation Planning Assistance, 33

disaster preparedness. *See* emergency preparedness

documents: gifts policy and, 41; handling instructions for, 303; storage environment for, 37

donors, policy and, 106

Dornak, Margaret, 145

dPlan, 33

Drost, Amanda, 179–88, 338

dry cleaning, *17*

dust, 5, 300

DVDs, 173–74, 260, 262–63

Eastside Genealogical Society, 159, 161, 164

eBay, and historical research, 322

Eden, Barbara B., vii–viii, 338

education of public: genealogical societies and, 164; on preservation, 296–304; on racial issues, 311–12; rationale for, 296–97; records retention project and, 142–43

Elder, Rebecca, 138, 144

emergency, definition of, 22

emergency information sheet, 26

emergency plan: development of, 25–26; reviewing, 32; testing, 31–32

emergency preparedness, 22–34; and archives, 155; and newspaper collections, 70; and photographs, 185; response outline for, 27–28

encapsulation, *18*

enclosures: for photograph preservation, 122; stabilization procedures for, *18*

encyclopedias, online, 323

environment: educating public on, 302; emergency procedures for, 28; for family history items, 36–37; low-cost options for, 5–6; for manuscripts, 120; for negatives, 207; and newspaper preservation, 66; for oral history materials, 277–78; for photographs, 185; for scrapbooks, 100

equipment: for digitization, 171–73; for in-house repair, 16–20; for oral histories, 264, 270–71, 280

erasure, 5

ethics: and local history collections, 124, 127, 132–35; and photographs, 181–82; and racial issues in collections, 313. *See also* copyright issues; privacy issues

external hard drives, 174; for oral history storage, 261

Facebook, and historical research, 321

fair use, of copyrighted work, 131

false light, 132

family history material: data storage for, 173–75; gifts policy on, 35–43; preservation of, 169–76

Federal Emergency Management Agency (FEMA), 23, 31

Feige, Dyani, 22–34, 338–39

Ferris State University, 312

film storage, 36–37; gifts policy and, 40

finding aids: for catablog, 241; definition of, 202

Fisseler, Brende Lincke, 137–45, 339

FitzGerald, Kerry A., 243–53, 339

flatbed scanners, 171

Fleming, Sarah, 162

Foley, Erin, 86–93, 339

Fortier, Rose, 189–98, 339–40

frames, 4–5

Fraser, Lisa, 159–68, 340

gelatin silver photographs, 99–100, 121, 200

genealogical societies, 243–44; educating on preservation, 297; meetings of, 163; partnerships with, 159–68

genealogy, 157–76; and local biographies, 224; obituary files, 243–53

geographic area: and collection development policy, 109; and newspaper preservation, 56–57

Georgia Historical Society, 223

Getty Conservation Institute, 33

gifts policy, 35–43; on archives, 148–49; and collection development, 111; recommendations for, 42–43

glass plate negatives, 183; care instructions for, 186, 207

Grand Haven Genealogical Society, 243–44

grants: for digital preservation project, 219–20; for oral histories, 271–72; for records retention project, 138, 141

Griffin, Emily, 316–24, 340

Gwynn, David, 127–36, 340

handling: educating public on, 302–3; scrapbooks, 101

Harbeson, Cyndi, 234–42, 340

Heinsohn, Holly, 145

Helling, William, 105–15, 341

HEPA vacuums, 5

Heritage Preservation (organization), 33

historical newspapers, selection for online access, 47–54

historical societies, 223, 270–71; educating on preservation, 298; partnerships with, 214, 216–17

Historical Society of Pennsylvania, 216

history. *See* family history material; local history; oral histories/interviews
Hopkinson, Caroline, 224
housing, for newspaper preservation, 68
Hudson, Alexia, 213–22, 341
Hughes, Richard, 313
humidifiers, 6
humidity, 300–301

Ifijeh, Goodluck Israel, 63–72, 341
Image Permanence Institute, 187
incident commander, 28
indexing: local newspapers on microfilm, 55–62; oral interviews, 278–79; photograph collections, 194–98, *196–97*; scrapbooks, 78
Indiana University of Pennsylvania, 266–74
informational value scrapbooks, 76–78
inherent vice, term, 301
inks, 16
integrated library system, 61
intellectual property issues, 128–32
Internet: catablog on, 234–42; and historical research, 318–24; indexes on, 198; local biographies on, 230
interviews. *See* oral histories/interviews
inventory: and catablog, 238; of oral histories, 273, 281; and policy development, 108; of scrapbook contents, 87–90
irreparable items, *15*
Ives, Edward, 269

Jackson, Athena, 47–54, 341
Jim Crow Museum of Racist Memorabilia, 312
Jimerson, Randall, 312

Kennedy, Joseph, 213
Kodachrome photographs, 121
Kouba, Elizabeth, 138, 144–45

labels, for photographs, 122
Lane, Henry S., 316

large-format scanners, 172
Lathrop, Suellyn, 275–83, 341
Lavaca County records retention project, 137–45
ledgers, repurposed as scrapbooks, 83
legal issues: and records retention project, 141–42. *See also* copyright issues
Leinaweaver, Chad, 3–10, 342
LeMaster, Rochelle, 35–43, 342
letter of agreement (LOA), 160; sample, 167–68
liability issues, and local history collections, 124
Library of Congress (LOC), 33, 129; Chronicling America, 319–20; and digital preservation, 219–20; and sheet music collections, 312; Subject Authority Headings, 57–58
light damage, 300
lignin-free, term, 77, 299
LOA. *See* letter of agreement
LOC. *See* Library of Congress
local authors, and collection development, 108
local biographies, 223–33; publication of, decision flowchart for, 230, *231*
local history, 103–56; archives in, management of, 146–56; catablog and, 234–42; collection development guidelines for, 105–15; diary preservation, 213–22; nontraditional methods in, 316–24; oral interviews, 257–65; privacy and copyright concerns, 127–36
local newspapers, on microfilm, indexing, 55–62
local writing clubs, educating on preservation, 298
LOCKSS theory, 303
Longenecker, Randall, 289
low-cost options: affiliations and, 287–95; catablog as, 235; for collections care, 3–10; and family history items, 38; for oral history storage, 261

Madden, Karl, 305–15, 342

Maine Memory Network, 82

manuscripts: gifts policy and, 41; by local authors, 119–20; storage environment for, 37

maps: gifts policy and, 41; storage environment for, 37

Massey, Georgia, 227

materials: collection development policy for, 109–10; for in-house repair, 16–20

McDevitt, Theresa, 266–74, 342

McKnight, Mark, 307

memorandum of understanding (MOU), for diary digitization, 217–18

Meredith, Judy, 161

message boards, and historical research, 318

microfilm: digitizing, title selection for, 47–54; life expectancy of, 67; newspapers on, 55–62, 66–67

Milwaukee Public Library, Historic Photo Archives, 189–98

minstrel songs, issues in preservation of, 305–15

miscellaneous, as heading, 194

mission, policy and, 106, 108

mobile devices, catablog and, 236–37

Morrow, Carolyn Clark, 7

MOU. *See* memorandum of understanding

multimedia, catablog and, 237, 241

music collections, 305–15; categorizing, 308–9

National Digital Newspaper Program (NDNP), 48, 319–20

National Endowment for the Humanities, 219–20

National Park Service, Museum Management Program, 303–4

natural collections, 192

NDCC. *See* Northeast Document Conservation Center

Nebraska State Historical Society, 270–71

negatives, 183–84, 207; care instructions for, 186

newspaper(s), 45–72; definition of, 63–64; in developing countries, preservation of, 63–72; gifts policy and, 41; on microfilm, indexing, 55–62; and obituaries, 244–45; online archives, 318–20; selection for online access, 47–54; storage environment for, 37

newspaper preservation: in local history collections, 118–19; methods of, 66–69; need for, 65–66; recommendations for, 69–70; and scrapbooks, 75–77

newsprint, characteristics of, 65–66

New York State Archives, 185

nitrate negatives, 184, 207; care instructions for, 186

Northeast Document Conservation Center (NDCC), 123, 303–4

Nykolaiszyn, Juliana, 257–65, 342

obituary files, 243–53; checklist for, 252–53

OCR. *See* optical character recognition

odors, *19*

offsite storage, for oral history storage, 261

online. *See* Internet

online newspaper collections: definition of, 48–49; selection for, 47–54

open reels, 36, 40, 123. *See also* reel-to-reel film

optical character recognition (OCR), 49, 60, 170, 224

oral histories/interviews, 255–83; best practices in collection of, 268–69; case study on, 134–35; copyright issues with, 130; preservation of, 123–24, 266–83; privacy issues and, 132–33; recommendations for, 269–70, 273–78

Oral History Association, 280

ownership rights: and collection development, 111; and family history items, 41–43; and local genealogical partnerships, 161–62; and scrapbooks, 87

pages, of scrapbooks, 96–97; attachment of, 95–96
paintings, handling instructions for, 303
pamphlet binding, *19*
paper: newsprint, 65–66; in scrapbooks, 96
paperback stiffening, *19*
paper repair, in-house, 11–21; procedures for, *17–18*
particulates, 300
partnerships: affiliation agreements for, 287–95; development of, 289–91; for digital preservation, 214; for emergency preparedness, 31; establishment of, 159–60; example of, 292–94; guidelines for, 160; with local genealogical societies, 159–68; for newspaper preservation, 69–70; for oral history preservation, 268
PAT. *See* Photographic Activity Test
patrons. *See* users
Pennsylvania State University Libraries, 217–18
permissions letter, for local biography publication, 229
persistent URL (PURL), 218
personnel: for local biography publication, 230; for newspaper indexing, 58–59. *See also* staff; volunteers
pests: damage from, 301; and newspaper preservation, 66; risk assessment on, 25; stabilization procedures for, *19*
phase boxes, 3–4, *18*
Phillips, Jessica, 296–304, 343
photocopying: for newspaper preservation, 67, 119; for scrapbook preservation, 90–91

Photographic Activity Test (PAT), 122, 204, 300
photographic scanners, 172–73
photographic societies, educating on preservation, 298–99
photographs, 177–209; collection management, 180–81, 189–98; digital, 186; gifts policy and, 40; handling instructions for, 302; in local history collections, 120–23; and oral interviews, 270, 276–77; organization of, 191–94; in scrapbooks, 98–100; storage environment for, 37; threats to, 121; types of, 121, 182–84; unidentified, 39; unusual types, 206–8
plastics, for photograph preservation, 122
platinotype photographs, 184; care instructions for, 186
Pocket Response Plan, 26
policy: on archives acquisition, 148–49; importance of, 105–7; and local genealogical partnerships, 161–63; on local history collection development, 105–15, 117–18; on newspaper preservation, 69; on photographs, 120–21; on preservation, 13–14; sample, 113–15; on scrapbooks, 78, *84. See also* collections policy; gifts policy
polyester film, 184; care instructions for, 186
polyethylene bags, 4
polyvinyl chloride (PVC), 97, 122
portfolios, *18*
posters: gifts policy and, 41; low-cost preservation options, 4; storage environment for, 37
pottery, handling instructions for, 302
prefaces, for sheet music collections, 306, 311
preservation: approaches to, 285–324; checklist for, 119; community education on, 296–304; definition of, 65, 299; process of, 118; versus

conservation. 185, *See also* digital preservation

preservation issues, 325–26; with genealogy, 157–76; with local history, 103–56; with newspapers, 45–72; with newspapers in developing countries, 63–72; options for, *15*; with oral histories, 255–83; prompt response to, 7–8; with scrapbooks, 73–102; selection for, 13–14; training, importance of, 12–13

pressing, *18*

prevention, low-cost options for, 6–7

privacy issues: and local history collections, 124, 127, 132–33; and photographs, 181–82

processing: definition of, 202; photographs, recommendations for, 204–5

provenance, of archives, 152–53

public disclosure, 132–33

public domain, 129

publicity: for catablog, 242; ethical issues and, 133; for historical research, 323–24; for local biography project, 232; for obituary file, 251; for records retention project, 143–44

PURL, 218

PVC, 97, 122

quilt guilds, educating on preservation, 298

racial issues: notes on, 311; preservation of Black history, 213–22; sheet music preservation, 305–15

RAID, 261

Really Simple Syndication (RSS), 236

rebacking, *19*

recording equipment, digital, 280

records retention project, 137–45

redundant array of independent disks (RAID), 261

reel-to-reel film, 36, 41, 264. *See also* open reels

Regional Alliance for Preservation, 33

repair, in-house, 11–21, *15*; advantages of, 12; procedures for, *17–18*; training for, importance of, 12–13

reproduction rights, and collection development, 111–12

research: historical, nontraditional methods for, 316–24; volunteers and, 165–66

resolution, of audio recordings, 259

resources: on community education, 303–4; on copyright issues, 132; on emergency preparedness, 32–34; for genealogical partnerships, 160–61; on oral history preservation, 265; on photographs, 187

retrieval, of data, 175–76

Richey, Nancy, 116–26, 343

rights. *See* copyright issues; ownership rights

risk assessment, 23–25; options for, *24*

RSS, 236

safety film, 184; care instructions for, 186

salted paper photographs, 121, 182; care instructions for, 186

salvage: basic techniques, 30; priorities for, 28–29; stabilization procedures and, *17–19*

Saunders, Janice, 145

scanning, 53; equipment for, 171–73; scrapbooks, 92–93. *See also* digitization

schedule: for family history digitization, 176; for indexing, 61–62; for obituary project, 248–49; for photograph organization, 193; for records retention project, 140–41

Schroeder, Patricia, 306

Schwieger, Hans, 236

scrapbooks, 73–102; with annotations, *81*; deteriorating pages, *79*; fragile, handling, 101; low-cost preservation options, 5; physical properties of, 94–102; policy on, 78, *84*; preserved

items, *80*; security and availability of, 86–93; users and, 75–85
security: and archives, 156; and local history collections, 124; low-cost options for, 7; risk assessment on, 25
SEE ALSO entries, 196, *197*
SEE entries, 196, *197*
servers, for oral history storage, 261
sheet-feed scanners, 171
sheet music collections, 305–15; categorizing, *308–9*
side-laced bindings, 95
silver gelatin photographs, 99–100, 121, 200
slides, 207; gifts policy and, 40; storage environment for, 36
social networking sites, and historical research, 321, 323–24
Society of American Archivists, 181; code of ethics, 313
software, for scanning, 173
solid state drives (SSDs), 174, 280
Sonenklar, Carol, 268
Soules, Aline, 325–26, 343
South King County Genealogical Society, 159
space: for in-house repair, 16–20; for interviews, 276; low-cost options for, 5–6; for scrapbook preservation, 87
spreadsheets: for newspaper indexing, 59; for obituaries, 247, 249; for photograph index, 197
SSDs. *See* solid state drives
stabilization procedures, 16, *17–19*
staff: and archive access, 156; and catablog creation, 239; and collection development, 110; and obituary project, 248; policy and, 106–7
storage: of audio recordings, 259–62; educating public on, 302
storage space: for archives, 155; and gifts policy, 39–41; low-cost options for, 5–6; for scrapbooks, 100–101
strap-hinges, 95

sub-Saharan Africa, newspaper preservation in, 63–72
subject headings: miscellaneous/unknown, 194; for newspaper indexing, 57–58; for photographs, 205
sulfited pulps, 96
suppliers: archival resources, 125; for in-house repair, 20
supplies: for emergency response, 29–30; for scrapbook preservation, 89
surveys, for historical newspaper selection, 51–52; methodology for, 52–53
Szwarc, Irene, 145

Tabah, Rebekah, 199–209, 343
Tagged Image File Format (TIFF), 82, 92, 218
Taylor, Tomaro I., 287–95, 343–44
telephone chain, 27
temperature damage, 301
Teper, Jennifer Hain, 94–102, 344
textiles, handling instructions for, 302
theater groups, educating on preservation, 298
theme, for catablog, 240
TIFF. *See* Tagged Image File Format
tintype photographs, 121, 183; care instructions for, 186, 207
tissue, acid-free, 4
training: for catablog, 235; for emergency preparedness, 31–32; for in-house repair, importance of, 12–13; for newspaper preservation, 70; for photograph processing, 200
transcription, of oral interviews, 279; equipment for, 271
Twitter, and historical research, 321

unbuffered, term, 300
United Nations Educational, Scientific and Cultural Organization (UNESCO), 291
United States Newspaper Project, 48
University of North Carolina at Greensboro, 127

University of South Florida, 292–94
unknown, as heading, 194
users: and archives, 156; and catablog,
    235–36; and collection development,
    110; and family history digitization,
    169, 176; and indexing, 195;
    interface, for obituary file, *250,* 251;
    and microfilm, 67; and newspaper
    deterioration, 70; and obituaries,
    248; and photographs, 192, 201; and
    scrapbooks, 75–85
UV film, 6

vacuums, low-cost options for, 5
value, of archives, 151
vendors, contacts for emergency, 30
video oral histories, 262–63
visual literacy, 200
Volkel, Theresa, 145
volunteers: genealogical societies and,
    165–66; and obituary project, 248;
    and records retention project, 138–39,
    145
vulnerability assessment, 23–25

waivers, and gifts, 42
Wallace, Lew, 316
Warlick, Roger, 223, 231
water damage, *19,* 301

Watkins, Maurine, 317
web address, 240
websites, and historical research, 318
Weiden, Jeannette, 253
Weigle, Anastasia S., 75–85, 344
Welland, Sarah, 146–56, 344
Western State & Territories Preservation
    Assistance Services, 33–34
wet books, salvaging, *19*
Whitehead, Kaye Wise, 216
women, preserving history of, 213–22,
    266–74
wooden frames, 4–5
word processing software, for newspaper
    indexing, 59–60
worksheets, for obituaries, design of,
    244–46
workshops, genealogical, 164
wrappers, 262–63
wrapping, for newspaper preservation,
    68
writing clubs, educating on preservation,
    298
written interviews, preservation of,
    123–24

Yale University, 312–13

Zackmann, Kelly, 55–62, 344

About the Editors
and Contributors

Carol Smallwood received her MLS from Western Michigan University and her MA in history from Eastern Michigan University. *Writing and Publishing: The Librarian's Handbook and Librarians as Community Partners: An Outreach Handbook* are 2010 ALA anthologies. *Lily's Odyssey* and *Contemporary American Women: Our Defining Passages* are new releases outside librarianship. *Pre-and Post-Retirement Tips for Librarians* is her twenty-fourth published book. Some magazine credits include *The Writer's Chronicle, English Journal,* and *Michigan Feminist Studies*; her library experience includes school, public, academic, and special libraries, as well as administration and consultation.

Elaine Williams is the branch manager and youth librarian at the Lynchburg (Ohio) Branch of the Highland County District Library. She received her master's degree in library science from Kent State University (1997) and was certified as an Ohio public librarian in 2002. Her poetry has appeared in *Scifaikuest, Snowy Egret,* and *Open Minds Quarterly,* and her nonfiction essays in *Open Minds Quarterly* and *Librarians as Community Partners: An Outreach Handbook* (2010) and *A Cup of Comfort for Fathers* (2010). Elaine is a member of the Lynchburg (Ohio) Historical Society and the Ohio Library Council, Southwest Chapter.

∼

Karen E. K. Brown, preservation librarian, University at Albany, SUNY, obtained her BFA from the Cooper Union, MAC from Queen's University, and

MLIS from Dalhousie University. Ms. Brown has written topical leaflets and developed workshops for the Northeast Document Conservation Center. She has also developed online workshops and programs for the American Library Association and published in *Library Resources & Technical Services.* She is co-author of a SPEC Kit for the Association of Research Libraries. In 2003, she won the Esther from ALCTS for leadership in the field of preservation.

Howard C. Bybee is the family history librarian in the Harold B. Lee Library, Brigham Young University, Provo, Utah. He is faculty advisor for the French section of the Immigrant Ancestors Project. He has taught Introduction to Family History at BYU. He has spoken about the Lee Library genealogy resources at conferences throughout Utah. He has master's degrees in French, anthropology, and library science, and has been employed in the Harold B. Lee Library since 1988.

Elizabeth B. Cooksey, academic reference librarian, just finished a year of post-retirement professional work at Armstrong Atlantic State University, Savannah, Georgia. She obtained her MLS (1977) and MA in history (1981) at the University of Oregon. Liz is a member of the American Library Association. She has appeared in *The Acquisitions Librarian, The Georgia Library, The Green Library Journal, The New Georgia Encyclopedia, Libraries & Culture, RQ, The Reference Librarian,* and *Science and Technology Libraries.*

Amanda Drost received her MLIS degree from Wayne State University. She is currently the Kentucky Library catalog librarian at Western Kentucky University, where she catalogs historical and modern materials for the library's special collection. Amanda spent a year volunteering in the archives at the Grand Rapids (Michigan) Public Library (GRPL), working with a local photograph collection under the supervision of the library's archivist. While at GRPL, she spent time digitizing and readying negatives with vinegar syndrome for long-term storage.

Barbara B. Eden is the director of the Department of Preservation and Collection Maintenance at Cornell University Library. Working at Cornell since 1985, Barbara has managed numerous grant-funded projects that have focused on digitization, conservation, microfilming, and education and training. Throughout her career she has participated in the many changes in the field and has served as a consultant to organizations as diverse as the Syracuse University Library, Union County Municipal Archives, the Brooklyn Museum of Art Library, and the History Center of Tompkins County.

Dyani Feige, preservation specialist at the Conservation Center for Art & Historic Artifacts (CCAHA), works with libraries, archives, museums, and other cultural organizations to conduct needs assessments and risk assessments, assists in emergency preparedness, and helps develop policy and planning documents and long-term preservation plans. She also helps develop and present preservation-related educational programs. Before joining CCAHA, Feige worked for the Brooklyn Museum Libraries and Archives, the New York Public Library's Preservation Division, the Conference Board, New York University's Bobst Library, and Kent State University's Special Collections and Archives.

Brenda Lincke Fisseler has been employed by the French Simpson Memorial Library in Hallettsville, Texas, for twenty-one years. Among her duties, Brenda is in charge of the library's local history/genealogical collection. She is the coordinator of the Lavaca County Record Retention Volunteers, a group that has been working with historic Lavaca County records for the past six years. Brenda has received training for this endeavor from Amigos Library Services and the Texas State Library and Archives Commission. She has also published nine finding aids for Lavaca County records and writes historical articles for newspapers and historical quarterlies.

Kerry A. FitzGerald serves as assistant director for Loutit District Library in Grand Haven, Michigan, and is a member of the Michigan Library Association. She received her MILS from the University of Michigan and a BA in anthropology from Western Michigan University. Specializing in technical services and information technology, Kerry catalogs the rare materials of the Local History and Genealogy Department and coordinates the library's digitization projects. Loutit District Library is currently digitizing its photograph, document, oral history, newspaper, and fragile monograph collections.

Erin Foley received her BA in archaeology from Yale University, followed by an MA in library and information studies from the University of Wisconsin–Madison. An archivist who specializes in photographic history, Erin worked with Civil War–era glass negatives at Washington & Lee University, one hundred years of Minneapolis ephemera and photography at Minneapolis Public Library, and the archives and artifacts of American Circus at Circus World Museum. Erin is currently the library director in Rio, Wisconsin, where she works with an active group of local historians.

Rose Fortier has been historic photo librarian and digital projects librarian at the Milwaukee Public Library since 2005. She obtained her MLIS from the University of Wisconsin–Milwaukee. Her digital collections have been featured in the *Milwaukee Journal Sentinel, Library Journal,* and on the American Library Association's I Love Libraries blog. She has presented programs on organizing and digitizing photos and other materials to patrons at her library and at the Wisconsin Association of Public Libraries and the Upper Midwest CON-TENTdm Users Group annual meetings.

Lisa Fraser is an adult services librarian at the Bellevue Library in Bellevue, Washington, the largest of the forty-six libraries in the King County Library System. She received an MLIS from the University of Washington and a master's of international administration from the School for International Training in Vermont. Lisa has administered library partnerships with museums, genealogical societies, human services organizations, and colleges. She contributed to *The Frugal Librarian* (2011). She teaches courses in marketing and advocacy for libraries at the Information School of the University of Washington.

Emily Griffin is a reference librarian at the Crawfordsville District Public Library in Crawfordsville, Indiana. She holds an MLIS degree from Drexel University in Philadelphia, Pennsylvania. In addition to reference duties, she is responsible for local history and genealogy research and maintaining the library's growing collection. She is active in integrating social networking and additional technologies in a modern library. She recently published a historical article in Wabash College's *Wabash Magazine* on one of its graduates who gained fame as a Hollywood actor and restaurateur before slipping into oblivion.

David Gwynn, digital projects coordinator for the University Libraries of the University of North Carolina at Greensboro (UNCG) since 2009, has worked extensively with local, regional, and university history collections. David earned his MLIS from UNCG in 2009 and is a member of the American Library Association, the Society of American Archivists, and the Society of North Carolina Archivists. Before entering the field of librarianship, David spent twelve years as a web designer and developer. He has completed numerous digital projects and has also had research published in *LIBRES*.

Cyndi Harbeson is the processing archivist in the Carol Grotnes Belk Library and Information Commons at Appalachian State University in Boone, North Carolina. Cynthia has a master of science in library science and a master of history from Simmons College in Boston and a bachelor of arts from Saint Joseph College in West Hartford, Connecticut. She is a member of the Society of American Archivists, New England Archivists, Society of North Carolina Archivists, and the North Carolina Library Association.

William Helling is the head of reference/local history at the Crawfordsville District Public Library in Crawfordsville, Indiana. He holds an MIS from Indiana University, where he is also an adjunct lecturer for the School of Library and Information Science. He designed and oversees the two dozen local history databases that the public library maintains. He has published in *Computers in Libraries*, *Indiana Libraries*, *Literature/Film Quarterly*, *The Great Circle* (journal of the Australian Association for Maritime History), and so on. His book *Crawfordsville* came out in 2011.

Alexia Hudson is reference and instruction librarian at Penn State (Abington) College. She is an alumna of the inaugural class of the American Library Association's Emerging Leaders Program (2007). Alexia is the recipient of several honors including the 2007 Pennsylvania Library Association's New Librarian of the Year award and was acknowledged as one of *Library Journal*'s "Movers and Shakers" in 2008. She received a MLIS degree from the University of Pittsburgh (2005) and a BA in English literature and African American studies from Temple University (1993). Part of her research focus is librarianship's role in preserving ethnohistory.

Goodluck Israel Ifijeh, serials librarian at the Center for Learning Resources, Covenant University, Ota, Nigeria, joined the university in 2007. Mr. Goodluck worked in public and school libraries between 2000 and 2006 and holds a diploma and bachelor's degree in library and information science from the Ambrose Alli University, Ekpoma, Edo State, Nigeria. He is currently studying for a master's degree in library and information studies from the University of Ibadan, Nigeria. Mr. Goodluck has published scholarly articles in local and international journals, including *Library Philosophy and Practice*.

Athena Jackson has worked in public archives and the e-publishing industry. At the North Carolina State Archives, she established specifications for historical newspaper digitization and assisted in coordinating grant funding and vendor relationships. As an editor for an e-publisher, Athena developed bibliographies, indexing specifications, and end-user platform requirements for online humanities collections. She is at the University of Miami Libraries as assistant professor and special collections librarian. Athena has presented to the K–12, academic, and public library audiences. She's a member of the Rare Books and Manuscripts Section of the Association of College and Research Libraries.

Suellyn Lathrop, university archivist and records officer at Western Kentucky University, Bowling Green, Kentucky, since 2007, obtained her MS in history from Illinois State University. A member of the Midwest Archives Conference and Kentucky Council of Archives, Suellyn has over twenty years' experience in academic, private nonprofit, and state archives in Illinois, Kansas, Missouri, North Carolina, and Kentucky. She received the Thornton W. Mitchell Service Award in 2005 from the Society of North Carolina Archivists.

Chad Leinaweaver is the assistant director at the Morristown and Morris Township Library, New Jersey. Previously, Chad cataloged, preserved, and exhibited the rare books, fine prints, posters, pop-up books, greeting cards, and other collections in the Special Collections Division of the Newark Public Library. He was formerly the director for the Library and Museum Collections at the New Jersey Historical Society and the director of Library User Access Services of the New England Historic Genealogical Society. Chad authored portions of the *Dictionary of New Jersey History* and has written numerous other articles.

Rochelle LeMaster is currently working with the American Memory Project through Cleveland State University, and often assesses photographic works for inclusion into various projects. She has also done preservation analysis and surveys for the Cleveland Museum of Natural History and the Cleveland Institute of Music. While attending Kent State University, Rochelle worked with the Cleveland Botanical Gardens, creating accession and de-accessioning policies for their 35mm slide collection along with other items to be included in their archives.

Karl Madden is assistant professor and academic librarian at Medgar Evers College, City University of New York, in Crown Heights, Brooklyn. He holds master's degrees in library science and music. He has been a professional musician and music teacher, and he taught English for several years in Japan. He has published articles and chapters on music, libraries, information, and film music. He is active in international academic conferences and is involved in performance and visual arts projects.

Theresa McDevitt, government documents/reference librarian and history and women's studies bibliographer at Indiana University of Pennsylvania's Stapleton Library, has worked there since 1986 and has also served as acting special collections and archives librarian, acting library dean, and acting library associate dean. She is editor or co-editor of books such as *Women and the American Civil War: An Annotated Bibliography* (2003), *Government Publications Unmasked: Teaching Government Information in the 21st Century* (2003), and *Let the Games Begin!: Engaging Students with Interactive Information Literacy Instruction* (2003).

Juliana Nykolaiszyn, assistant professor/oral history librarian, joined the Oklahoma Oral History Research Program at the Oklahoma State University Library in May 2007. From interviewing narrators to processing oral history collections, Juliana's work involves not only the creation but preservation and online access of oral histories. A native of Miami, Florida, she earned her MLIS from Florida State University. Prior to entering librarianship, Juliana worked in media relations and marketing along with radio and television production.

Jessica Phillips, head of the Preservation Department at the University of North Texas, Denton, Texas, since 2007, studied preservation management at the University of Pittsburgh, where she earned her MLIS in 2006. Before joining the University of North Texas, Phillips interned in special collections at Marietta College and the University of Pittsburgh and also at The Castle, a historical house museum. She has given presentations about preserving personal collections for libraries and genealogical societies as part of ALA's National Preservation Week initiatives.

Nancy Richey is a graduate of the University of Kentucky and Western Kentucky University in Bowling Green, where she received degrees in information science and Southern history. Richey is currently reference and image librarian at the Kentucky Library and Museum. Richey is also a board member of the Janice Holt Giles Historical Society, where she acts as a docent at the Kentucky author's home, now a house museum near Columbia, Kentucky. She also serves as registrar for the Samuel Davies Chapter of the Daughters of the American Revolution.

Aline Soules, a library faculty member at California State University, East Bay, earned her MSLS at Wayne State University, her MA at the University of Windsor, and her MFA in creative writing at Antioch University, Los Angeles. She has worked in a variety of public and private academic libraries in the United States and Canada. Her recent articles appear in *New Library World* and *Library Hi Tech,* and her chapter on "The Balance of Authority and Responsibility in Middle Management" appears in *Middle Management in Academic and Public Libraries* (2011).

Rebekah Tabah holds an MA in photographic preservation and collections management from Ryerson University (Toronto, Ontario, Canada) and George Eastman House (Rochester, New York), She is responsible for collection development, donor relations, appraisal, reference, cataloging, exhibits, preservation, copyright, web content, reference, visual literacy instruction, fund-raising, and internships and outreach programs pertaining to photographs for a private, nonprofit repository. The management of backlogs and orphan and unidentified photos is a strength; and large, complex nineteenth- and twentieth-century photograph collections are a specialty. She also serves as a consultant for private collectors, academic repositories, galleries, historical societies, and museums.

Tomaro I. Taylor, associate university librarian at the Louis de la Parte Florida Mental Health Institute Research Library, Tampa, Florida, received her master of arts in library and information science from the University of South Florida in 2002 and archival certification from the Academy of Certified Archivists in 2005. She has worked extensively with the Society of Florida Archivists, the Florida Library Association, the Ybor City Museum Society, and the Society of American Archivists, primarily focusing on museum-library collaborations and diversity in libraries and archives.

Jennifer Hain Teper has served as head of conservation for the University Library at the University of Illinois, Urbana-Champaign, since 2001 and as interim head of preservation since 2009. She graduated from the University of Texas at Austin in 2000 with a MLIS and CAS in the conservation and preservation of library and archival materials. Before her current appointment she worked at the University of Texas's Harry Ransom Humanities Research Center, the University of Pittsburgh Library, the New York Botanical Gardens Library, and the University of Kentucky Audiovisual Archives.

Anastasia S. Weigle, director of Teti Library and Special Collections at the New Hampshire Institute of Art, obtained her MSLIS in archives management from Simmons College. She is adjunct faculty at the University of Maine, where she teaches Introduction to Archives and Manuscripts. She served as processing archivist for the Maine Maritime Museum in Bath and Harmon Museum in Old Orchard Beach, Maine. She is a member of the American Library Association, New England Library Association, New England Archivists, and Maine Archives and Museums.

Sarah Welland is a qualified archivist with a postgraduate degree in archives administration from the University of New South Wales and more than twenty years' experience as an archivist and records manager. She currently works as an archives and records consultant to both public and private organizations, and develops and teaches distance courses in records and archives to undergraduates at the Open Polytechnic of New Zealand (Auckland). Sarah has also set up a local history collection from scratch in her local community, and understands the issues facing librarians in this area.

Kelly Zackmann is the local history librarian for the Robert E. Ellingwood Model Colony History Room at the Ontario City Library in Ontario, California, where she is responsible for day-to-day operations and preservation management. Kelly earned her bachelor's degree in English from the University of California, Riverside, and her master's degree in library and information science from San José State University. In addition to her formal education, she has continued to attend training activities in archives and preservation, including the Western Archives Institute in 2009.